A LOVE OF READING

Reviews of Contemporary Fiction

ROBERT ADAMS

M&S

Cloth edition published 2001
Trade paperback edition published 2002

National Library of Canada Cataloguing in Publication Data

Adams, Robert, 1937-
   A love of reading: reviews of contemporary fiction /
Robert Adams. – Trade pbk. ed.

ISBN 0-7710-0660-8

1. English fiction – 20th century – Book reviews. I. Title.

PR881.A32 2002   823'.91409   C2002-903222-9

We acknowledge the financial support of the Government of Canada through the Book Publishing Industry Development Program for our publishing activities. We further acknowledge the support of the Canada Council for the Arts and the Ontario Arts Council for our publishing program.

Pages 307 and 308 represent a continuation of this copyright page.

Design by Sari Naworynski
Typeset in Times by M&S, Toronto
Printed and bound in Canada

This book is printed on acid-free paper that is 100% ancient-forest friendly (100% post-consumer recycled).

McClelland & Stewart Ltd.
The Canadian Publishers
481 University Avenue
Toronto, Ontario
M5G 2E9
www.mcclelland.com

1 2 3 4 5   06 05 04 03 02

For Pearl Brownstein Adams

For Jonathan Ann
Thank you for coming home
for Christmas — the very
best gift we could have.
Love Dad.
Dec/02.

CONTENTS

PREFACE

I find great joy in reading. It was the most wonderful gift my parents gave me.

My mother and father had little formal education, but they were both widely read and had a great love of the written word. My mother taught me to read when I was four. By the time I was six, my two much older brothers had left to fight in the Second World War, and so I became, in effect, an only child. I had friends in my little town and I played with them after school every day, but after I came home the rest of the evening was always the same. My parents and I each had our own comfortable chair by the fire, and we sat and read after dinner until it was time for me to go to bed.

I don't know how much of that routine was for my benefit. I suspect that at least some of it was a deliberate sacrifice by my parents of other possible leisure activities. It was part of their lifelong effort to teach by example.

It was certainly effective. Reading has always been associated in my mind with love, security, and warmth. I was about fifteen before I discovered that not everyone read for two or three hours every day. When I went into the homes of friends and saw no books, I always assumed that they were in another room and that the family would take up their reading at some time after I left.

I was a teacher for thirty-six years, at every level from Grade Seven to third-year university, and like every other teacher I was often asked by parents how best they might encourage their children to read. My answer was, and is, always the same. If you want to buy books for your child, buy books. If you want to read to your child, read. It is a good start. But if you are serious about helping your child, *let the child see you read*. Children listen to a distressingly small portion of what we say, but they pay great attention to what we do. I am convinced that the habit of reading is the greatest legacy a child can receive, and I remain deeply grateful to my parents, Haldane and Edith Sarah Adams.

Every year I prepare a series of five reviews, each of a contemporary novel, to be delivered on stage in Montreal and Toronto. I choose novels that have caused me to see some part of my world or some aspect of the human condition in a new light. I am particularly attracted to novels set in cultures or times other than my own. Much of what I believe about writing and reading and the duty of the reader to discover the writer's intention I cover in the talk I gave to the Writers' Trust of Canada, which begins this collection, but there are a couple of other points I would like to address.

Reviewers are often criticized for rehashing too much of the plot and offering too little close analysis of the text. Sometimes the charge is justified. A university lecturer is allowed to assume that everyone has just studied the material under consideration. I, on the other hand, know that up to half of my audience has not yet read the novel under review and many of the others may have read it some months ago. Some readers have told me that they read the novel twice, once before and once after my review. Others wait until after my review for their first reading. They tell me that they find my comments and my setting the novel in its historical or literary context very helpful in engaging the novel more closely. In any event, because I feel a responsibility to make sure that my remarks have meaning for as many people as possible, I see some kind of plot summary as unavoidable. As much as I can, I always try to blend it in with a discussion of character, but I always feel like Ferlinghetti's man on a tightrope, trying desperately not to lose my balance, and I know that sometimes I slip and spend too much time on the plot.

I freely confess that in my reviews I always reveal the end of the novel, and for this I make no apology. I am not a newspaper critic reviewing a novel only recently published, essentially offering an informed opinion as to why a potential reader may or may not enjoy the work. I wait until a novel is in paperback before I review it so that the subscribers to my series have at least a year to read it if they wish to. It seems clear to me that I have no choice but to examine in detail the last pages of a novel. The end of a narrative is not only a part of the narrative, it is a condition of the narrative. If Macbeth had accepted Macduff's offer of life, albeit as a sideshow freak, instead of certain death on the battlefield, then the whole Scottish play becomes a satire and not a tragedy. If Anna Karenina had finally begged for forgiveness instead of choosing to die under the wheels of a train, then our perception of the whole novel would have changed. It is absurd even to consider discussing a novel or a play without paying attention to its defining moment.

It remains only for me to thank the very many people who have helped me. I thank Naomi Richer, whose idea it was that I begin my own lecture series and who went with my wife, Pearl, to find the right locations in Montreal and Toronto. I thank my dear cousins, Florence and Shirley Brown, for their wonderful contribution, from research and feedback to their devoted practical help at every Montreal review. I thank Joe March of McClelland & Stewart for his enthusiasm and his expert marketing advice as we were setting up the Toronto series. I thank Judy Stoffman of the *Toronto Star* for flying to Montreal to hear me speak, for writing so generously about the review, and for her kindnesses since. I thank Doug Gibson, the president and publisher of McClelland & Stewart, for offering to publish this collection, and I thank my M&S editor, Alex Schultz, for his expertise and gentle guidance.

I must also thank Abe Bogen, Léo Gervais, Sam Gesser, Sari Greenberg, Judy King, Clayre Kogan, Annie and Bernard Michot, Florence Parnell, and Linda Twight, all of whom have helped me in so many ways.

Above all, I thank my beloved wife, Pearl Adams, who had her own distinguished career as a teacher, for turning my life around when I met her, for being my agent and manager and very fine editor, and for being my best friend.

Note: All the page references in the reviews are to the paperback edition indicated under the title.

THE RELATIONSHIP BETWEEN WRITER AND READER

(from a lecture delivered to the Writers' Trust of Canada at its 14th annual Great Literary Dinner Party, Toronto, November 9, 1999)

Reading of course comes to us first. From our earliest moment of consciousness we are obliged to decipher the world around us: we must read signs, signals, faces, danger. We must read so that we can impose order on a confusing world and know how to survive in it. After that stage comes *real* reading, as Alberto Manguel points out in his delightful *A History of Reading*. The child who learns to read is admitted into the communal memory and shares in the communal past.

But why do people write? For most people it is such agony. I am reminded of a joke I heard only two days ago. A writer had died and was awaiting reassignment to some future existence. But before the reassignment he was permitted a tour of heaven and hell. First he went to hell, and hell was full of writers, tearing their hair out in frustration, crippled with writer's block, unable to get a word onto the page. And then he went to heaven, and heaven was full of writers, racked with frustration, tearing their hair out, unable to get a word onto the page.

The dead writer turned to St. Peter and said, "I'm puzzled. Heaven and hell seem identical." And St. Peter replied, "No, no, no; the agony is the same, but in heaven they get published."

What is this innate need to write? Because it is innate – the human animal has demonstrated that, ever since the first Sumerian chipped in stone six thousand years ago and left his observation for others to decipher.

Edward Gibbon gave one answer to the Duke of Gloucester, an eighteenth-century illiterate who demanded to know why, with Gibbon, it was always "scribble, scribble, scribble." Gibbon – I paraphrase his answer – said it was because he enjoyed writing; it permitted him to give shape to chaos, to know what was not known before, and to enter into communion with humanity. But he prefaced all that with the comment, "I write because I must."

I have put the question "Why do you write?" to many authors. Rohinton Mistry told me that if he didn't write he felt incomplete. Last year in Tokyo, Haruki Murakami gave me exactly the same answer.

But the answer really begs the question. Why *must* they write?

Of one thing we can be sure. They write to be read. I don't care what Kafka said to Max Brod. If Kafka had really wanted his work destroyed, he would have destroyed it himself. It seems clear that an anticipated reader is part of the writing process. Jean-Paul Sartre took it even further: "*Le roman, c'est l'entreprise d'un homme seul: lire, c'est participer aux risques de l'entreprise.*" To read is to share the writer's risk. Because, in both writing and reading, there *is* a risk, and I will come to the nature of that risk in a moment.

But first, what is it that the writer wants so desperately to communicate to his or her unknown reader?

There are so many theories. François Mauriac, for example, argued that for the writer writing is an ongoing process of self-discovery, a re-examination of the writer's childhood, embellished, rearranged, enlarged, changed beyond easy recognition, but a re-examination of the author's childhood nonetheless. "For the novelist," Mauriac said, "the door closes at twenty." It's an attractive idea, and one thinks immediately of so many authors – Mordecai Richler, Charles Dickens, Brian Moore, at least in his early work.

Another theory is that proposed by my friend the late Harry Slochower, a New York psychoanalyst and the editor of the literary magazine *Imago*. In his great book *Mythopoesis*, Harry argued that there are only so many stories to tell and that those stories are the myths that inform our whole Western civilization. He made a kind of Jungian argument that we all know these myths, that we are born with them already in our collective memory, and that the retelling of them, and the rereading of them, with whatever particularities they are endowed, are acts of comfort, of reassurance that we are not alone, that we are participants in a great collective ongoing past. Perhaps.

The theory that I personally find most persuasive is that argued by Northrop Frye in his masterpiece *Anatomy of Criticism*. I like it especially because it does not exclude the simultaneous validity of other theories.

Frye suggests first that every narrative contains within itself the author's vision of the individual and his relationship to the universe. Second, Frye suggests that the writer has an innate need, not always consciously felt, to communicate that vision to the world outside.

Frye also argues that there are only four visions available to the writer. He calls them the four mythoi: Romance, Comedy, Tragedy, and Satire.

In the unlikely event that the serious writer sees the universe as benevolent, then the author's vision will be Romantic in the case of a strong protagonist or Comic if the protagonist is fallible and out of step with his world.

Since they are unrealistic visions of existence, Romance and Comedy tend to be the stuff of cinema rather than of literature. Think of *Pretty Woman* and the admirably positive Miss Julia Roberts finding a happy ending because fate and her new client are both ultimately benevolent – the perfect Romance.

For Comedy, think of James Stewart in the Frank Capra movie, bumbling, stumbling, but finally redeemed by heaven itself in the person of Clarence the Angel.

If the author's vision is one of a hostile universe – the only realistic perception – then we have Tragedy or Satire. Tragedy is the rarer vision since few of us are capable of the tragic defiance of Lear or Macbeth.

Thus Satire is left as the commonest vision, the narrative of the weak and imperfect individual making the best of existence in a fallen world. It is the bleakest of Frye's mythoi, and the one that informs most of our fiction.

Why should we readers be so interested in the author's vision? And what are our responsibilities as readers?

My own belief is that the reader has two duties. The first is to discern as clearly as possible the author's vision. Once that vision, usually satiric in Frye's sense of the word, is apprehended, the reader will then challenge both the writer and himself by matching the author's vision to his own. In that juxtaposition lies the tension – the excitement – of reading.

This is what I think Sartre meant by the reader sharing the writer's risk. The writer has already risked the truth of his vision by encapsulating it in the prison of words, words that might betray his intention.

By matching his own vision to that of the author, the reader must now undertake his own risk. In effect, he is negotiating with the author's vision to produce a new, refined vision of his own.

In recent years, I have been reviewing novels alone on a theatre stage. What is rewarding is that, in Montreal and Toronto, I have found a combined audience of nearly three thousand people also willing to take a risk. For an hour and a half, five times a season, they listen as I examine the tension between the author's vision and my own. Then the audience and I enter into a dialogue and there is real excitement as the three visions of existence clash – the writer's vision, my vision, and the vision of each member of the audience.

It doesn't matter that each member of the audience and I may have reacted differently to the novel. What matters is our engagement with it. As Kafka said, "A book must be the axe for the frozen sea within us . . . if the book we are reading doesn't shake us awake like a blow on the skull, why bother reading it in the first place?"

The novel offers the excitement of competing visions, but there are joys available to the reader other than those offered by the novel. The thrill of visiting another place, another time. Recently, I've had the illumination of seeing China through the perceptive eyes of Jan Wong. I have reread *Vimy*, Pierre Berton's wonderful recreation of that incredible, defining, Canadian moment. I confess happily to the sin of pride that it was my own cousin Claude who won the toss to lead the Canadian machine-gunners out of the trenches and over the top.

There is so much reading pleasure available to us: a background so fascinating that it becomes a character in the narrative; the quality of the prose, spare and minimal or lush and evocative; the sudden insight in which we recognize our shared humanity; the felicitous phrase that resonates. I remember, for example, how I could never define exactly, even to myself, the great joy I find in my grandchildren. And then I came across a grandfather in one of the novels of Amos Oz. He said that his grandson was "the delight of his soul." I have used that expression ever since.

Perhaps it is true that authors no longer have the authority they once enjoyed. Perhaps it is true that the power of novels to shape the national conversation has declined. People now speak of seeing *Star Wars* as a formative experience equivalent to my own boyhood memories of reading Dumas, Dickens, and Zola. Perhaps George Lucas and Steven Spielberg have already replaced our great writers as the shapers of our collective dreams. A recent piece in *The Futurist* suggests that books are dying as a form of communication. It points out that verbal and visual transmission is a thousand times faster than the creation and consumption of written text. The prophecy is that, by the year 2070, the only people using text as literature will be an elite and very elderly priesthood.

Well, by the year 2070, I expect that my wife, Pearl, and I may be slowing down a bit, but until that happens I promise the writers in this audience that you will have my full attention and my total devotion to our great, shared enterprise.

THE TORTILLA CURTAIN

T. Coraghessan Boyle
(Toronto: Penguin, 1996)

T. Coraghessan Boyle puts the accent on the second syllable of his unusual middle name, a name all the more unusual because he adopted it in adolescence.

He was born Thomas John Boyle in upper New York State in 1948, which meant that he was an adolescent in the sixties. Those of us who remember the decade will recall that it was a time of great unrest: the Vietnam protest, militancy in the black and women's movements and, perhaps most important of all, the protest of the young against the older generation.

The rebellion of the young was largely a reaction against the complacency and self-satisfaction of their parents, and it was as part of that rebellion that Boyle rejected one of the names his parents gave him and adopted Coraghessan. It was a deliberate attempt to assert his selfhood against his parents, to cry out his own individuality. He said exactly that in a recent interview: "I suppose my name is an affectation of a sort, but what the hell. There are five billion of us on this planet all screaming for attention." I suppose we're lucky, really; we could be reading a novel by T. Starship Boyle, or T. Moonchild Boyle.

T. Coraghessan Boyle's was a working-class Catholic family. He had a very sixties adolescence which, as well as his troubled relationship with his family, included heroin addiction. One can't really blame him for the troubled relationship; his father, a school bus driver, and his mother, a high

7

school administrator, were alcoholics, and both died of the disease before he was thirty. He was also typically sixties in that he became a teacher only in order to escape military service in Vietnam.

But – and it's a big but – he found that he liked teaching. His drug habit overcome, he returned to university to qualify himself more thoroughly for a teaching career. He took a Master's and a Ph.D at the University of Iowa, specializing in Victorian literature, particularly the works of Ruskin and Dickens. However, his actual doctoral dissertation was made up of his own original short stories, published as his first book in 1979. Since then he has never looked back. He has published altogether five collections of short stories and six novels, of which *The Tortilla Curtain* is the most recent.

Boyle, a drug-addict hippie of the sixties, is now a fully tenured professor of English at the University of Southern California with a house in the San Fernando Valley, a wife, three children, and two cars, of which one is a BMW.

The only two remnants of the sixties about his appearance are the gold earring in his left ear and his middle name, Coraghessan.

Strange how life turns out, isn't it?

What about his writing, and how much of it reflects his adolescence?

Only in one short story, "If the River Was Whisky," from a 1989 collection, is there anything autobiographical. In everything else, all his other short stories and the five novels that preceded *The Tortilla Curtain*, T. Coraghessan Boyle wrote what is usually called satire. But it was not satire in its true literary sense, as I understand the term.

What Boyle did in all his work before this was to poke fun at the icons, the sacred cows, of American middle-class culture. He took on the Hemingway myth, the cult of machismo, the American as warrior, and the deification of John Wayne. His writing was funny, full of frenetic energy, and always, always, very, very cruel. Over and over again I have heard him called one of America's greatest comic writers, even one of America's greatest satirists.

With that opinion I have never agreed. What T. Coraghessan Boyle did in all his works until this one was to ridicule, to fix on a target, whether it be artistic pretension or health food nonsense or psychiatric babble, and make fun of it. And to make fun of it, he had to exaggerate it, to make the weaknesses of his target a little larger than life, to blow the balloons up a little bigger so that, when he pricked them, the bang would be a little louder. I always enjoyed his ridicule of our sacred cows. I like seeing the pretentious brought low. But I always felt there was something missing. When a writer ridicules something, he always distorts it, and so, even as we laugh, we know the writer is not describing real life; he is describing an exaggeration of real life, a parody of real life.

Until *The Tortilla Curtain*, I always held that Boyle was not a satirist but a caricaturist, which made him, in my view, no more than a first-class second-rate writer. First class because of his control of language, the sheer energy of his writing, the wonderfully inventive situations he created, the sharpness of his ridicule. I was interested too in a notion that runs through all his work, that humankind is divided into two groups, the hunter and the hunted, the exploiter and the exploited.

But I never felt that what he was writing was satire. True satire is more delicate than ridicule, more difficult, more profound. Satire, in its purest literary sense, has a dimension that was never present in any of T. Coraghessan Boyle's work until now.

In true satire, the writer looks at an imperfect world, a fallen world, the world we live in. The writer fixes on our central character and records all the failures, together with the compromises the protagonist must make in order to survive. There is anger in satire at both the fallen world and the weak protagonist, but it must be informed by pity, even compassion. And a part of that compassion will be for ourselves, for we too live in a fallen state and we too are less than we might be.

It is to this level, the compassion of true satire, that T. Coraghessan Boyle has finally aspired in this, his sixth novel. If he had written it in the manner of his earlier work, then all we would have had was ridicule, ridicule of the Californian yuppie lifestyle. He would have done it well; we would have laughed at the yuppie pretensions of Delaney and Kyra Mossbacher, the rich couple who are two of the four main characters, but that would have been the end of it. We would not have thought more deeply than our own sarcastic laughter; there would have been none of the insights into the human condition that real satire provides, that this novel provides. There would have been no touching of our deeper feelings, no probing of the terrible moral dilemmas that face us all in the real, satiric, fallen world in which we live.

One last word on satire.

A novel or play that contains the satiric vision must include four elements. First, there must be an imperfect world. Second, we must see a weak protagonist compromising with the imperfections of its fallen state. Third, we – and the author – must experience a fellow feeling, a compassion, for the struggling individual. Fourth, and this is essential, there must be a character in the novel who represents the ideal in order that we may see how far the world and the protagonist have fallen below that ideal.

Now we can move to *The Tortilla Curtain*, which I hold to be a pure and exquisite satire, infinitely superior because of its pity and compassion to anything Boyle has previously written. He has said in the past about his work, "I've always written about man as an animal species among other animals, competing for limited resources." In his earlier books all he did was to mock his characters, the greed of those who hunt and the stupidity of those who are hunted. In this novel he demonstrates, for the first time, compassion for his characters, whether they are the exploiters or the exploited. He demonstrates an understanding of the complexity of their motives and the complexity of their actions, and compassion for the failures of their lives. And because of this he touches the profound depths of the human psyche.

The Tortilla Curtain was written in 1995 when T. Coraghessan Boyle was forty-seven. As its basic structure, as befits a student of literature, Boyle used one of the most traditional devices, that of high plot/low plot, a literary device that dates back to Shakespeare and the seventeenth century and even before. Shakespeare used it most effectively in three of his Falstaff plays, *Henry IV* parts I and II and *Henry V*. In each of the three plays there are two parallel plots, one in high society at the king's court, and one in low society at the tavern. Occasionally the two worlds touch, usually in the person of Falstaff, and the two worlds illuminate each other. We also begin to realize how each of the worlds, whether high or low, is driven by much the same emotions: greed, love, hate, and ambition.

So it is with *The Tortilla Curtain*. We are going to explore two worlds: one at the top of the hill, rich, white, and American, and one at the bottom of the hill, poor, Mexican, and illegal immigrant. The hill is not just a metaphor in this novel, it is a physical reality.

The action is set in Topanga Canyon on the California coast, a little south of Los Angeles. Let us begin with the low plot.

At the bottom of the canyon, hidden in the brush and the trees, beside a stream, a man and woman are camping. They are Mexican and they are illegal immigrants. Throughout the novel, through their own memories, we learn their history.

The man is thirty-three years old and his name is Cándido Rincón. He comes from a tiny Mexican village, Tepoztlán, in the province of Morelos. It is a desolate little place and Cándido often thinks about it.

> For three quarters of the year the villages of Morelos became villages of women, all but deserted by the men who had migrated North to earn real money and work eight and ten and twelve hours a day instead of sitting in the *cantina* eternally nursing a beer. (p. 50)

The novel tells us that Mexico has an *official* unemployment rate of 40 percent, with a million new people entering the labour market every year. It has a government and a bureaucracy riddled with corruption ever since the overthrow of President Diaz in 1911 by the Institutional Revolutionary Party, whose one purpose for the last eighty-six years has been to remain in power.

The poor, especially the rural poor like Cándido, have no choice. They can starve or they can travel to *El Norte* to work, slipping across the border to find menial domestic work or to pick fruit. However miserable the conditions, they will earn some money to send home.

And so Cándido has several times come north, illegally, into the United States and worked. During one of his absences his wife, Resurrección, leaves him for a handsome alcoholic. On his return Cándido finds himself cuckolded, humiliated. This is after all Mexico, the world of machismo.

Cándido is a little man and he can't even beat up his wife's lover. He tries, gets beaten up himself, and becomes a drunk on the streets. And then Resurrección's little sister, sixteen years old, comes to him and says she would like to go up north with him as his wife, as his common-law wife. Her name is América. She also dreams of a life in the Golden Land. With aching simplicity the dream is spelled out.

> "I want one of those houses," she said, "A clean white one made out of lumber that smells like the mountains, with a gas range and a refrigerator, and maybe a little yard so you can plant a garden and make a place for the chickens."

A house, a yard, maybe a TV and a car too – nothing fancy, no palaces like the *gringos* built – just four walls and a roof. Was that so much to ask? (pp. 28-29)

And the answer of course is no, it's not much to ask. And so Cándido Rincón brings América with him, first to the border at Tijuana and then across the border, eventually to Topanga Canyon.

Even before they begin that journey, Cándido knows that the risks are far greater for América than for him. The worst that can happen to him is that he will be caught by the U.S. Immigration Control, *La Migra*, and sent back to Mexico. Far worse can happen to América, at sixteen beautiful with her tiny figure and the huge eyes that come with her Aztec Indian heritage. It is a terrible world that Cándido and América must journey through.

Cándido remembers what happened on one of his earlier trips to the north when he was waiting in Tijuana for a chance to cross. There was a twelve-year-old girl and many Mexican men like himself, waiting to cross the border:

The girl's parents had a shack made out of wooden pallets nailed together, a surprisingly sturdy little thing set amid a clutter of tumbledown shanties and crude lean-tos, and when they went off in the morning, they padlocked the girl inside. But those animals – they howled outside the door and pounded at the walls to get at her, and nobody did a thing. Nobody except Cándido. Three times he snatched up a length of pipe and drove them away from the shack – junkies, *cementeros,* bottle suckers – and he could hear the girl sobbing inside. Twelve years old. One afternoon they managed to spring the lock, and by the time Cándido got there, it was all over. The sons of bitches. He knew what they were like, and he vowed he'd never let América out of his sight if he could help it, not till they had a real house in a real neighborhood with laws and respect and human dignity. (p. 27)

The passage shows us Boyle's mastery of simple, powerful, brutal prose to match the stark brutality of the world he describes. There are few adjectives and fewer adverbs. The strength is in the nouns and the verbs and thus in the action. This kind of writing is unbelievably different from the witty, facile sarcasm of his earlier work. In this novel he is not engaging in ridicule, he is looking at a world whose imperfections he has no need to exaggerate. We feel the author's anger, and more important we feel his compassion for the victims of that world.

We note one more thing. T. Coraghessan Boyle does not fall into the liberal trap of vilifying the rich and glorifying the poor. Given his belief that humanity is divided into the hunter and the hunted, it would have been easy to stereotype the poor as good and the rich as bad, but Boyle shows us that within the world of the poor, there are also the hunters and their victims. Suffering in general, says Boyle, does not ennoble, it degrades. Those cast to the bottom of society invariably victimize one another.

And so Cándido, thirty-three, and América, by now seventeen, begin their dangerous journey to the Promised Land. On their second attempt to cross the border at night, they are waylaid by other Mexicans. Cándido is robbed and América is stripped naked. Only the arrival of *La Migra*, of a U.S. border patrol, saves her from gang rape. They are turned back to Mexico, but a third attempt to cross is successful and they end up on the California coast, camping miserably without food or money at the bottom of Topanga Canyon.

Cándido must find food. To do that he has to get to the nearest store, and to do that he must cross the highway.

After he makes his pathetically few purchases, he runs back across the highway with his tortillas and is hit by a car. His cheek is smashed, his left arm is broken, and he is thrown over the side of the canyon. With that accident we meet the other half of the narrative, the high plot.

The car is a freshly waxed Japanese car, an Acura, with personalized licence plates. It is a yuppie car. It is a car driven in a world that Cándido and América do not even dare to dream of.

The driver is Delaney Mossbacher. He lives in Arroyo Blanco Estates at the top of the canyon. We are told later that his parents had left Delaney enough money for him to spend most of his time writing and thinking and experiencing nature. His wife, Kyra, is a real estate agent, utterly devoted to her work and very successful. She brought into their marriage a son, Jordan, who attends a fine private school.

We have a marvellous description by Boyle of the couple at the top of the canyon.

He and Kyra had a lot in common, not only temperamentally, but in
terms of their beliefs and ideals too – that was what had attracted them
to each other in the first place. They were both perfectionists, for one
thing. They abhorred clutter. They were joggers, nonsmokers, social
drinkers, and if not full-blown vegetarians, people who were conscious
of their intake of animal fats. Their memberships included the Sierra
Club, Save the Children, the National Wildlife Federation and the
Democratic Party. They preferred the contemporary look to Early
American or kitsch. In religious matters, they were agnostic. (p. 34)

Here is a perfect portrait of the ultimate modern couple. Equal and politically correct and at the top of the canyon and of the Californian social scale.

The old Coraghessan Boyle would have left it at that. There is in the
description a distinct touch of the ridicule that used to inform his work.
But the new Coraghessan Boyle, the Boyle who wrote this novel, goes
further. While, throughout the novel, he continues to poke fun at the
lifestyle, he adds another dimension to their characters – complexity.
Describing the wife, Kyra Mossbacher, he says,

Her headache was gone now, but it had been replaced by a fatigue
that went deeper than any physical exhaustion, a funk, a malaise she
couldn't seem to shake. . . . It was ridiculous, she knew it. There were
people out there going through Dumpsters for a scrap to eat, people
lined up on the streets begging for work, people who'd lost their
homes, their children, their spouses, people with real problems, real
grief. What was wrong with her? (p. 74)

Kyra suddenly becomes, not a stereotype of American success, but a real
person with all the angst and self-doubt that goes with being human.
Delaney, her husband, is just as real. He's not just a self-indulgent
Californian with enough private means to stay home and write about
nature, he is actually capable of a tremendous awareness of beauty.

It was a Sunday in mid-August, seven in the evening, the sun fixed
in the sky like a Japanese lantern. There was music playing somewhere, a slow moody piano piece moving from one lingering faintly
heard note to the next, and when Delaney looked up from turning

the kebabs he watched a California gnatcatcher – that rare and magical gray-bodied little bird – settle on the topmost wire of the fence. It was one of those special moments when all the mad chittering whirl of things suddenly quits, like a freeze-frame in a film, and Delaney held on to it, savored it, even as the fragrance of ginger faded into the air, the piano faltered and the bird shot away into nothingness. (p. 183)

The tableau is truly marvellous. It reminded me of those moments of tranquillity in Wordsworth's poetry, what the poet called "spots of time," and nowhere does Boyle suggest that Delaney is anything but sincere in his wonder at the loveliness of the world around him.

Delaney also has a social conscience. In the Arroyo Blanco Estates, the wealthy white project at the top of the canyon, there are two ongoing struggles. One is particular to the Delaneys. They have a chainlink fence around their house, in spite of which their beloved dogs keep getting eaten by the coyotes who roam the hills nearby. Heightening the fence doesn't seem to keep the coyotes out. Delaney is torn between his admiration of the coyotes' ability to survive and the havoc they are wreaking on his household.

The second conflict is general to the community. The value of the project would be enhanced if a wall were built around the property with a guard at an entry gate. The object is to keep out undesirables. And undesirables means Mexicans. There are frequent community meetings on the topic. Delaney Mossbacher makes the liberal argument: "'Immigrants are the lifeblood of this country – we're a nation of immigrants – and neither of us would be standing here today if it wasn't.'" (p. 101) Further, Delaney

wanted to tell Jack that he was wrong, that everyone deserved a chance in life and that the Mexicans would assimilate just like the Poles, Italians, Germans, Irish and Chinese and that besides which we'd stolen California from them in the first place. (p. 102)

Jack Jardine, Delaney's lawyer, offers a reasoned argument against unlimited immigration. It is an argument repeated throughout the novel, elaborated, developed, but fundamentally this:

"The ones coming in through the Tortilla Curtain down there, those are the ones that are killing us. They're peasants, my friend. No education, no resources, no skills – all they've got to offer is a strong back, and the irony is we need fewer and fewer strong backs every day because we've got robotics and computers and farm machinery that can do the labor of a hundred men at a fraction of the cost." (p. 101)

Other neighbours offer arguments that are less reasoned and more clearly racist: " 'The more you give them, the more they want.' " " 'I resent having to wade through them all every time I go to the Post Office.' " (p. 192)

The children of the wealthy whites are often even more racist than their parents. The son of the lawyer Jack Jardine, Jack Junior, is a particularly poisonous example. Delaney Mossbacher overhears him making obscene references to Mexican girls and reflects that the wall that would keep the Mexicans out would keep the racist white youth in. We, the readers, feel the bigotry of the wealthy white youth even more keenly because we know it is they who write Spanish-language graffiti on walls to promote anti-Mexican feeling; it is they who destroy the poor little camp of Cándido and América at the bottom of the canyon.

And so we have the high plot/low plot, the two little worlds, one rich and white at the top of the canyon, where Delaney Mossbacher fights a losing battle with his neighbours for tolerance, and the Mexican world at the bottom of the canyon, where Cándido and América are preyed upon by other Mexicans, notably two dangerous men who are also camping out and who rob and rape América.

Boyle contrasts the two worlds so delicately. Consider evening meals. Sometimes for the Mossbachers, dinner is at home. On one such evening, "Smoke rose from the barbecue in fragrant ginger-smelling tufts as Delaney basted the tofu kebabs with his special honey-ginger marinade." (p. 183)

"Tofu kebabs" – that says it all, doesn't it?

Sometimes, at the end of the evening, Kyra is waiting in bed for Delaney, particularly if something went wrong during the day – a coyote took another of her dogs for example, or a favourite house failed to sell. On page 65, Kyra is in bed, waiting and eager: "There was something about the little tragedies of life, the opening of the floodgates of emotion, that seemed to unleash her libido. For Kyra, sex was therapeutic, a release from sorrow, tension, worry, and she plunged into it."

Then, in contrast to all their elegance and tension and sexual sophistication, we have the situation at the bottom of the canyon with Cándido and América. It's one of the days when they've earned enough money to buy food:

> They sat side by side in the sand, warmed by the fire, and shared the tin of sardines and ate half the loaf of store bread, North American bread baked in a factory and puffed up light as air. She held the last sardine out for him and he put his hands on her breasts and let her feed it into his mouth, the fire snapping, the night wrapped round them like a blanket, all his senses on alert. He took the sardine between his lips, between his teeth, and he licked the golden oil from her fingers. (pp. 126-27)

Not since the eighteenth-century novel *Tom Jones* have I read such a perfect marriage of food and sex. How different in its fullness and naturalness from the elegant stress in the white American world a few hundred yards above. Delaney, liberal pro-immigrant as he is, has only been aware of Mexicans in theory, in the abstract, in general. He has enough self-knowledge to see that, and to admit that

> he'd never really thought about it before, but they were everywhere, these men, ubiquitous, silently going about their business, whether it be mopping up the floors at McDonald's, inverting trash cans in the alley out back of Emilio's or moving purposively behind the rakes and blowers that combed the pristine lawns of Arroyo Blanco Estates twice a week. Where had they all come from? (p. 12)

He even tries to imagine the life of a Mexican:

> [T]he cramped room, the bag of second-rate oranges on the street-corner, the spade and the hoe and the cold mashed beans dug out of the forty-nine-cent can. Unrefrigerated *tortillas*. Orange soda. That oom-pah music with the accordions and the tinny harmonies. (p. 10)

But the world is too far from his own for him to picture it with any accuracy.

Then comes the fateful accident when his car hits Cándido on the highway.

Delaney gets out of the car and finds the crumpled body thrown over the edge of the canyon. Suddenly, for Delaney Mossbacher, Mexicans have an individual face. He sees "the frail scrambling hunched-over form of a dark little man with a wild look in his eye . . . red-flecked eyes, the rictus of the mouth, the rotten teeth and incongruous shock of gray in the heavy black brush of the mustache." (p. 3)

What is Delaney's reaction when, for the first time, he comes into intimate contact with one member of the great Mexican masses? "To his shame, Delaney's first thought was for the car . . . and then for his insurance rates . . . and finally . . . for the victim." (p. 4)

Cándido comes to, and Delaney asks, "'Can I help you?'" and twenty dollars change hands. Cándido limps away, badly injured, and Delaney drives off.

When Delaney takes his car to the dealership to get it fixed, Kenny Grissom asks him, "'So what'd you hit – a deer? Coyote?'" (p. 13)

When Delaney phones his wife to tell her what has happened, she panics and suggests he call their lawyer. Delaney replies, "'I gave him twenty bucks . . . I told you – he was *Mexican*.'" (p. 15)

But the incident isn't over for Delaney. He thinks of Cándido constantly; sometimes he sees him in the supermarket parking lot by the post office, waiting with other Mexicans at the unofficial labour market at the side of the highway. His own guilt transforms itself into a hatred of the man who makes him feel unworthy. He begins to argue less vehemently against bigots and racists, and accepts the building of a wall with a guarded gate around the project. He begins to blame Mexicans in general and Cándido in particular for all of California's ills, from the crime rate to litter to graffiti. Mexicans begin to frighten him, and by the time he meets the same two Mexicans who so menace Cándido and América his reaction is knee-jerk redneck.

All he could think of was the sheriff and getting these people and their garbage heap out of here, of hustling them right back to wherever they'd come from, slums, *favelas*, *barrios*, whatever they called them. They didn't belong here, that was for sure. (pp. 116-17)

The Mexicans, including this particular Mexican, become the scapegoat for all of Delaney's white fears. The last straw is when his car is stolen and his lawyer friend Jardine says to him, " 'What do you expect . . . when all you bleeding hearts want to invite the whole world in here . . .?' " (p. 146)

Never mind that Delaney's intellect tells him it is far more likely that white people stole the car, he doesn't even argue with the lawyer.

There is another fascinating process going on in Delaney's mind. He is a nature-lover with a particular admiration for the coyote. He writes about nature and he writes about the coyote: *"The coyotes keep coming, breeding to fill in the gaps, moving in where the living is easy. They are cunning, versatile, hungry and unstoppable."* (p. 215)

Gradually, he comes to have the same view of Mexicans and the twin threats to his well-being begin to blur and eventually become indistinguishable in his mind.

Strangely, Delaney has a remarkable degree of self-knowledge in spite of his fixation on Cándido not as his victim but as his oppressor. In the final discussion with Kyra on the wall about to be built around the estate, he says, " 'This isn't about coyotes, don't kid yourself. It's about Mexicans, it's about blacks. It's about exclusion, division, hate.' " (p. 220)

While the affluent WASP couple live their fearful, selfish, but not unthoughtful existence behind the wall of the Arroyo Blanco Estates, things go very badly for Cándido and América at the bottom of the canyon.

After being hit by the car, Cándido is too sick for days to walk up the canyon. He cannot work. The same nature that inspires such beautiful thoughts in Delaney Mossbacher evokes a very different response in Cándido. Boyle puts it in a superb paragraph:

> He looked round the little clearing by the stream, and the leaves, the rocks, the spill of the slope above him and even the sun in the sky seemed unchanging, eternal, as dead as a photograph. For all its beauty, the place was a jail cell and he was a prisoner, incarcerated in his thoughts. (p. 49)

Now it must be América and not he who will struggle up the hill to the unofficial Mexican labour exchange at the post office. It is América who will walk eight miles to take a bus to a non-existent job. It is América who will earn a few pitiful dollars for cleaning little statues, ironically

of Buddha, with a cleaning material so corrosive that it strips the flesh
from her fingers because the white boss forgot to give her gloves. It is
América who will be robbed of those few pitiful dollars by Mexicans as
poor as she is, but not as good, and it is América, five months pregnant
by Cándido, who is raped by those same robbers. As I read about América
and as I winced at each of the hurts inflicted upon her, at the same time I
felt an overwhelming admiration for the incredible courage of this seventeen-year-old girl, homeless, hungry, living by a stream in one torn
dress with a common-law husband twice her age and badly hurt, going
off to a place she does not know to try to get work in a language she does
not speak. I marvelled at her strength.

And I was touched when she modified her little American dream. She
had hoped for a house and a yard. Now she would settle for "a single room
with a hot shower and a toilet, some trees on the street and a market, some-
place she could buy a dress, some lipstick, a brush for her hair." (p. 127)
It's such a little dream; it's not so much to hope for.

At one point, Cándido looks down at her and sees that

> she was seventeen years old and as perfect and beautiful as an egg in
> its shell; she was América, hope of the future, his wife, his love,
> mother-to-be of his first child, the son who was even now taking
> shape in that secret place inside of her. (p. 24)

As I read that I focused on the phrase "América, hope of the future." I
thought about the promise of the Statue of Liberty, "Give me your tired,
your poor, your huddled masses yearning to breathe free," and I thought
how good it would be if this little América with her willingness to work
and her love and her decency and her strength were in truth the picture of
America's future.

In contrast to the resilience of his tiny wife, Cándido is in physical
misery. Already humiliated by the desertion of his first wife and by what
América has had to undergo, he must now lie sick while his wife labours.

This is not the easy, fashionable, politically correct gender equality of
Delaney Mossbacher who stays at home to work. This Mexican, Cándido
Rincón, is a man whose whole value system, whose whole dignity, whole
selfhood, is based upon his role as provider and protector. Now he can

neither provide nor protect and his agony is total and we share that pain, however foolish we may find his machismo.

But there is growth in Cándido, wonderful growth. In spite of his initial resentment as he looks at América, in spite of his initial violence towards her, born out of his own frustration and self-hatred, more and more he sees not only her beauty but her strength. He loves her so much that even the loss of his traditional male role will not essentially diminish that love. He bursts into rage at his own impotence, his own helplessness, but the love is dominant and the love grows into something like respect.

I watched fascinated as Cándido's macho attitude changed. But then comes one blow after the other, each blow more terrible than the last. Cándido, recovered and working, is robbed of his savings by other Mexicans. Both he and América are cheated by various of their employers. The labour exchange is closed. América is increasingly homesick. Her baby will come soon and she yearns to show it to her mother.

Cándido also becomes aware as their paths cross that the American who hurt him with the car hates him.

Even an apparent stroke of good luck turns into disaster. Trying to cook a turkey at Thanksgiving, given to him by two "good old boys" who'd got it free at a supermarket giveaway, Cándido causes a canyon fire that threatens the Arroyo Blanco Estates and burns what little savings he and América had buried.

Then, even worse, their baby, a little girl, Socorro, is born blind. She was born on American soil, but the advantages that Cándido and América dreamed of for their American child will not come easily to her.

After the fire, Cándido is reduced to begging, to stealing from garden sheds to make a lean-to for his wife and child, and to luring away the neighbourhood cats to make a stew. But even worse is to come. While Delaney is driving down the highway he sees Cándido and slows to a halt – incidentally causing an accident. All Delaney's agonies come together in his mind – the coyotes taking his two beloved dogs, the two Mexicans in the area who so frighten his wife, the theft of his car, the disappearance of his cat, the graffiti, the fire that nearly destroyed his house, the accident he's now involved in – and he sees the little Mexican as the author of all evil. He rushes home to get a revolver to track the Mexican down.

By chance, the hidden video camera he's set up to trap the graffiti artist chooses that moment to reveal the real culprit, the vicious, racist son of Delaney's lawyer friend Jack Jardine. But by now blind bigotry has taken over; reason has fled. Forget the graffiti, "the Mexican was guilty of so much more than this." Thus the hunt begins, and Delaney tracks Cándido down to the little shack with América and little blind Socorro.

We see how delicately the writer has blurred the distinction in Delaney's mind between the coyote and the Mexican. Initially both admired for their resilience, they have become intertwined predators who menace his fragile security.

We have seen the even-handedness with which Boyle treats the problem of illegal immigration. The arguments are presented, I think, fairly and we, the readers, are left in a moral dilemma. We are commanded by our various religious faiths to welcome and nurture the stranger – the Parable of the Good Samaritan comes to mind, as do the words of the Passover Seder, that we must welcome and comfort the stranger for we too were strangers in the land of Egypt. Yet is our hospitality to reach the point where our society will be overwhelmed? Wisely, T. Coraghessan Boyle presents the problem but goes no further. As Thornton Wilder once told me, it is the business of literature to ask questions, not to give answers. The question Boyle poses is troubling to me, and it is one that I have not yet resolved.

I admired the novel for the force of its language, for the brutality of some moments and the tenderness of others, and the perfect match of language with each.

I admired the restraint, the realism, the absence of stereotyping: there are good Americans and there are evil Mexicans.

I admired the detailed picture of the stresses and ultimate emptiness of the life of the rich and the miseries and ultimate hopelessness of the life of the poor.

I admired the courage of Cándido and América, who can pick themselves up and continue after each separate and distinct terrible blow.

And I admired the brilliance of the climax of the novel.

As an armed Delaney threatens Cándido and his wife and child at the bottom of the canyon, they face a flood and a mudslide, brought on by the recent heavy rains. Always a physical possibility in California, this particular mudslide is also a metaphor for the fragility of a society based on privilege for the few and hardship for the many.

All of them, Delaney, Cándido, América, and the baby, are swept away in the flood. For Cándido, it seems the last straw.

> What was it about him? All he wanted was work, and this was his fate, this was his stinking *pinche* luck, a violated wife and a blind baby and a crazy white man with a gun, and even that wasn't enough to satisfy an insatiable God: no, they all had to drown like rats in the bargain. (p. 353)

But they don't all drown. América catches hold of the post office roof and draws Cándido up after her. But the baby is gone and, apparently, Delaney.

The novel, the satire, seems to have come full circle. América and Cándido are where they started, wretched, poor, homeless, and alone.

And then we have the very last paragraph. With reference to Cándido:

> The dark water was all around him, water as far as he could see, and he wondered if he would ever get warm again. He was beyond cursing, beyond grieving, numbed right through to the core of him. All that, yes. But when he saw the white face surge up out of the black swirl of the current and the white hand grasping at the tiles, he reached down and took hold of it. (p. 355)

Cándido sees a white face and he grasps a white hand and Delaney Mossbacher is saved. With instinctive goodness, he has reached out to save the person who has been the author of his pain, who represents the white majority who refuse to share their bounty.

It is this single, shining, beautiful action that makes clear how imperfect the world we have examined has been, how fallen, how much less than it could be.

Now, in this last paragraph, we have the fourth essential element of the satire, the yardstick of goodness against which the imperfect world and its imperfect people may be measured.

In this superbly constructed novel, Boyle has achieved maturity as a writer. He has looked upon his world, described it movingly and accurately without exaggeration, informed it with his compassion and understanding, and left us with powerful images, the dilemma of immigration to think about, and an ideal to reflect upon.

Some readers, I know, found the novel painful, but think how beautiful it is to put down the book and dream of a world where that last shining action might become the norm.

Think, too, how beautiful it is to see a writer move from the easy laughter of ridicule to the profound, compassionate, moving vision of true satire. How beautiful it is to see a writer move from competence into greatness.

A PRIVATE VIEW

Anita Brookner
(Toronto: Vintage, 1996)

I would like to begin my analysis of Anita Brookner's novel *A Private View* by going back in time more than three hundred years. We must go back to the year 1667, when the great blind English poet John Milton sat in his study and finished dictating to his daughters the thousands of lines of poetry he had composed in his mind. The incredible epic was his vision of the beginning of the world, from the fall of Satan out of the heavens to the expulsion of Adam and Eve from the Garden of Eden. John Milton, perhaps the greatest intellect the world has ever seen, the last man to know everything, was a Puritan, intensely religious, and it was his intention in his great work, *Paradise Lost*, "to justify the ways of God."

But after he had finished *Paradise Lost*, and after it had been printed and circulated, he realized that he had done a terrible thing: he had created a narrative of which Satan was the hero.

Milton knew as he reread his epic in his mind's eye that the reader would not see the glory of God or the weakness of mankind as its main thrust. The audience would be lost in admiration for the energy of Satan, the fallen angel. It was not God's eternal goodness that would hold the reader, it was Satan, who could declare in Hell, "'Here at least we shall be free . . . / Better to reign in Hell than serve in Heaven.'"

So the central character of *Paradise Lost*, whatever Milton's first intention, is Satan, once God's first lieutenant, still defiant after his fall from Grace:

"What though the field be lost?
All is not lost. The unconquerable will
And study of revenge, immortal hate,
And courage never to submit or yield."

What grips us now, as it gripped Milton's readers three hundred years ago, is the excitement of energy, the excitement of freedom outside goodness, the excitement of action. Goodness is bland; action, even evil action, is exciting.

One hundred and fifteen years after Milton, at the beginning of the nineteenth century, the English Romantic poets took up the same theme – the glorification of action, the excitement of energy. And they, unlike Milton, did not feel bound by Christian teaching of the virtue of goodness. Perhaps the greatest of all the English Romantic poets, the visionary William Blake, put it most clearly: "The road of excess leads to the palace of wisdom." If you do not act, if you do not act to excess, then how will you know what you are capable of? If you do not use your energy to its limits, how will you know what you can do and who you are?

Blake said again: "He who desires but acts not, breeds pestilence," and "No bird soars too high, if he soars with his own wings." And, "You never know what is enough until you know what is more than enough."

But Blake knew how we fear to act, to live, to go to our extremes: "The weak in courage is strong in cunning." He knew how easily we rationalize not acting, taking the safe way; that we can always find reasons to act carefully, moderately, prudently. When we contain our passions, our freedom, our energy, it is usually not out of a sense of goodness, but rather fear of where our energy might take us.

We leave the Romantic poets and their glorification of action, of energy, even of Satanic energy, and we move another hundred years forward. The year is now 1915. The poet T.S. Eliot has just written the poem "The Love Song of J. Alfred Prufrock." Seven years later he will publish his second great poem, "The Wasteland."

Since the first, "The Love Song of J. Alfred Prufrock," is my favourite twentieth-century poem, indulge me for a moment or two while I talk about it. For those who have read A Private View, the connection between that novel and Eliot's poem and my previous remarks on Milton and Blake will become very clear.

Eliot's poem begins with a fashionably dressed man in his sixties standing alone in a corner at a cocktail party. Hypnotized by the repetitive, meaningless cocktail chatter, he allows his mind to begin an inward journey. For ten or twenty minutes, he makes a journey into his own soul. He sees himself for what he is, a neat, fastidious, careful man who has lived his whole sixty-odd years without ever taking a single risk, without ever once running at life and ripping it off in large chunks. Never once has he felt free, never once has he let his ego, his selfishness, rip. As he says, he has often longed "to murder and to create," in other words to act, to explore the road of excess without thought of consequence, to face the universe and ask the overwhelming questions, *Who am I?* and *What am I capable of?*

In these few minutes of the internal journey, he faces the truth about his life in that most terrible of all lines of modern poetry: "I have measured out my life in coffee spoons."

At the same moment in his reverie, he realizes that he will never call up his energy and roll the universe into a ball. He will continue to live a carefully controlled life, measured out in discreet and careful quantities. He will never act out his desires, never follow Blake's road of excess, never feel the heroic energy of the fallen angel. We end the poem with the most profound pity for J. Alfred Prufrock. In the last lines, he says, "I grow old . . . I grow old," and of the mermaids he has glimpsed far off, he says, "I have heard the mermaids singing, each to each. / I do not think that they will sing to me."

And so we leave J. Alfred Prufrock in his corner at the cocktail party, safe, neat, precise, careful, and desperately sad.

Now we come to the year 1994 and Anita Brookner and her novel *A Private View*. Brookner is a supremely well-educated person. She must know Milton and Blake and Eliot. I am convinced that whenever she writes, and she has written fifteen novels of which *A Private View* is the fourteenth, she has "The Love Song of J. Alfred Prufrock" at the back of her mind. She went to university in England, as I did, in the 1950s. At a British university, there is no way she could not have undertaken a close analysis of Eliot's poem. I am convinced that it has remained with her always as part of her being, her psyche, as it has remained with me.

That comment made, let us now move to a consideration of her chief character in the novel, the protagonist George Bland.

George Bland is sixty-four years old when we meet him. He is the recently retired Head of Personnel at a medium-sized paper and box company. The time is now, and he lives in his own excellent apartment, what we call a mansion flat, in a pleasant part of West End London, not too far from Marble Arch.

He is fastidious, has exquisite taste, is unmarried and, when we meet him on the very first pages, he is in France on an unexpected holiday in Nice. He has just retired. George Bland had not planned to take this holiday, but his greatest friend, Michael Putnam, has just died of cancer. The two of them, both bachelors, had worked for the same company, George Bland in Personnel and Michael Putnam as an accountant. What the two men had planned for their retirement was to take a trip together, to go and explore the Far East by the slowest means possible. Neither had a family and each had made the other his beneficiary in case of death. George, even more comfortably off than before because of Michael's unexpected demise, has gone to Nice for the first time to find a little comfort in the sunshine.

The two men had developed a lifelong friendship based on a very odd foundation. Each of them was afraid of life and each of them remembered childhood poverty in a dysfunctional family.

We are told that they shared a secret. From "shabby beginnings," each had made "a slow upward rise to middle-class affluence." (p. 5)

As he spends his four days in Nice, George Bland reflects on his life and we learn the details.

He was born in Reading, an exceptionally undistinguished small city about an hour to the west of London. His father was a sports journalist and his mother a nurse. Because of his father's addiction to drink and gambling, the family lived in ever poorer circumstances. George's whole memory of childhood was of his parents' squabbling and his mother either reading – the house was full of books – or fighting with her sister. When he was twenty and his father dropped dead, he had to leave Reading University after only one year to live at home to care for his mother until she died. While caring for his mother, he found a job as a clerk in a cardboard-box factory.

After his mother died, the family house was sold and George transferred from Reading to London, still with the same company, to which he would give forty-four years of service. It was there that he met Michael Putnam.

George has spent his entire forty-four-year career slowly building a middle-class life. Like his friend, he lives in fear of falling back into the poverty and misery of his childhood. Both are intent on constructing a safe middle-class oasis, a secure fortress to protect themselves from the harshness of the world each had seen in childhood.

Every Monday for forty-odd years, George Bland and his friend would have lunch together and discuss two topics, the trip to the Far East when they retired and their success in building a solid, solitary, financially safe life with a celebration of middle-class values. How does the novel put it? For both of them, "from an initial bedrock of misgiving and suspicion had flowered charity and judicious benevolence and hard-won fair-mindedness." (p. 5) Each sees himself as a good man, giving carefully measured sums of money to good causes, living carefully measured lives. Neither of them ever wants excitement; excitement would endanger their careful routine. George Bland remembers his friend saying to him, "I wouldn't give a thank you for a fatal passion. A fatal passion can turn nasty, you know." (p. 223)

Each of the two men kept the world at bay, or at least kept at bay extremes of feeling. Michael Putnam built his protection by being the office Romeo, by having discreet little affairs with many of the staff. By having myriad little affairs, he kept himself safe from any one passion that might blaze up and cause him to lose control. And so Michael Putnam kept himself safe and isolated and calm and controlled: "[I]n spite of these random friendships, in spite of the women who entered his flat, for however brief a period, he remained prudent, oddly chaste, trans-parently honest." (p. 193)

George Bland has protected himself from excess in a different way. He had had a childhood sweetheart in Reading, Louise, to whom he was engaged for twenty years. They made love sedately and regularly, but not excessively, and George was surprised when she suddenly married an older man, a retired doctor, for financial security. She continued, however, to sleep occasionally with George. As she said, reasonably I thought, " 'I knew you before I met Dennis,' " and now the doctor, her husband, has died and she and George are firm friends. They speak on the phone every Sunday and Louise occasionally visits when she comes up to London from the country. George feels safe with Louise. She does not intrude upon his inner self. She demands no action. She leaves "his inner life undisturbed."

(p. 94) When we meet George, on holiday in Nice, he reflects on why he never married Louise: "She was, he knew, very slightly boring; perhaps that was why he had never married her." (p. 15)

Her lack of passion notwithstanding, Louise, plus George's brief encounters on his annual holiday, has satisfied all his sexual needs for the last forty-four years.

He can also look back on his good deeds. He was exceptionally kind to his employer's private secretary after her breakdown, and to his employer himself after his stroke. Indeed, those acts of kindness were in part responsible for his promotion. He is healthy and reasonably wealthy after his inheritance from his friend. He is wildly afraid of approaching old age and its possible humiliations, but he has a store of sleeping pills just in case incapacity should make life too difficult to bear. Thus he has made every possible arrangement for his future well-being. Like his friend Michael Putnam, he has no belief in an existence after death, no comfort in the idea of a better life beyond. "He had come to terms with the fact that there was no consolation. He was an unbeliever." (p. 27) The hypocritical behaviour of some of his employer's religious relatives when he was a young man had convinced him that "the comforts of religion . . . sounded more like torments." (p. 27)

Only one memory disturbs his tranquillity. After the death of his father, when he first took on the care of his mother, he had "longed for her to die and had suffered ever since, had done penance for this longing." (p. 42)

A part of that penance had been his good deeds, the care he gave to his employer's private secretary and to his ailing employer himself. It is only now that he is retired, without his like-minded friend, that the memory rises up. His days are long, unfillable, and as he reflects on his life, he realizes that his whole life "had been based on flight . . . flight from an uncomfortable childhood, an unfairly victimised adolescence, an atmosphere of tension and contention, his father drinking too much, his mother ever handy with reproaches." (p. 15) His whole life has been an attempt to create an opposite, safer world. And in that creation of safety, he realizes that there is "the sadness of loss . . . for his whole past life, for his refusal of adventure, excitement, commitment." (p. 18)

Now that he no longer has his work, the comforting centre of his life, he panics. He cuts short his holiday in Nice and rushes back to his apartment. It's a lovely apartment and we are told how he sees it: "When he was away from it he thought of it longingly, as the place which would always provide him with a refuge from the world. When he was actually inside it, safe and warm and quiet . . . it exasperated him . . . [for] those same qualities." (p. 21)

We are told how he had carefully moved up through the years from a small flat to a larger one and then finally to this gem, kept immaculate by his cleaning lady, Mrs. Cardozo.

We are given the details of his routine, his walks through West End streets, his visits to the Royal Academy exhibitions in Piccadilly, his purchases at the Food Hall at Selfridge's, his browsing at the London Library, his whole life lived in carefully controlled segments, all taking place in upper-middle-class London, in those ever so precise, ever so fastidious, ever so genteel surroundings that the British critics call Brooknerland. It's where the women are always in twin sets and pearls and the men wear handmade shoes and ties in quiet good taste. Brooknerland had been enough for George Bland until now, but there have been changes. He now must contend, not just with a memory of an unkind feeling towards his mother, but with a great expanse of time that his work used to fill and with what Brookner calls the "gusts of longing that frequently swept over him." (p. 111) The longing is not for sex; he had always had enough of that from Louise and his casual affairs. Rather it is for something undefined. There is something missing, some excitement, something dangerous.

He has friends, not intimate friends, but friends. He is invited to parties, even to spend Christmas; he gives parties; he chats to the concierge at his apartment block. He has human contact. And still he has these "gusts of longing." Longing for what?

He is not without self-knowledge. Early we are told that he thought of himself "quite accurately, as an honest but fairly colourless man, not lacking in courage but disinclined to take risks." (p. 22)

On his walks through London streets, he once passes a group of boisterous children coming out of school. "How strong they were! They looked mythical in their confidence, a future race of giants." (p. 139) George Bland becomes convinced that there is something other people have which is denied him, something missing in his exquisitely ordered life. His taste is perfect – he can appreciate a first edition of Hans Christian Andersen with its delicate Arthur Rackham illustrations. But it is not enough. Those noisy, vulgar children have something that he doesn't – even Louise's dreadfully coarse and vulgar grandson Stuart has something he does not have. He feels alienated, unconnected to life. He occasionally wonders "whether he were dead already." (p. 113)

Brookner conveys all this marvellously. Lights are always subdued, there are no bright colours; everything – furnishings, carpets, everything – is in shades of grey. On one of his walks through London, we have the following superb psychological landscape:

> [T]hese closed silent little houses, facing each other imperviously across wide blank streets, thrilled him with a mystery of real strangeness. They were the stuff of his Sundays. In the fading light of a suburban afternoon they had often seemed to him to be deserted, uninhabited, so still were they, so undisturbed by any sign of life. He had been born in such a house, but in another town, where afternoons seemed to stretch into infinity, and where only a rare passer-by had hinted at a human presence. He had never been back, but occasionally his own comfortable metropolitan life seemed to him an aberration, as if he were still a stranger, a newcomer. (p. 133)

Brookner has created a person who moves through life but who is absolutely unconnected to it in any way that gives meaning.

I was reminded again of J. Alfred Prufrock, who also wandered through half-deserted streets, the half-deserted streets of his own mind.

When George Bland says that he has learned the trick at parties of going into a light, contemplative sleep while still able to respond automatically to any superficial questions, I thought of Prufrock at his cocktail party, able to make a journey into his own soul while not missing a beat of the meaningless cocktail party chatter.

When George Bland says he feels an "oceanic desire for validation," for meaning in his life, I am reminded of Eliot's Prufrock and the lines "Should I, after tea and cakes and ices / Have the strength to face the moment to its crisis?"

Anita Brookner's George Bland and T.S. Eliot's Prufrock, men of exquisite taste and ordered lives, both know they have missed the boat. The boat may be nearby – there may still be room in the boat of authentic living – but they don't know how to get into it.

And then, in *A Private View*, there is a development.

George has a surprise phone call from Mrs. Lydiard, one of his neighbours from the floor upstairs. Mrs. Lydiard is divorced with grown-up children, confident, independent, slightly glamorous. She has made her own safe, independent world, as George Bland has, and "he had applauded her . . . for so spectacularly not needing his help." (p. 38)

Mrs. Lydiard tells George there is a young woman waiting outside the flat of the Dunlops, a couple away in the United States on holiday. She knows that George has the spare key.

And so George meets Katy Gibb. He gives her the Dunlops' key after she tells him that Mrs. Dunlop is a close friend. (This he discovers later to be a lie.) He invites the two women, Katy Gibb and Mrs. Lydiard, out for dinner, where Katy Gibb reveals herself as an English girl totally taken with Californian culture. She claims to have spent time at a California stress workshop and wants to spread the gospel of nature healing, essential oils and aromatherapy. All she needs is the money to start the project. She has all the jargon of Californian nonsense. After she meets Mrs. Lydiard and, later, Louise, she says, " 'I was getting a lot of negativity back there. I could feel my stress levels going up.' " (p. 101) Once she's outfitted herself in Mrs. Dunlop's clothes, she says, " 'I'm feeling very good about myself . . . I'm in the moment.' " When Katy talks about getting in touch with one's feelings, George tries to follow her: " 'And I suppose the first step is to get in touch with the child inside you?' " Katy replies, " 'Within. We say within.' " (p. 55)

For a while, I thought Anita Brookner was doing a Henry James, bringing together the European sophisticate George Bland and the American naïf, represented here by Katy Gibb. There is certainly some of that. George Bland, never fooled for an instant by Katy's hard sell of Californian truths, can be very perceptive. Katy has been explaining the mutual reinforcement in the stress workshop she attended in California under the guru Howard Singer. George reflects,

[I]f all Howard Singer's acolytes spent their time telling each other how great they were then no information of any importance was ever likely to be exchanged. This seemed to him an excellent idea for keeping people happy on a fee-paying basis, providing that those people were rather stupid or lonely. (pp. 115-16)

Again, when Katy Gibb tells him about the advantage of supervised exercise combined with essential oils and stress reduction, claiming that she knew six or seven people with a personal trainer, George answers, "'You mean they pay good money to be exercised when they could just as easily go for a brisk walk on their own?'" Katy is shocked: "'I'm afraid you just don't understand the modern ethos.'" (p. 151)

Well, like George Bland, I don't understand the modern ethos either, and I must say I enjoyed those Henry James-like passages.

Katy deceives no one. As George notices later, "Mrs. Lydiard had soon seen sense and vanished from the scene." Certainly George feels sorry for the girl, "so gamely repeating her mantras in an uncaring world." (p. 123)

He sees her, as he always sees everything, including himself, with perfect accuracy. He is not even slightly physically attracted to her. He notes dryly, coldly, objectively, that she has a little roll of flesh on her stomach that would give her trouble later on. He describes her as "infinitely disadvantaged . . . there was not the slightest danger that her efforts would succeed." (p. 137) He is careful to tell her that "what money I have is all tied up." (p. 151) He has no doubt that she has earmarked him for future use in her "flimsy enterprise."

He notes her greed when he takes her and Mrs. Lydiard for that first meal; she orders snails and prawns and champagne. He notes her verbal digs at both Mrs. Lydiard and Louise – both of whom react – and understands that "she brought everyone to the brink of bad behaviour, simply by dint of behaving rather badly herself." (p. 57)

But, all this notwithstanding, he is drawn to her. As he puts it clearly, he "had been stimulated by the sight of the girl's appetites." (p. 61)

He knows the careful life he has constructed is in danger. "He had better steer clear of the edge . . . avoid the occasion of sin . . . barricade himself if necessary behind the walls of his accustomed habits and routines." (pp. 65-66)

George is not immediately sure of exactly what danger Katy represents, and he has no idea, initially, of how great the danger is. As she rearranges the furniture in his flat, he tells himself that he "could restore order once she had gone." He still feels in control.

It is not until two-thirds of the novel has passed that what Katy Gibb might represent becomes clear to him.

He dreams of throttling her, of using his whole energy to destroy her. And when he concentrates his attention on the meaning of that vision, he experiences a revelation that is overwhelming.

> [I]n visiting some kind of violence on her . . . he might experience a powerful erotic satisfaction . . . a hostility, the factor that had always been missing in his too correct, too considerate lovemaking. . . . The knowledge hit him like a stone hurled by an unseen assailant. (pp. 120-21)

It is a moment of truth, an epiphany. For a brief moment, "he was afforded a glimpse into the heart of hedonism, something ancient, pagan, selfish. . . . To live like that would be to know true freedom." (p. 121)

George feels as if he has emerged from a long sleep. He sees now what has attracted him to Katy Gibb. She is purely selfish, utterly indifferent to the needs of others, greedy, totally outside goodness; even more important, completely outside middle-class conventions and morality.

He sees his last chance of knowing freedom – freedom, not happiness. He looks at himself, his old self, for what may be the last time. "He had been a man in the prime of life, and he had subjected that manhood to an anaesthetic of routine and small indulgences." (p. 158)

He makes Katy Gibb an incredible offer: "'How would you like to spend Christmas in Rome?'" (p. 154) He even contemplates marriage to her. She permits him no illusion, saying, "'My time does not come cheap.'" (p. 201) But his offer stands: "What really tempted him . . . was the idea of jettisoning his careful tedious life and of surrendering to the idea of venality, vulgarity. . . . He would take a perverse joy in letting her ruin him." (pp. 156-57) He says, in a lovely phrase, "They would travel, live elsewhere, a perpetual elsewhere." (p. 162)

She would deceive him of course, yet there was a weird excitement in the thought that "he would always be on the verge of losing her." (p. 165)

He would know no peace – he would feel pain, jealousy, angst – but they would be full emotions, not like the half-life he has lived so far. He is still able to stand outside himself, to see himself and Katy Gibb objectively. "[H]e had been overcome with passion for a woman half his age, whom he hardly knew, and who was hard, cunning, venal, and an opportunist to her fingers' ends." (p. 205) He knows objectively that "the reality would be far shabbier." But, knowing all this, his offer of Rome stands.

While he waits for her decision, he lives fully, authentically, painfully: "He was on the edge . . . face to face with the action of a lifetime. In that moment he left his previous life behind." (pp. 215-16)

And then her decision comes. She decides to return to America. He gives her money for her ticket and expenses. He owes her that for the few days of existential living she has given him, the few days of dreams and joy and pain as he waited for her decision.

After she leaves and George surveys the chaos she has created in the Dunlops' apartment, he says, with admiration, "This is freedom . . . freedom is to take what one wants." (p. 226)

Now he has his Mrs. Cardozo restore order to the apartment that Katy Gibb has ravaged. As for himself, "He would be left with his dry memories and his small routines, obliged to make his peace with what remained to him . . . he would no doubt salvage a little outward dignity." (p. 231-32)

But, as he says himself, "he would never know it, that madness of which the poets wrote." (p. 231) We know which poets he refers to: Milton, who wrote of Satanic freedom; Blake, who glorified action whatever the cost; and Eliot, whose Prufrock dreamed of being free to murder and create.

On the last page of the novel we have the sadness of "I have had my adventure. . . . Now I must live my life as I have always lived it." And then comes the usual phone call from Louise, full of the routine trivia of her life. George suggests a spring cruise as his birthday gift to her. The cruise will be pleasant and Louise will not intrude upon his inner self. But this will not be anarchic freedom. It will not be madness.

What is the attraction of this novel? Is it no more than a restatement of Eliot's "Prufrock" in prose? Well, there is humour. Consider the exchanges between Katy Gibb and the two women, the neighbour Mrs. Lydiard and Louise. The fencing between the two generations is delicate and perfectly observed. When Katy lauds nature healing, Mrs. Lydiard says, " 'I think I'd rather trust my doctor.' " (p. 55) When Katy urges unexciting Louise to seek colour counselling, Louise says, only semi-ingenuously, " 'I don't think we have it in Lymington. Is it very expensive?' " (p. 99)

Consider the exquisite attention to detail. In her description of George's apartment, Brookner gives us the perfect blueprint of a perfectly appointed home. If you don't trust your own taste, don't hire an interior decorator, use this novel as your textbook. If you want a fabulous tour of upper-middle-class London, Brooknerland, follow George on one of his walks.

But surely that is not enough.

What is then the attraction, not only of *A Private View*, but of Brookner's fourteen other novels? Because Anita Brookner never changes her theme. All her novels have been about genteel individuals living lives of careful routine, never experiencing the "madness of which the poets wrote." Many of her protagonists have devoted a large part of their lives to unapprecia-tive parents, and all of them have a sense that they have missed out on life because they fear risk. All of them have protected themselves by retreat-ing into a quiet world of subdued colours. Each of Brookner's novels deals with one final opportunity for her protagonist to break out, "to murder and create." It is understandable that some unkind critics have labelled her "Last Chance" Brookner.

Her success lies I believe in her understanding of the conviction each of us has that someone out there is living a fuller life than we are, of the temptation that each of us must feel from time to time to know the extremes of our emotions.

But why does she keep doing it? After she won the Booker Prize for her fourth novel, *Hôtel du Lac*, about Edith Hope, a female George Bland, why didn't she stop and turn her attention elsewhere?

The answer I think is in two parts. The first is the clue she gives in her second novel, *Providence*. A young woman says to a professor of art, " 'I like your drawing. But why do you always do the same one?' " The answer: " 'That is called stylistic mastery.' "

No two treatments of the same subject are exactly alike. George Bland is not Edith Hope or Blanche Vernon or Lewis Percy or any other of Brookner's protagonists. Each is rendered differently, each is shaded differently, each has established a different routine to shield him- or herself from a hostile, threatening, external world. What they all have in common is perfect self-knowledge and a profound feeling of loss.

The second possible answer as to why Anita Brookner has dealt with the same theme fifteen times lies in her own life. Anita Brookner was born in London in 1938 to Jewish parents who had come to England from Poland. She has talked about her childhood and she says, openly, that she left her family to study because she found her family both eccentric and suffocating. I have no idea whether she saw them correctly or not, I am just passing on to you her perception.

It seems to me significant that she has used a Jewish family as background in only two of her novels, most notably her fifth, *Family and Friends*, where she analyzes the domination of four children by a matriarch. In her other novels, there are no Jewish references and I defy anyone to see any Jewish theme in *A Private View*. In fact George Bland could be seen as the perfect stereotype, at least outwardly, of the super-WASP.

Most of Brookner's studies took place in France, where she came to love the work of Stendhal for his wit, the perfect self-knowledge of his characters, his lack of sentiment, and his irony. All those qualities, I suggest, are to be found in her own work. She also became an expert on French art of the eighteenth and nineteenth centuries, notably de Greuze and David, and she has written extensively on Utrillo and Gauguin.

At the age of thirty she became the first woman to hold a named chair as a Professor of Art at the University of Cambridge. She also lectured in London at my favourite art gallery, the Courtauld Institute.

She did not publish her first novel, *The Debut*, until 1981, when she was forty-three. After a further seven years of writing, and six more novels, including the Booker Prize-winning *Hôtel du Lac*, Anita Brookner retired from teaching to write full time.

Her life in London is governed by a strict routine. She writes for a fixed number of hours each day and takes a long annual holiday in Europe.

She has declared that she is heterosexual not homosexual, but she has never married. She has said, "I always wanted to get married but, as it is, I've never really left school."

I am not a psychiatrist and I do not like amateur psychiatry. I also do not subscribe to the autobiographical theory of literature, that every writer is telling his or her own story, either directly or indirectly. This seems to me an absurdity. It is reasonable to assume that a writer draws some part of the material from his or her own life, but how much we can never know, and how much it has been transformed we can never know. It is absurd to suggest that Saul Bellow is Herzog or Christopher Marlowe is Tamburlaine or Mordecai Richler is Duddy Kravitz. To do so is to take Freudianism at its most simplistic. If the autobiographical theory were true, then who is Shakespeare? King Lear, Othello, Shylock, Pericles, or Hamlet? But having said all that, I am prepared to reverse myself.

It is not enough, I think, that Anita Brookner has read the poets Milton and Blake and Eliot and been profoundly affected. I believe that to be true, but it seems to me not enough to explain her devotion to the one theme.

Consider how close her own life is to that one theme. She had a family life she found oppressive. So did George Bland, and so did most of Brookner's central characters.

Brookner chose a life in academia that would afford her both a routine and a degree of protection from the outside world. She admits as much when she says, "I've never really left school."

I do not wish to slander her or to make up unfounded gossip, but I am reasonably sure that, during all those summer holidays in Europe, there must have been discreet relationships.

I do not know if there is a male counterpart of Louise in Anita Brookner's life, someone steady, sound, understanding, who meets the basic needs but who does not intrude. I do not know, but it would not surprise me.

I do know that the novel left me with a great sadness for all of us who have asked the question "Do I dare disturb the universe?" and who, after careful and methodical deliberation, have decided not to.

JACK MAGGS

Peter Carey

(Toronto: Vintage, 1999)

Although *Jack Maggs* is set in London in 1837, the novel contains so many references to Australia, particularly the state of New South Wales, and to the nineteenth-century punishment of transportation, that I thought a few explanatory remarks might be in order.

The land mass of Australia was not discovered by Europeans until 1770, when Captain James Cook, escorting a scientific party to the South Pacific to observe an eclipse, found land that did not appear on any maps. It reminded him of the Welsh coast he had sailed along as a boy, so he named it New South Wales and claimed what turned out to be a continent in the name of the British king.

Now for an apparently unrelated fact. Six years later, in 1776, the thirteen British colonies in North America declared their independence from King George III. The American colonists fought for seven years, won their independence, and became in 1783 a sovereign country.

The independence of the United States presented the British authorities with a difficulty. In what had seemed an ideal solution to its crime problem, Britain had been dumping its criminals in the American colonies since shortly after 1600. No one at the time would have dreamed of housing criminals in prisons at the public expense for long periods of time; prisons existed mainly for debtors and those awaiting trial or execution. It was much more sensible, went the conventional wisdom, that the offender be sent far, far away to a place where he or she would be forced to labour in the development of a new colony, a colony they would never be allowed to leave. Transportation, as the punishment was called, could be for life or for as few as seven years. In the case of the shorter sentences, once one had served one's time one was freed. Sometimes, if the penal colony became a little too crowded, one might be freed early with a "conditional pardon" – our protagonist in Carey's novel, Jack Maggs, was given one. As a free man, one could go into commerce or farming or mining; one might even prosper. But one had to stay in the colony. Return to England meant arrest and execution.

Naturally, after the United States became independent in 1783, Americans no longer wanted to be the waste receptacle for the English criminal classes. What now were the law-abiding folk of Great Britain to do with all their malefactors? And there were many. Transportation was the punishment for the most minor of transgressions. My father, who had a great taste for history, took me for a walk when I was a little boy to see an old iron bridge near our village in South Wales. He wanted me to read the plaque on the bridge. Rusting but still legible, the inscription read: "Punishment for defacing this bridge seven years transportation."

Then some unknown British civil servant had a wonderful idea. Why not send criminals to the newly claimed land in the South Pacific?

And so, in 1787, the first boatload of convicts went off to the other side of the world, forbidden under pain of death to return. Between 1787 and 1868, when transportation ended and prisons as we know them were established in England, more than one hundred and seventy thousand convicts, male and female, had been sent to Australia.

When one considers that the whole population of Australia, according to the 1851 census, was only four hundred thousand, it meant that at least 80 percent of the Australian population in 1851 were convicts, the children of convicts, or the grandchildren of convicts.

All this began to change after the discovery of gold in Australia in 1851. Free men started pouring in from all over the world. Soon the Australians, like the Americans before them, began to refuse to be a dumping ground, and the system of transportation came to an end in 1868.

Peter Carey, a native-born Australian, has spoken very clearly about the effect its early history had on Australia: "We're the only country in the world, as far as I know, that has its beginnings in a concentration camp, a penal colony. And a genocide too. That affected us forever." (Undated interview with the author, *PowellsBooks* online)

The genocide Peter Carey refers to is that perpetrated by white Australia against the aborigine people. He refers to it in great detail in his third novel, the Booker Prize-winning *Oscar and Lucinda*. Both the genocide and Australia's identity crisis vis-à-vis the United Kingdom have preoccupied Peter Carey for all his adult years.

A very peculiar love-hate relationship has always characterized the Australian attitude to the Mother Country, a relationship that has persisted to this day. Peter Carey has compared it to the way an abused child loves the abusing parent. On the one hand, Australians resent the England that punished their ancestors so cruelly; on the other hand, they still yearn for its approval. Peter Carey believes that, because of this peculiar relationship, Australians all too often feel an obsessive need to prove themselves, to show that they are first-class Australians and not second-class Englishmen.

In the fifties and sixties I lived for years in the Earl's Court area of London, heavily populated by expatriate Australians on the British leg of their two-year walkabout. I found them a very friendly lot, but I agree with Peter Carey that they are a people not at ease with their identity. They took such great pains to explain to me how much culture there was in Australia, contrary to popular misconceptions abroad. I lost count of how many times the plans for the Sydney Opera House were described to me in overwhelming detail.

Jack Maggs, the protagonist of Carey's novel, for example, has grown rich in Australia but longs for nothing more than to return to the England where he was so mistreated and from which he was cast out. When he does dare to return and is later urged to leave London, where his life is at risk, and go back to Sydney, he says, "'I *know*. God damn. I do know, Sir. But you see, I am a fucking *Englishman*, and I have English things to settle. I am not to live my life with all that vermin. I am here in London where I belong.'" (pp. 140-41)

Peter Carey himself was born in 1943 near Melbourne. At the age of ten he was sent away to a private boarding school, where he stayed for seven years. The memory of leaving his parents must have been a long-lasting trauma, since his four novels before *Jack Maggs* are full of lost babies and neglected children. Even *Jack Maggs* is about a child cast out by the Mother Country.

After a brief career in advertising, Carey published his first novel, *Bliss*, in 1981. It won Australia's top literary prize, the Miles Franklin Award, and he began to write full time with great success.

Peter Carey has come to terms with what it means to be an Australian, but like Thomas Keneally, who wrote *Schindler's List*, he believes that Australia should declare itself a republic and cut its last ties with the United Kingdom.

Peter Carey and his wife and two sons have lived for the last several years in Greenwich Village, New York City, where his wife is a successful theatre director. He explains his expatriate situation:

> But I do really like being here. For God's sake, I've got a son who's an American. And when I talk about New York, I suppose that I'm talking about an America that is in its daily practice really – no matter what tensions there are in New York – sort of racially toler-ant. People really do work together and accommodate each other. (*PowellsBooks* interview)

But given the concerns he has always felt, Peter Carey must surely experience an occasional homesickness, and it is that homesickness which produced *Jack Maggs*. It was first published in 1997 and won the Commonwealth Writers' Prize in 1998.

The novel derives from a number of sources. Peter Carey had been reading a book by Edward Said, *Culture and Imperialism*, about how difficult it is for ex-colonies to define themselves. Said mentions the Dickens novel *Great Expectations* and the convict Magwitch. The refer-ence pricked Peter Carey's interest and he remembered the marvellous movie of the novel made in England in 1946. (*ibid*) You will of course remember that superb production by David Lean, completely faithful in mood and spirit to Dickens's text. It starred John Mills, Valerie Hobson, Alec Guinness, Jean Simmons, and an absolutely magnificent Finlay Currie as the convict Abel Magwitch.

A decade ago, Peter Carey said that he had read no Dickens except for the first thirty pages of *Bleak House* and a biography of the writer. (*New York Times Book Review*, February 12, 1998) More recently, however, he claims to have read not only *Great Expectations* but a number of other novels by Dickens. (*PowellsBooks* interview) In any event, I am convinced that the movie left an unforgettable impression on Peter Carey, as it did on me.

Let me outline the main points of *Great Expectations*, as we must have them in mind if we are to appreciate just how brilliantly Peter Carey is going to turn them on their head.

Philip – Pip for short – is an orphaned country boy being brought up by his terrible sister and her saintly husband, the local blacksmith. Nearby are the "Hulks," the prison ships in which convicts wait to be transported to Australia.

One early evening, while the young Pip is visiting his mother's grave, he is surprised by an escaped convict, Abel Magwitch, who demands the boy find him a file for his chains and food, "wittles" as he calls it. It's one of the great scenes of cinema when the huge, hulking convict springs on the boy out of the evening mist. I'll never forget his threat to the boy to stay silent:

> You fail, or you go from my words in any partickler, no matter how small it is, and your heart and your liver shall be tore out, roasted and ate. Now, I ain't alone, as you may think I am. There's a young man hid with me, in comparison with which young man I am a Angel. That young man hears the words I speak. That young man has a secret way pecooliar to himself, of getting at a boy, and at his heart, and at his liver. It is in wain for a boy to attempt to hide himself from that young man. A boy may lock his door, may be warm in bed, may tuck himself up, may draw the clothes over his head, may think himself comfortable and safe, but that young man will softly creep and creep his way to him and tear him open.

I love it! I love it! It's Dickens at his very best. No one ever understood the fears of childhood the way he did.

Pip brings the convict a file and even more food than he could have expected, but Magwitch is recaptured and sent to Australia.

Years later Pip is told he has a secret benefactor who desires him to go to London to become a gentleman. He assumes it to be the local eccentric, the rich Miss Havisham, with whose ward Estella he has fallen in love. So imagine his horror when he finally discovers his benefactor is the convict Abel Magwitch, who had become rich in Australia after

serving his time. Risking death, Magwitch returns in secret to London to
see "his boy." Pip has become something of a snob and is initially
revolted that his benefactor is a convict and not a rich lady. His natural
goodness eventually comes to the fore, however, and when Magwitch is
betrayed and arrested, Pip visits the dying man every day in the prison
hospital. The death scene is particularly wonderful. Bear in mind that
Pip has found out that Miss Havisham's ward, Estella, is in fact
Magwitch's daughter, taken from him in her infancy because Magwitch
was a convicted criminal.

"Dear boy," he said, as I sat down by his bed: "I thought you was
late. But I knowed you couldn't be that."

"It is just the time," said I. "I waited for it at the gate."

"You always waits at the gate; don't you, dear boy?"

"Yes. Not to lose a moment of the time."

"Thank'ee, dear boy, thank'ee. God bless you! You've never
deserted me, dear boy."

I pressed his hand in silence, for I could not forget that I had once
meant to desert him.

"And what's the best of all," he said, "you've been more comfortable alonger me, since I was under a dark cloud, than when the sun
shone. That's best of all. . . ."

"Dear Magwitch, I must tell you, now, at last. You understand
what I say?"

A gentle pressure on my hand.

"You had a child once, whom you loved and lost."

A stronger pressure on my hand.

"She lived and found powerful friends. She is living now. She is a
lady and very beautiful. And I love her!"

With a last faint effort . . . he raised my hand to his lips. Then, he
gently let it sink upon his breast again, with his own hands lying on
it. . . . and his head dropped quietly on his breast.

Magwitch had to die, although Dickens allows him to cheat the hangman.
The Victorian reader would never have accepted that a criminal escape his
punishment.

And then of course we have the end of the novel, where Pip and Magwitch's long-lost daughter Estella walk hand-in-hand out of a garden into the sunset.

Whatever Carey rehearsed in his mind, the novel or the movie, he realized that as an Englishman and a social reformer Dickens had cast the ultimately noble Pip as the central character. Magwitch was no more than an example of Victorian cruelty to the London poor. Carey decided to retell the story. But this time Magwitch, now called Jack Maggs, would be the protagonist and he would end the novel as an Australian free man and not as an English criminal. Carey would put a modern, post-colonial spin on the Dickens story. Instead of being a pitiable convict, serving only to show how noble the Englishman became, Jack Maggs would become a deeply complex and admirable hero.

A "mag" by the way was nineteenth-century criminal cant for a thief: it comes from the magpie, the bird that swoops down to steal shiny objects. However, Jack Maggs claims his foster mother gave him the name because he chattered like a magpie and talked too much. (p. 83)

With Jack Maggs at centre stage, Carey's novel begins on April 15, 1837, with true Dickensian mystery. A huge man, with hooded eyes and hawk nose, and the two middle fingers of his left hand missing, lands at Dover and takes the coach for London. We learn his story piece by piece as the novel progresses. He is forty-four years old when we meet him, twenty years younger than the Dickens original, and Carey reveals his earlier life through two ingenious narrative devices.

First, Jack Maggs will be put under a series of hypnotic trances by a writer called Tobias Oates, during which Maggs will speak of the events of his youth. Second, Maggs will write a series of letters to Henry Phipps, the young man for whom he is searching and whom he calls his son. These letters by Maggs will build up to a kind of confessional autobiography, an apologia.

To make for clarity, I'm going to rearrange the events of Jack Maggs's life, as he reveals them in his letters or under hypnosis, into chronological order.

At three days old, Maggs was thrown off London Bridge by his birth mother and found on the mud below by street urchins. The mudlarks sold the baby for a few pennies to Silas Smith, a local thief who lived with

"Ma" Mary Britten, the matriarch of a criminal clan and the neighbour-hood abortionist.

By eight years old, Jack Maggs was an accomplished thief. Silas Smith, Ma Britten's lover, would lower him down the chimney of rich houses. (Shades of *Oliver Twist*! Peter Carey saw that movie as well.) Maggs would then let in his accomplice Sophina, Smith's daughter, and together the children would ransack the house, delivering the loot to the waiting Smith or to Ma Britten's half-witted son, Tom.

When not engaged in burglary, the eight-year-old Jack Maggs and Sophina Smith had to clean up the blood and fetuses left behind after Ma Britten's primitive abortions. The details of child abuse are more terrible than any Dickens ever dared to commit to the printed page.

It's not too difficult to see "Ma Britten" as a variation of "Mother England." There are not many certainties in history, but one is that the great industries of England and the great wealth of the nineteenth-century upper classes and the great British Empire itself were all built upon the broken bodies of little children.

But of course, like the abused dog or the abused child who never stops loving the abuser, Jack Maggs wants desperately that both Ma Britten and Mother England will love him and call him son.

As Jack Maggs will much later write in one of his letters to Henry Phipps, by the time he and Sophina were fourteen,

> *We were fast at our work, faster than those who depended on us could ever guess, and when we had filled our sack, and I had placed it care-fully beside the kitchen door, I would mount the stairs and set off, in all that great house, to find my "wife" who had gone on ahead of me.*
>
> *And, who was in bed, of course, and waiting for me.*
>
> *My dear boy, I pray I do not shock you with this tale or that you . . . will doubt me when I say, what innocents we were.* (p. 235)

The two children had created a little Eden in the agony of their lives, a demi-paradise of only a few minutes duration, and at great risk.

On one fateful occasion, they sleep too soundly and too long. Tom, waiting outside, panics and runs home to fetch his mother. Ma Britten enters the house to find the two children naked and fast asleep in each other's arms.

Jack Maggs she will flog, and then she will induce a miscarriage in five-month-pregnant Sophina. Tom, mad with jealousy, takes Maggs to the cesspool behind the Britten house and shows him the aborted fetus floating among human waste.

That sad little love between the two children, Jack Maggs and Sophina, could rip your heart out. Of all the love affairs of the novel, it was the one that affected me the most, I suppose because it was the innocent love of children who could find love nowhere else in a family and a country that had turned their backs on their own little ones.

To complete his revenge, Tom later betrays both Sophina and Jack Maggs to the authorities for stealing silver. Sophina will be hanged. The law, then as now, was always more severe on a female than on a male. A woman, thought to be born with more delicate sensibilities, was presumed to have fallen further from grace. Maggs will receive a lighter sentence: transportation to New South Wales for life.

On its way to the convict ship, the prison coach will stop at a smithy, where the blacksmith's boy will give Maggs a portion of his own poor food. It is then that Maggs makes a promise similar to that of his Dickensian predecessor.

> [W]hen I finished my meal, I made this solemn promise to the little boy. I knew exactly what I said. I spoke it out loud . . . I would come back from my exile . . . I would spin him a cocoon of gold and jewels . . . I would weave him a nest so strong that no one would ever hurt his goodness. (p. 287)

The irony is that Maggs will elevate the boy, whom we come to know as Henry Phipps, to the very class that had so abused him and his beloved Sophina and all their like.

Seven years after his arrival at the dreaded penal colony of Moreton Bay, Maggs receives a grant of a strip of barren land and a "conditional pardon" to make space for new arrivals. Under the land he is given he finds clay. From clay he can make bricks, and from his brickworks he makes a fortune. "I am a vermin who made ten thousand pounds from mucky clay. I have a grand house in Sydney town. There is a street named for me, or was when I sailed. I keep a coach, and two footmen. I am Mr. Jack Maggs Esquire." (p. 306)

"Mr. Jack Maggs Esquire"! So why does he call himself "a vermin"? Because, according to his lights, there is no virtue in being a rich Australian; virtue is to be found only in the English gentleman. To that end he has sent much money, secretly, back to England to the boy who showed him kindness.

Now, more than two decades after England sent him away, Maggs has come back to be with "his boy," the English gentleman he believes he has created. Unlike Dickens's Pip, Henry Phipps has always known that it was Jack Maggs, the ex-convict, who was sending him the money. He had even replied with syrupy letters in order to get more. What he had never expected was that Maggs would risk his life by coming back to London. As soon as Maggs writes to say he's coming, Henry Phipps runs away. He is not the gentleman of whom Jack Maggs dreamed, he isn't the noble Pip of the Dickens novel, he is a selfish, weak, depraved fop, and he goes to hide in his gentlemen's club in Covent Garden. It is an interesting club, of a type common in the London of the day. It's a club where rich men could entertain children and servants of either sex who sold their sexual favours for money. Henry Phipps's particular taste is for very young men and boys of the lower economic classes, but nineteenth-century England catered to every orientation. Whichever sex was involved, it was still part of the same exploitation of the poor, the young, and the defenceless.

Anxious to find "his boy," Maggs inquires at the house next door to the empty Phipps house, and here Carey makes an exquisite point. In spite of his fine clothes, Maggs is mistaken for a servant applying for a vacant position as footman. It is a beautifully made observation. Money and clothes did not make a gentleman in nineteenth-century England any more than they do today. To pass as a gentleman, one must also have the arrogance, the belief in one's own genetic superiority, that comes only with being born into a family with many generations of social position and money.

The neighbour, Percy Buckle, faces the same problem as Jack Maggs. Buckle was a seller of fried fish who inherited a fortune from a distant relative. Now he has money and a big house and servants and can indulge his passion for buying books and reading. But it doesn't make him a gentleman as the English understand the expression. He lacks the air, the accent, the attitudes, the natural arrogance. And his servants recognize this; they treat him with familiarity, even with contempt.

The novel has a third character in the same boat, Tobias Oates the writer, always ill at ease because of his humble origins.

Jack Maggs takes the footman's job offered him, because it puts him next door to the house of "his boy," a house he can explore at his leisure to find some clue as to Henry Phipps's whereabouts.

The household Maggs enters is a fascinating one, full of splendidly drawn characters worthy of Dickens himself. An outstanding example is the dictatorial housekeeper, Mrs. Halfstairs. What a gorgeous name for a Victorian housekeeper! Maggs is taken on as footman only because he is exactly the same height as the other footman and the delicious Mrs. Halfstairs wants them to look like matching bookends.

And of course there is the maid Mercy Larkin. Until she was thirteen she had led an upper-working-class life, the daughter of an East London mechanic and a beautiful part-time lace worker. She even went to school. All that changed when her father died. Without the protection of a male, essential in nineteenth-century England, she and her mother tried baking to make a living, but all their efforts were in vain and the mother sank into prostitution. Even this was insufficient to sustain the two, and Mercy's mother had no choice but to dress her thirteen-year-old up in tawdry finery and take her down to the Haymarket, just off Piccadilly. Within minutes, a tall gentleman came up, and the innocent child, supposing him to be an old friend of her parents, went off with him to endure a vicious, loveless penetration.

It is just one more example in the novel of England's abuse of her children. At thirteen Mercy Larkin would have been by no means the youngest prostitute on the street.

Mercy's mother was soon saved from the nightmare by going insane, and Mercy was taken in by the friendly neighbourhood fried-fish seller, Percy Buckle. He was kind to her, he read stories to her, and when he inherited his great fortune, she came with him as the maid. As she grew older she also came into his bed. Buckle is essentially a decent man, but even he could not avoid the temptation of all male employers with female servants. Mercy, for her part, is grateful to Buckle for saving her from the streets and, with the encouragement of Mrs. Mott the cook, even dreams of becoming Mrs. Percy Buckle.

But, when the powerful, brooding Maggs joins the staff, Mercy is immediately attracted to him. She knows she is "spoiled goods" in his eyes but reasons that the suffering he has evidently undergone might induce him to accept her.

Mercy is playing a dangerous game. Maggs gives her no guarantees and Buckle becomes increasingly jealous as her feelings become more evident. Her friend the cook warns her:

> "You get up there and get back in the master's good books or God knows what sort of life you're going to have."
> She knew what sort of life. She knew it exactly. She saw the stinking little room in Fetter Lane. She saw the Haymarket, the vile dress with its gaudy ribbons. (p. 277)

Mercy knows that she must have a man to protect her from that stinking room and that vile dress. But with whom will she stand the better chance? It's one of the great questions of the novel.

There is one more fascinating character at the Buckle house. Not a member of the household but a frequent guest, he is the popular writer of newspaper serials and reporter of sensational events, the bloodier the better, Tobias Oates.

Oates is clearly modelled on Dickens himself. Each of them grew up in poverty and each of them is terrified of debt and ending up in a debtors' prison. Each of them also had a father who incurred debts for which the son was held responsible.

While both the fictitious Tobias Oates and the real Charles Dickens were popular guests at upper-crust dinner parties, both were really invited as entertainers, as curiosities. Neither was ever accepted as a gentleman.

In the novel, Tobias Oates gets his eighteen-year-old sister-in-law pregnant. In real life Dickens had an affair with his sister-in-law Mary Hogarth, with whom he later asked to be buried, and before his separation from his wife in 1858 it is very probable that he had another affair with his other sister-in-law, Georgina Hogarth. Both Tobias Oates and the Dickens after whom he is fashioned felt deprived of love in their poverty-stricken childhoods, and both tried to compensate later by having as many physical relationships as they could cram into their busy schedules. Tobias Oates himself calls it "an unholy thirst for love."

Finally, both the character Tobias Oates and the real Charles Dickens were profoundly interested in science. To the nineteenth century, this

meant not only the serious studies of people like Darwin, but also spiritu-
alism, magnetic fluids and, especially, hypnotism. Tobias Oates is thrilled
when the new footman falls to the ground in agony during a dinner party
at the Buckle household. It is a wonderful opportunity for Oates to demon-
strate his hypnotic talent. The pain in Maggs's cheek is relieved, and this
becomes the first of several sessions where Tobias Oates will put Jack
Maggs into a hypnotic trance. In one of the sessions, Oates will induce
Maggs to remove his shirt. Thus the horror is revealed: his back is "a
brooding sea of scars, of ripped and tortured skin." (p. 95)

All those who see Maggs's back know of only one place where such
punishment could have been inflicted, a penal colony in Australia where
they had perfected a very particular instrument of torture. The "double cat-
o'-nine-tails" was a whip with nine thongs, each of which had knots along
its length with a sharp piece of metal fixed into each knot. A hundred lashes
had mutilated Maggs's back, torn two fingers from his left hand, and cut
the nerve in his cheek that causes him such torment.

Now Oates and the whole Buckle household know Maggs's secret: he is
a returned convict, what they call an "NSW bolter."

For a long time Tobias Oates has been convinced that there exists such
a thing as the hereditary criminal mind. Here is his chance to explore
one. He intends to use the information gleaned to write the great novel
that has so far eluded him. As Maggs once mined the ground for his clay,
so Oates will mine the very essence of Jack Maggs to find the material
for his book.

Believing Oates intends only to relieve him of pain, Maggs agrees to let
Oates hypnotize him every day for two weeks. That will still allow Maggs
to slip out nightly through a window, over the rooftop, and into the house
of "his boy," where he searches endlessly for clues and writes mighty but
undelivered letters to his missing gentleman.

The action now becomes complicated. In return for the sessions, Maggs
demands that Oates help him track down the elusive Phipps. Desperate for
money, the debt-ridden Oates demands sixty pounds from Maggs for a trip
to Gloucester, where they visit the legendary thief-catcher Partridge, who
is believed to be able to find anybody. The visit turns sour and Maggs is
forced to kill Partridge in self-defence. Realizing he has been tricked,
Maggs turns on Oates, "'You have betrayed me, Tobias,'" and becomes
even more enraged when he discovers notes Tobias Oates has made on

Maggs's most secret thoughts, even the details of his true love, his Sophina:
" 'You stole my Sophina, you bastard.' " (p. 305)

Oates is frightened – Maggs is a powerful man – and in an effort to win
back Maggs's trust offers him a confession as proof of his friendship.
Tobias confides that he has impregnated his young sister-in-law.

Maggs agrees to help him and obtains pills from a seventy-year-old Ma
Britten, still in business. Unfortunately, Tobias's wife, Mary, knowing of
her sister's predicament, also obtains pills from the same source. A double
dose of pills causes the death of the sister-in-law. Tobias, racked by guilt,
is a crushed man.

It's a beautifully handled little subplot, one of many in the novel, but
Jack Maggs is no nearer finding his beloved boy. The irony of course is that
everyone has known almost all the time exactly where Phipps is hiding.
The footman Edward Constable, a reluctant part of the rent-boy system,
saw him at the gentlemen's club and told Mercy Larkin, who told Percy
Buckle, who told Tobias Oates.

Everyone, except Mercy Larkin, is becoming increasingly afraid of
Maggs. Percy Buckle, the social upstart, initially sympathetic to Maggs's
suffering, is both jealous and afraid; harbouring a returned transportee is a
capital crime.

It is in almost everyone's interest that Maggs be got rid of, and so Percy
Buckle and his lawyer, Mr. Makepeace, go to Henry Phipps to plot Maggs's
death. They cannot just inform on him to the authorities, because then all
Maggs's property would be seized by the crown, including the house Henry
Phipps lives in. But if Maggs were killed during a burglary, say by Henry
Phipps while defending his residence, then all Maggs's property, including
the house, would devolve upon Henry Phipps, Maggs's heir. And Percy
Buckle would make a tidy sum in commission on the sale of the house,
which Phipps wants never to see again.

Thus it is that Phipps and Buckle wait in the empty house for Maggs to
come as he does every night, looking for traces of "his boy."

And when Maggs comes, with him is Mercy Larkin, who has finally
decided to throw in her lot with the returned transportee and is trying to
warn him of the plot she has overheard.

Now we have the meeting between Maggs and the English gentleman
he has created. As Jack Maggs finally looks upon the face of "his boy,"
he sees, not the nobility of Dickens's Pip, but the vicious, corrupt face of

the upper-class England that had cast him out and hanged his beloved Sophina so many years before. How far are we from the death scene in *Great Expectations*, when Pip and the dying Magwitch hold each other in reciprocated love!

Phipps's bullet misses Maggs and takes away the ring finger of Mercy Larkin's left hand, the hand she raised to protect Jack Maggs. Now they will be linked by missing fingers, the vivid, living emblem of what England has done to them both.

The rest of the novel is inevitable. After escaping London that very night, Maggs accepts Mercy Larkin's offer to return with him to New South Wales and look after his two motherless sons. They will marry and she will bear him five more children, "real Australian children" as Mercy calls them. Maggs will continue to prosper and proceed from civic honour to civic honour until at last he passes away in 1857 in the bosom of his weeping family.

It's a lovely, happy, Dickensian ending. But Dickens could never have written it. A Victorian audience would never have permitted a convict and an ex-prostitute to go unpunished and find happiness together. Of course, it isn't perfection. Maggs would never rediscover the idyll he shared with Sophina in childhood, and there is a pragmatic quality in Mercy's decision to choose Maggs. But it's still happiness, and as much happiness as real people can aspire to.

What happened to Tobias Oates?

We are told that he published his *Death of Maggs* three years after the "real" Maggs dies in Australia. It took him twenty years to get over the death of his sister-in-law. The novel he finally puts out is no more than melodramatic trash, with Maggs cast as a murderer who meets a cruel death. Tobias Oates is Dickens without the talent. I thought it was a nice touch by Carey to have Oates's novel published in 1860. That's the date of *Great Expectations*.

We learn nothing of the fate of Henry Phipps, and that is as it should be. That petty, worthless gentleman deserves no further mention.

What is it that we have enjoyed in the novel? We have been rushed through the squalid, fetid world of Victorian London's poor. We have witnessed an exquisite examination of the English class and penal systems with all their attendant cruelties. We have looked at every kind of neglected child in a great catalogue of abuses. We have seen a power struggle between an author determined to steal another man's secrets and a man intent on preserving his story and his integrity. We have seen the movement by Jack Maggs from an English to an Australian identity that mirrors the odyssey of the whole Australian people.

It is a triumph of a novel. Peter Carey took on the master himself. Dickens was an Englishman who wrote about the nobility of an English boy; Carey began at the same starting point but changed the focus. We end the novel with Maggs a successful Australian, the father of seven and the ancestor of many.

Peter Carey was asked by an Australian newspaper to sum up in one sentence his intention in *Jack Maggs*. His answer: "I wanted to give Mother England a kick up the arse."

My surprise is that he did it so brilliantly and that I, with my strong emotional attachments to the Great Britain of my birth, should have so enjoyed reading about it.

Dickens's pathetic Englishman, Abel Magwitch, and Carey's proud Australian, Jack Maggs, have both entered my internal world, peopled by characters I can never forget and whom I visit from time to time. I cannot pay either author or either character a greater compliment.

WISE CHILDREN

Angela Carter
(London: Vintage, 1992)

Usually, when I review a novel, I make some general remarks about the nature of the novel, followed by a brief biography of the author and then a commentary on the work itself. It's a good approach and one that has worked for me for the past several years.

But this time is different. This is my first examination of a deconstructionist novel, and I will have to go about it very differently. A radically new treatment seems appropriate.

First I want to discuss for a moment my definition of a novel. Let us go back almost three hundred years in English history to the time of the first factory, an innovation that would change England from an agricultural economy to a modern industrial state. Beginning in the early eighteenth century there was an explosion of energy, creativity, commerce, and trade that we call the Industrial Revolution.

There were many results of this fantastic expansion of economic activity after 1711 – the growth of cities around the new factories, the creation of industrial slums, great fortunes, social problems like overcrowding and child labour, and England's economic domination of the whole world. But the result of the Industrial Revolution that touched most directly upon the evolution of literature was the creation of a large middle class. It was a class that had never existed before in any significant numbers. It was a class that had risen out of the poor and had prospered in the new industrial economy. It was a class that owed its existence to its intelligence. The middle class was made up of the people who knew how to make the new system work; they were the shopkeepers in the new cities, the factory managers, and the engineers who looked after the new inventions.

They were intensely curious and they were uneasy in their new social position. The most popular books in the early eighteenth century were travel books and how-to books: how to write a correct letter, how to give a party, how to manage a big house, how to deal with servants. Out of those how-to books came the first true English novel in 1740, *Pamela*, by Samuel Richardson. It's a collection of letters, a popular genre at the time. Sample letters that they could use as models for their correspondence were very popular with members of a class only just learning the social niceties. But this collection was different. Taken together, the letters tell a story about a poor girl who goes to work as a maid in a great house. Mr. B., the master of the house, first tries to seduce her and then, impressed by her virtue, offers marriage. The subtitle of the novel says it all, "Virtue Rewarded." Thus the novel is not only a full portrait of Pamela, far more devious than she seems at first sight and well aware that marriage is her only avenue to move upmarket, it is also blatant propaganda for middle-class values and middle-class morality. The message is clear: marriage is the ideal goal and the traditional family is the ideal structure. This is what deconstructionists call the novel's hidden agenda. The novels of Jane Austen are an excellent illustration: suitors may be acceptable or unacceptable, obstacles may block the path of true love, but there is never any question that the ideal to be realized is a middle-class nuclear family. There are few surprises in Miss Austen's work; the delight is in the detail.

Pamela was wildly popular and there were many imitations. Writers began to explore variations on the theme, particularly the terrible consequences visited on those who deviated from the implicit morality contained in the new form.

There was a great deal of experiment in the early days of the novel. There were novels with the occasional black page, novels with two stories written on alternate pages, and, only twenty years after *Pamela*, Laurence Sterne's incredible *The Life and Opinions of Tristram Shandy* (1760-67), a multi-volume opus consisting almost entirely of wonderful digressions. The reader of today might be astounded to learn how much of the technique of the avant-garde modern novel had already been tried by the end of the eighteenth century. Tried and, in most cases, rejected.

Permitting myself a Sterne-like digression, I have noticed the same phenomenon in the theatre. Robert Lepage is hailed as the innovative genius of the stage. I would be the last to deny Lepage's enormous creative talent, but nothing I have seen of his work – the brilliant special effects, the acrobatic movement, the use of startling lights and sounds – might not be found already blueprinted on the pages of Antonin Artaud's *Le Théâtre et Son Double* (1937).

The sad truth is that almost everything has been done before.

In spite of all the experimentation, the definition of the novel has undergone very little change since *Pamela*. First, the novel is always a prose fiction about a world that seems as tangible and complex as our own. Second, within that real world there moves a central character, a protagonist, as psychologically complicated and as human as we are ourselves. As we follow the life of the protagonist we must feel a shared humanity. We must believe in him or her. The truly great novel creates a character who becomes real in our mind and who becomes a permanent resident of our internal world. Who can forget Emma Bovary, Ebenezer Scrooge, Sherlock Holmes, or David Copperfield?

As well as creating a real person moving through a real world, the novel will teach: it will have a strong didactic element. Remember that the novel was created for a new class, anxious to learn and very curious about the world and about themselves. The novel is for the middle class, about the middle class, and is generally by the middle class. Even in the heyday of experiment with the new genre in the eighteenth century, the experiment was always with the form, the structure; there was never a serious questioning of the underlying bourgeois morality. Until recently.

I am referring to the advent of the deconstructionist movement and its high priest, the French philosopher-critic Jacques Derrida. The movement's greatest exponent, at least among British novelists, was the late Angela Carter. Salman Rushdie called her "the most brilliant writer in England" before she died, all too soon, in 1992 at the age of fifty-two. Following Derrida's teachings, Angela Carter's objective in her novels was to shatter not only the traditional structure of the novel, with its respect for chronology and logical cause and effect, but to reveal the traditional novel's underlying morality, its middle-class propaganda, and substitute a new moral underpinning more appropriate to our chaotic age. What, the deconstructionists argue, is the point of proselytizing for a Jane Austen world in a Western society where more than half of all marriages turn out to be no more than temporary arrangements and where women demand, and are clearly entitled to, a destiny other than waiting for Mr. Darcy?

The narrator of *Wise Children*, Dora Chance, warns us that we are in for a rocky ride, although appropriately enough in a deconstructionist novel, the warning is given at the end.

> Hard to swallow, huh?
>
> Well, you might have known what you were about to let yourself in for when you let Dora Chance in her ratty old fur and poster paint, her orange (Persian Melon) toenails sticking out of her snakeskin peep-toes, reeking of liquor, accost you in the Coach and Horses and let her tell you a tale.
>
> I've got a tale and a half to tell, all right! (p. 227)

The first lines of the novel are revealing: "Good morning! Let me introduce myself. My name is Dora Chance. Welcome to the wrong side of the tracks."

The book is set, not in middle-class London north of the Thames, but in a working-class district south of the river, the side the tourist rarely sees. This was certainly how London was divided when I lived there in the fifties and sixties. The division was one of the givens one could count on in looking for a place to live, but Dora undermines our certainty immediately: "But you can't trust things to stay the same. There's been a diaspora of the affluent, they jumped into their diesel Saabs and dispersed throughout the city." (p. 1)

When we meet her, Dora is seventy-five years old. She and her twin sister, Nora, are preparing to attend the hundredth birthday of their father, the great actor-manager Sir Melchior Hazard. But before we attend the party, Dora is going to tell us the story of her life as she flits from past to present to past, to a different past, back to a different present, from reality to imagination to reality.

Do forgive me if I violate the very essence of deconstruction and rearrange the events in some kind of chronological order; I really have no choice. If I don't impose a semblance of order, we will lose each other very quickly.

Let us begin with Ranulph Hazard – possibly, just possibly, Dora and Nora's grandfather. He was a Shakespearean actor at the end of the nineteenth century. He was one of that great breed of actor-managers, dedicated to the Bard of Avon, who took their companies to small cities and towns all over the world to share with audiences their worship of Shakespeare. They were as theatrical in life as they were on stage, scenery-chewers to a man, but they loved what they did.

(The last of the line was Sir Donald Wolfitt. His *Merchant of Venice*, on a temporary stage in the local cinema in my little Welsh town, was the first play I ever saw. Hopelessly overacted, his Shylock was both the worst and therefore most memorable of my life. I remember my mother quoting some unknown wit, "While Olivier and Gielgud present *tours de force*, Wolfitt is forced to tour." Wolfitt was very much in the tradition of Ranulph Hazard.)

Hazard is enjoying much success in his international tour of small towns. Lear is his favourite role and his much younger wife, Estella, is his Cordelia. They are a success on the stage, but Estella is having sex during the intermissions with Cassius Booth, another member of the company. She gets pregnant and delivers twins – father uncertain. Ranulph shoots her, her lover, and then himself. The twins, Melchior and Peregrine, are taken in by an elderly Scottish aunt, a Dickensian character who is the warden of a workhouse. Peregrine runs away to America, and Melchior, much later, runs away to London.

Melchior stays in London at a boarding house specializing in a clientele from the theatre. It is run by Mrs. Chance, later known as Grandma. Melchior seduces a maid at the boarding house, Pretty Kitty, who dies while giving birth to another set of twins, Dora and Nora. Melchior leaves, and Dora and Nora are brought up by Grandma Chance, who gives them her name. You will have noticed the two family names used so far are Hazard and Chance. That surely speaks volumes about Angela Carter's belief in a foreseeable future. Much of middle-class living is based on the belief that tomorrow will be much like today. It is that belief which permits us to plan, to invest in the future, to educate our children, and to prepare sensibly for retirement. The problem is that the future is much less certain than it was even a generation ago. The old assumptions no longer hold true, and Derrida and Angela Carter are putting the case that we need a new set of assumptions, or possibly no assumptions at all, to respond to a new, more chaotic age.

With Grandma Chance, Angela Carter has introduced a new social structure: that of the "chosen" family. "Grandma invented this family. She put it together out of whatever came to hand." (p. 35) Angela Carter clearly believes this new structure to be far more appropriate to the needs of the late twentieth century than the traditional nuclear family. Grandma Chance will build quite a large family over the years. At the request of Peregrine Hazard, she will take in a fourteen-year-old orphan, Cynthia, known as "our Cyn" (the pun intended). As time goes by, our Cyn gives birth to Mavis, who gives birth to Brenda, who gives birth to Tiffany. Tiffany grows up to be a very tall, gorgeous black woman, the beloved godchild of Dora and Nora. There are, significantly, no recorded fathers in the line from our Cyn to Tiffany. It is true that Brenda married a certain Leroy, but only after Tiffany was born, and he is almost certainly not her father. In *Wise Children* it would be a very wise child indeed who knows his or her own father. As a matter of fact, there is a joke in the novel told by a Brighton Pier summer comedian that is very much to the point:

> "I want to get married to the girl next door, Dad."
> ". . . you can't marry the girl next door, son, on account of she's your sister."
> . . . "Looks like I'll never get married, Mum." "Why's that, son?" He told her all about it, she says: "You just go ahead and marry who you like, son –"
> Split-second timing. That pause. Perfect.
> "*E*'s not your father!" (pp. 64-65)

Let us for a moment leave Grandma Chance and her chosen family and see what has been happening to Melchior Hazard. Since he abandoned his illegitimate daughters, Nora and Dora, to the care of Grandma Chance, he has been contributing financially to their upkeep, but now his circumstances have changed. He has moved into the first rank of his profession and he is about to marry an aristocrat, Lady Atlanta Lynde. He no longer wants to acknowledge his two bastard children, so his twin brother, Peregrine, out of the goodness of his heart, takes over financial responsibility for Dora and Nora and sends them a weekly allowance until he's wiped out temporarily in the Wall Street Crash of 1929. When the support stops, Dora and Nora have to earn a living, and they go into vaudeville at the age of fifteen. By the way, Dora and Nora are identical except for the perfume they use. As a matter of fact, they are so identical that they switch perfumes so that Dora can enjoy Nora's boyfriend as her seventeenth birthday present.

Melchior has by now become a country squire, and he invites Dora and Nora to his country home for a costume ball. Unfortunately, the house burns down, although everybody is copulating too much to really notice. I cannot even begin to describe the level of sexual energy of which every character, whatever the age, seems capable. What on earth do these people eat? Their diet must be very different from mine.

Melchior's wife, Lady Atlanta, gives birth to twin girls, Saskia and Imogen, Nora and Dora's half-sisters, and Melchior seems more prepared to acknowledge his first set of twins, asking them, as a favour, to carry with them a piece of Shakespearean earth from Stratford-on-Avon so that he can sprinkle it on the set of the Shakespearean film he's making in Hollywood.

This permits Angela Carter to move much of her cast to Hollywood, and unbelievably we move to a higher level of sexual activity. Dora sleeps with Irish O'Flaherty, a drunken scriptwriter (his name alone is worth the price of the novel), and Nora finds herself an Italian boy. Nora and Tony actually marry, but Tony's possessive mother pours marinara sauce all over Nora at the wedding, reclaims her little boy, and gets the marriage annulled. This is not a novel where the action flags.

We also get to meet a gorgeously grotesque Hollywood producer known only as Genghis Khan, who has just abandoned the wife of his early days to marry the film star Delia Delaney, née Daisy Duck. It's not too unusual a situation, where an immigrant producer marries a young woman of the established culture. Genghis – I know him by no other name – makes only one miscalculation. Daisy Duck, now Delia Delaney, was actually born on Hester Street, New York's equivalent to Mordecai Richler's St. Urbain. She is not the white Anglo-Saxon Protestant of whom he had dreamed.

Not surprisingly, the marriage doesn't last. What is surprising is that it is our old friend Melchior Hazard who becomes Delia's lover. Having established himself in Hollywood as a morsel of England's upper crust, Melchior is prepared to ditch Lady Atlanta, just as Delia is prepared to ditch Genghis Khan. They marry, and Genghis, furious, decides to marry

Melchior's daughter Dora. What sweeter revenge than to take a man's daughter in a society that sees women as property? It is then that Genghis's original wife, a Brooklyn lady, turns up at Dora's door. She has undergone extensive plastic surgery to become a replica of Dora, and now she begs to take Dora's place and be once more married to her errant husband. With a compassion typical of most of the women in the novel, Dora acquiesces. She and Nora go back to London free of both Tony and Genghis.

You may well wonder how the first Mrs. Genghis was able to achieve such a make-over in what was a relatively short period of time. Do not concern yourself with the passage of time. In the world of the deconstructionist, the bourgeois concept of time has very little relevance.

Back in London, Dora stars in a series of nudie shows with her sister. They both return to live with Grandma Chance. When the old lady is killed in the Blitz, the family needs a replacement mother. Dora and Nora decide to take in their former stepmother, Lady Atlanta, Melchior's first wife. She is now better known as "Wheelchair," ever since her daughters, Saskia and Imogen, persuaded her to sign over all her property and then pushed her down the stairs.

Again to no one's surprise, Melchior – now Sir Melchior – announces that his marriage to Delia Delaney is over; he is taking a third wife, the twenty-one-year-old who has been playing Cordelia to his Lear. (Melchior is a real chip off the old block.) His new wife is also the best friend of his daughter Saskia, not too uncommon a triangle in our new world of ever-dissolving and re-forming relationships.

In the fullness of time, Sir Melchior's third wife, known to Dora and Nora as Lady Margarine (she's best known for her TV commercial for that product), gives birth to twins, Gareth and Tristram. Gareth goes on to become a priest, and Tristram has an absolutely repulsive TV game show called "Lashings of Lovely Lolly." The hostess is Tiffany, the beautiful black goddaughter of Dora and Nora. Tristram is having an affair with Tiffany. Unfortunately he's also sleeping with his half-sister Saskia, so much older than him that he always calls her "Auntie."

If, for the sake of following the plot, you wish to make a genealogical chart of Melchior's family, please do so. If you want to do the same for the generations of Grandma Chance's chosen family, please do so. But do not put them side by side and expect them to make sense. There is no absolute universal chronology. The two charts will not fit on the same timeline. I've tried it and it doesn't work. Two generations of one family are matched by five or six generations of another in what, in our traditional world, would appear to be the same time frame. I repeat what I said earlier, the bourgeois concept of time has no place in a deconstructionist novel.

We are now coming to Sir Melchior Hazard's one hundredth birthday party, the one for which Dora and Nora were preparing when we met Dora at the beginning of the novel. It will be a magnificent celebration. All three of Melchior's Lady Hazards will be there: Wheelchair, Delia Delaney, and Lady Margarine.

Tristram and a pregnant Tiffany will continue the very public confrontation they began earlier on the television tribute to Sir Melchior. Tristram asks Tiffany for forgiveness, but instead of Angela Carter arranging the comic reconciliation, the reuniting of the lovers, which has ended the comic novel for more than two hundred years, the author has Tiffany refuse Tristram on the grounds of immaturity. For good measure he will also get a beating from Tiffany's mother, Brenda. In this novel, men are not the source of power, of strength, of sexuality. Women are. The women of this novel are earthy and sexual and full of life. The novel is a call to energy, to action, in a world of marvellous women.

But there are exceptions. Saskia tries to poison Sir Melchior's birthday cake. She and Imogen are angry because he discontinued their allowance when they became twenty-one. But Saskia confesses before anyone actually eats the cake. Oddly enough, the attempted poisoning is not the major event of the party. It is overshadowed by at least three other happenings.

First, Sir Melchior's long-lost twin brother, Peregrine, also one hundred years old, makes a miraculous entrance surrounded by butterflies and carrying two babies in his pockets. They are twins, a boy and a girl. He says that they are the children of Tristram's twin brother, Gareth the priest. Dora and Nora agree joyfully to bring them up. (Louis de Bernières was right when he told me that magic realism made plotting much too easy for the novelist!)

The second major event of the party is almost as startling. In a magnificent act of copulation on top of Saskia's fur coat in the upstairs bedroom, Peregrine and his niece Dora make the chandeliers shake at the ball below. Their combined age is one hundred and seventy-five.

The third surprise at the party, a more eventful celebration than those to which I am invited, is Wheelchair's revelation that Peregrine and not her then-husband, Sir Melchior, was the father of Saskia and Imogen. This leads Dora, *after* she has had sex with him, to ask her uncle, "'[Y]ou're not, by any chance, my father, are you? . . . seeing as how you're everybody else's.'" (p. 222) It's no more than a matter of idle curiosity to her; she doesn't appear to be concerned about any immorality.

Dora's question caused me to reflect on a number of mysterious parentages in the novel. At the very beginning, we were never certain who fathered Melchior and Peregrine. Was it Ranulph Hazard, Estella's husband, or her lover, Cassius Booth? Who knows who fathered our Cyn's daughter Mavis, and who the fathers were of the succeeding generations? Paternity is always a mystery, and even the identity of a mother is questioned. Peregrine suggests to Dora that perhaps Pretty Kitty, Grandma Chance's maid, was not Dora and Nora's mother. After all, the girls only have Grandma Chance's word for it; perhaps they were the result of Grandma's own "last fling." (p. 223)

The novel ends with Peregrine producing the twins he says are Gareth's. Who on earth is the mother? Dora is no help; all she does is comment on Gareth's role in the matter: "[T]o add to the hypothetical, disputed, absent father that was such a feature of our history, now you could add a holy father, too. Put it down to liberation theology." (p. 227)

This is indeed a revolutionary novel. Through all the repeated acts of incest, the most profound taboo of patriarchal society is violated. The biological family, the basic unit of middle-class life, ceases to have any relevance for Angela Carter's characters. The only relationships that last are those based on love, not on the chance, the hazard, of birth. As Tiffany points out to Tristram, "'There's more to fathering than fucking, you know.'" (p. 211)

The cry of the novel is *carpe diem!* – seize the day! – or, as Grandma Chance put it, "'Pluck the day! You ain't dead, yet! You've got a party to go to!'" (p. 190)

Angela Carter has created a wonderful, vibrant, pulsating anarchy. This is not a novel with a clear vision and a clear moral certainty for one generation to pass on to the next. While shattering the traditional structure of the novel and its underlying moral didacticism, *Wise Children* is a celebration of energy, love, laughter, and sexuality. Nobody expects anybody, including the reader, to follow the family connections.

It is also a celebration of language. Open the novel at random and you are likely to find one of Dora's glorious one-liners, although it would be hard to top one of her earliest aphorisms. As she applies her party makeup to her seventy-five-year-old face, she reflects that "the habit of applying warpaint outlasts the battle." (p. 6)

Her sister, Nora, can give her a run for her money. Consider this exchange as Dora waxes nostalgic for the railway stations of yore:

> Even the railway stations, changed out of recognition, turned into souks. Waterloo. Victoria. Nowhere you can get a decent cup of tea, all they give you is Harvey Wallbangers, filthy cappuccino. Stocking shops and knicker outlets everywhere you look. I said to Nora: "Remember *Brief Encounter*, how I cried buckets? Nowhere for them to meet on a station, nowadays, except in a bloody knicker shop. Their hands would have to shyly touch under cover of a pair of Union Jack boxer shorts."
>
> "Come off it, you sentimental sod," said Nora. "The only brief encounter *you* had during the war was a fling with a Yank behind the public convenience on Liverpool Street Station."
>
> "I was only doing my bit for the war effort" I replied sedately, but she wasn't listening, she started to giggle.
>
> "'ere, Dor', smashing name for a lingerie shop – Brief Encounter."
> She doubled up. (p. 3)

Do you wonder that Angela Carter is the most studied English writer at English universities, and I am not excluding Dickens and Shakespeare?

As the novel ends, Nora and Dora are creating their own chosen family, just as Grandma Chance did. They will go into the future with Gareth's little twins, a boy and a girl, the first twins of the novel not to be of the same sex. The children are the inhabitants of a brave new world, a secular Eden. Whatever it will be like, if the deconstructionists have any say, it will have discarded the patriarchal morality that has been at the heart of our society and our novels for so long.

It is incredible to me that in spite of her militant deconstructionism, Angela Carter has created characters as memorable as any created in more traditional fare. Surely we are all drawn to the energy of these two wonderful women.

Let us remember them as they enter that wonderful birthday celebration and see themselves in a great mirror:

. . . two funny old girls, paint an inch thick, clothes sixty years too young, stars on their stockings and little wee skirts skimming their buttocks. Parodies. Nora caught sight of us at the same time as I did and she stopped short, too.

"Oooer, Dor'," she said. "We've gone and overdone it."

We couldn't help it, we had to laugh at the spectacle we'd made of ourselves and, fortified by sisterly affection, strutted our stuff boldly into the ballroom. We could still show them a thing or two, even if they couldn't stand the sight. (pp. 197-98)

Dear heavens, I wish that they were real and I had met them. I would have given anything to have heard them say

. . . and we'll go on singing and dancing until we drop in our tracks, won't we, kids.

What a joy it is to dance and sing! (p. 232)

THE FARMING OF BONES

Edwidge Danticat

(Toronto: Penguin, 1999)

Before I begin my review of *The Farming of Bones* by Edwidge Danticat, let me tell you about a little mystery that has been at the back of my mind for years. It may seem at first that it has nothing to do with the novel, but in fact it has everything to do with it.

The plight of Germany's Jews had become intolerable by 1938. Accordingly, in July of that year, Franklin Delano Roosevelt called a meeting of thirty-two nations to be held in the French town of Evian. These Countries of Asylum, as they called themselves, were to discuss ways to alleviate the suffering.

But no one wanted the Jews. The British argued that a sudden influx of Jewish refugees would provoke anti-Semitism; the French claimed that they were already "inundated" with Jews; and, of course, for Canada "none was too many." The United States refused to increase its quota.

Only three small nations offered any help. Tiny, overcrowded Denmark, to its everlasting honour, said it would accept fifteen hundred more Jews. Holland offered refuge, but only on a temporary basis. It was the third nation that presented me with the mystery. The little dictatorship of the Dominican Republic, half of a small island in the Caribbean, said that it would accept a hundred thousand Jews. But the Dominican Republic made one very strange condition – the Jews had to work as agricultural labourers.

Because of the obstacles set up by the German government, and because of the lack of funds of the German Jewish refugees, only six hundred and forty-five Jews finally benefited from the offer of the Dominican Republic. They did very well by the way; the little community they established at Sosua still produces most of the Dominican Republic's butter and cheese.

But the question always nagged at me – why was the offer made in the first place? Why would a tinpot little dictatorship on half a Caribbean island behave more decently than countries like Canada, Britain, and the United States?

In all the years I spent reading about *Ha Shoah*, the Holocaust, I never found an answer to this one nagging little question. When my wife, Pearl, trained as a docent at the Montreal Holocaust Memorial Centre, I did the reading with her. I learned a lot, but I never found the answer to my one little question.

And then recently the strangest thing happened. I found the answer while doing my research on *The Farming of Bones*. And the answer to my question explains in large part the events of that novel. But before I can give the answer, I first have to deal with the history of the island of Hispaniola.

After Cuba, Hispaniola is the largest island in the Caribbean, and it is divided into two countries, Haiti in the west and the Dominican Republic in the east. Today they each have a population of about seven million. *The Farming of Bones* deals with the atrocity that took place in 1937 in the Dominican Republic, near its border with Haiti. I want to explain the events that led up to the horror of 1937. Without an overview of the history of the two nations that share the island of Hispaniola, I don't believe the novel is fully comprehensible.

The island was discovered by Christopher Columbus in 1492. In 1496, Columbus's brother, Bartolomeo, established a little settlement on the southeast coast. He called it Nueva Isabela – later it became the city of Santo Domingo. As a matter of fact, Christopher Columbus is buried beneath the city's cathedral.

The Spanish colonizers established coffee and sugarcane plantations. The original inhabitants, Arawak Indians and Caribs, were soon worked to death, and the Spaniards replaced them with black slaves brought over from the west coast of Africa.

The development of the island by the Spanish took place mainly in the east, spreading out from the settlement of Santo Domingo. The western end of the island was a haven for French pirates, who began their own coffee and sugarcane plantations and who also brought in their own African slaves.

After two hundred years of both French and Spanish colonization of Hispaniola, Spain was forced to recognize the reality that the western third of the island was under French control, and in 1697, by the Treaty of Ryswick, Spain formally conceded the territory to France. After 1697 we have two nations on the island, French-speaking Haiti in the west and the Spanish-speaking Dominican Republic in the east.

In 1804, in the French colony of Haiti, the slaves rose up against their French masters in what was the first victorious slave revolt in history. Other than England, Haiti was the only country in the world to success-fully defy Napoleon.

The Haitian ex-slaves, all of African descent, massacred the whole of the French ruling class. Although the French captured the initial leader of the revolt, Toussaint l'Ouverture, and starved him to death, they were unable to defeat the other two generals, Jean-Jacques Dessalines and Henri Christophe.

Unfortunately, the new leaders of Haiti, who declared themselves emperors, were intoxicated by the freedom they had won from the French. They spent the whole of the Haitian treasury on citadels, fortresses, and palaces to their own glorification, and in 1822, out of pure greed, attacked and occupied their Dominican neighbours, who had just won their own independence from the Spanish. For twenty-two years the Haitians domi-nated the whole island of Hispaniola. In 1844, the Dominicans rebelled against the occupiers and begged the Spanish to come back and protect them from the Haitians. The Spanish agreed, and ruled the Dominican Republic until 1865, when it again won its independence from Spain.

Even as an independent country, the Dominican Republic maintained strong ties with Spain. The Dominicans encouraged Spanish and other European immigration and investment. So great was the interest of Europe in the Dominican Republic, with its coffee and sugarcane plantations, that the United States actually occupied the country for eight years, beginning in 1916, to prevent a complete European takeover. When the United States moved out, they left behind a pro-business and pro-American right-wing government. In 1930 there was a military coup and General Rafael Leonidas Trujillo Molina became President and Generalissimo. Careful never to offend the United States, he would rule the country harshly but efficiently for thirty-one years until his assassination in 1961. Since then, the Dominican Republic has been run by a series of pro-American governments.

Any attempt at upsetting this, like the election of the socialist Juan Bosch, has been promptly quashed by the Dominican Army with American support.

In Haiti, meanwhile, things had been going from bad to worse. Through the nineteenth and twentieth centuries one dictator had succeeded another, usually by assassination. The country was so unstable that there was no investment from the outside. The Haitian plantations were taken over by the American United Fruit Company, but they put nothing back into the country except bribes to whoever happened to be in power. There was so much chaos in Haiti that the U.S. Army occupied the island for nineteen years from 1915 to 1934 just to protect American interests, but when they departed they left an island desperately poor and with no political infrastructure. There was so little work that thousands of Haitians slipped over the border to work on the sugarcane plantations of the Dominican Republic.

This is the point at which our novel begins, in 1937 in the Dominican Republic, in the seventh year of the regime of General Trujillo.

The plantations are full of Haitian immigrant workers. Some have been in the Dominican Republic for only a few years, some have been there for generations. The Haitian workers in the Dominican Republic are unwelcome guests, a hated minority. A part of that hatred is racist. More than 90 percent of Haitians are of pure African ancestry, the French having been wiped out in the rebellion of 1804.

It was different in the Spanish-speaking Dominican Republic. It was Trujillo's proud boast that 80 percent of the Dominican population, although of varying shades of brown, could claim at least partial Spanish ancestry. Ten percent could and still do claim pure Spanish descent.

In the novel a Haitian priest, Father Romain, is imprisoned in a Dominican jail. And what do his jailers, imbued with the racism of Trujillo, shout at him? " 'Our motherland is Spain; theirs is darkest Africa, do you understand?' " (p. 260)

In 1937, Generalissimo Rafael Trujillo decided to solve the problem of the unwanted Haitian workers. He decided to murder them. He needed their labour, but he already knew where to get replacements. Within months, at the Evian Conference, he would invite one hundred thousand European Jews to come to the Dominican Republic as agricultural workers. With one massacre and one invitation he would get rid of the Haitians and make his own country even more European. He literally wanted to whiten the country. And that explains what I had never understood, the offer to the Jews at the Evian Conference of 1938.

Trujillo put the first part of his plan into action in August of 1937. He would murder ten or twenty or thirty thousand Haitian workers. No one knows the exact figure. The perpetrators of genocides do not issue death certificates. That massacre is the focus of *The Farming of Bones*.

But first a word about Edwidge Danticat herself. She was born in 1969 in the capital of Haiti, Port-au-Prince. Ironically, the slum of her childhood had a pretty name, Bel Air. When Edwidge was two, her father left to try to prepare a new life for the family in New York. Two years later her mother joined her husband, leaving Edwidge and her younger brother in the care of an aunt.

The family was reunited in Brooklyn when Edwidge was twelve. There were now two more younger brothers. Her father worked as a taxi driver and her mother worked in a garment factory, as they both still do. Her parents made great sacrifices for Edwidge's education. She took a degree in French Literature at Barnard College in 1990 and her Master's in Fine Arts at Brown University in 1993. Of her three brothers, one is a teacher and the other two are students. She is unmarried and still lives with her parents and her brothers in a little house in East Flatbush. Brilliant, beautiful, successful, she is the embodiment of every parent's dream.

In 1994 she published her first novel, *Breath, Eyes and Memory*, based on the years of the Duvalier dictatorship during her childhood in Haiti.

The novel was well received, but Danticat still had to eke out a living where she could. Then came her well-deserved stroke of luck. She was an extra on the filming of Toni Morrison's novel *Beloved*, starring Oprah Winfrey. Danticat and Oprah met, talked, and became friends. Oprah made *Breath, Eyes and Memory* her Book Club choice. And the rest is history.

A year later Danticat published a collection of stories called *Krik? Krak!*, whose title is the phrase traditionally used by Haitian storytellers. "Krik?" asks the teller of tales, "Krak" answers the audience, and the bond is established. One of those short stories is "1937." A preview of today's novel, it also deals with the 1937 massacre in the Dominican Republic.

Finally, we come to *The Farming of Bones*, published in 1998 when Edwidge Danticat was twenty-nine years old.

Our protagonist is a young Haitian woman, Amabelle Désir, the child of Haitian labourers in the Dominican Republic. When she was eight, her parents were swept away in the river that forms the boundary between Haiti and the Dominican Republic. They had been trying to get back into Haiti to attend a market day at a nearby town. The river is called, oddly enough, the Massacre River, after a clash centuries before between Spanish colonists and French pirates, but the name is very appropriate to the events of 1937. The accident that orphaned Amabelle Désir at the age of eight, however, was just that, an accident, but she witnessed the deaths and the river will play a great part in her thoughts and her dreams.

She is found on the riverbank by Don Ignacio, a Dominican landowner, who takes her back to his estate to be the companion and maid to his daughter, whom we meet much later as a married woman, Señora Valencia. The two girls sleep in the same room and grow up together, but live in very different social worlds.

Don Ignacio's daughter will marry Colonel Pico, one of Trujillo's most fanatical admirers, always away from home at the Generalissimo's head-quarters, always attending assiduously to the Generalissimo's orders.

Amabelle's life will be divided between the household of Don Ignacio, his daughter and son-in-law, and Alégria, the nearby community of Haitian expatriate workers. The name is one of the many bitter little jokes in the novel. The word means "joy" in Spanish, but it isn't easy for the Haitian workers to squeeze joy out of their lives as unwelcome but necessary guests in the Dominican Republic. Most of the Haitians in Alégria have been there for generations. They call themselves in their own Créole French "*non-voyagé* Haitians," Haitians who don't travel. Some of them have moved up from the brutal work of cutting sugarcane, like Urèl the stonemason; they have even produced a priest, Father Romain. But they have no civil rights and are even denied access to Dominican schools. As one old Haitian woman puts it: "'Not me, not my son, not one of us has ever seen the other side of the border. Still they won't put our birth papers in our palms so my son can have knowledge placed into his head by a proper educator in a proper school.'" (p. 69)

When we meet Amabelle at the beginning of the novel, she has fallen in love with one of the sugarcane cutters, a recent Haitian expatriate named Sebastien Onius. Like Amabelle, he has suffered his own family tragedy. His father died in the great hurricane that swept both countries of the island of Hispaniola in 1930. It was then that Sebastien came to work in the Dominican Republic to earn money to help support his mother, Maman ("Man" for short) Denise, back in Haiti.

Sebastien has his own memory of witnessing death very close. He had tried to save his dying father, "'trying not to drop the father, not crying or screaming like you'd think, but praying that more of the father's blood will stay in the father's throat and not go into the muddy flood.'" (p. 34) And then Sebastien makes a revealing remark: "'If you let yourself, you can see it before your eyes.'"

Sebastien is a man of very powerful will. The reality he works in is very harsh, but he will not permit that harshness to invade his mind with sad memories. He is in strong contrast to Amabelle, who relives her parents' death every night in her dreams.

As he and Amabelle fall in love and begin to heal each other, Sebastien tries to give her a strategy for replacing her nightmares with a gentle peace.

> "I don't want you to dream of that river again," he said. "Give yourself a pleasant dream. Remember not only the end, but the middle, and the beginning, the things they did when they were breathing. Let us say that the river was still that day."
>
> "And my parents?"
>
> "They died natural deaths many years later."
>
> "And why did I come here?"
>
> "Even though you were a girl when you left and I was already a man when I arrived and our families did not know each other, you came here to meet me." (p. 55)

The innocence of Amabelle's simple questions – "And why did I come here?" – and the sweetness of Sebastien's advice – "Let us say that the river was still that day" – I really found quite overwhelming, especially the last line: "You came here to meet me."

Amabelle tries to turn the nightmare of her parents' drowning into gentle dreams, happy memories. The truth is that her mother "had always spoken so briefly and so sternly," (p. 208) but in the dreams inspired by Sebastien's love, everything is transmuted.

"'Her name was Irelle Pradelle and . . . she was always smiling. Except of course when she and my papa were drowning.'" (p. 14) The latter

sentence is a marvellous touch by the author – the forced concession to
reality. Dreaming as therapy has limits beyond which we cannot push. But
in general the dreams become happy memories of her father playing games
with her, making lanterns for her in the shape of General Toussaint's plumed
hat, the shape of the cathedral at Cap Haïtien. And sometimes she dreams
up images of strength to nourish her, including her childhood memory of the
great citadel looming over her birthplace at Cap Haïtien, the citadel built by
Emperor Henri Christophe at the time of Haiti's early greatness.

Amabelle is not stupid. She knows exactly what she is doing, using her
dreams to force away an unwanted memory. She says so clearly: "You may
be surprised what we use our dreams to do, how we drape them over our
sight and carry them like amulets to protect us from evil spells." (p. 265)

This ability to dream positively will sustain her later as she runs from
Trujillo's massacre. She will be able to conjure up her mother, who in truth
never smiled: "'I was saving my smile for when you needed it. . . . You will
be well again, ma belle, Amabelle. I know this to be true. And how can you
have ever doubted my love? You, my eternity.'" (p. 208)

The ability to control her dreams, which she learned from Sebastien,
seems to run in Sebastien's family. Later in the novel, Man Denise,
Sebastien's mother, who believes her son and daughter have been massacred, will say to Amabelle in two exquisitely simple and touching sentences, "'Leave me now. I'm going to dream up my children.'" (p. 243)

When Juana, the long-time housekeeper for Don Ignacio and his
daughter, challenges Amabelle, it is small wonder that Amabelle gives
this answer: "'Yesterday Juana called me a nonbeliever because I don't
normally pray to the saints,' I said. 'She asked me if I believed in anything, and all I could think to say was Sebastien.'" (p. 65)

The centrality of Sebastien in the life of Amabelle Désir is made clear
in the first lines of the novel. "His name is Sebastien Onius. He comes most
nights to put an end to my nightmare." It's a wonderful opening, drawing
us right into the novel. It's on a par with "Call me Ishmael." And then,
fittingly, comes a love scene that develops into a tender love poem, beginning with Amabelle intent on her lover's body:

[T]he cane stalks have ripped apart most of the skin on his shiny
black face, leaving him with crisscrossed trails of furrowed scars. His

arms are as wide as one of my bare thighs. They are steel, hardened
by four years of sugarcane harvests. (p. 1)

We recognize here not only Amabelle's adoration of her lover's body but
also the genesis of the novel's title, *The Farming of Bones*. Cutting the sugarcane is a brutal kind of farming that strips the skin and flesh from the
body, bringing the bones closer to the surface. There is also a grim foreboding in the word "bones" of the massacre that is to come.

Even more important is the poetry, the love in her voice when she says,
"He is lavishly handsome by the dim light of my castor oil lamp."

The powerful Sebastien reciprocates:

"Look at your perfect little face," he says, "your perfect little shape,
your perfect little body, a woman child with deep black skin, all the
shades of black in you. . . ."

He touches me like one brush of a single feather, perhaps fearing,
too, that I might vanish.

"Everything in your face is as it should be," he says, "your nose is
where it should be." (p. 3)

All the senses are involved. Amabelle remembers:

In the morning, before the first lemongrass-scented ray of sunlight,
he is gone. But I can still feel his presence there, in the small square
of my room. I can smell his sweat, which is as thick as sugarcane juice
when he's worked too much. I can still feel his lips. . . . And I can still
count his breaths and how sometimes they raced much faster than the
beating of his heart. (p. 3)

It is a lovely erotic scene, involving all the senses. It made me run back
to read again the most beautiful of all love poems, The Song of Solomon.
That poem too was sung by a woman both black and comely. You will
remember how the Biblical woman praises her lover's body, just as
Amabelle praises that of Sebastien. You will remember also that The Song
of Songs contains those exquisite phrases "His mouth is most sweet: yea,
he is altogether lovely. This is my beloved, and this is my friend."

I am absolutely sure that Danticat had The Song of Solomon in mind when she wrote this opening scene. She dwells too long on the sweetness of Sebastien's mouth for the resemblance to be no more than a coincidence.

A brilliant beginning, I thought, as I first read the novel. Without any detail of physical lovemaking, the scene manages to achieve a high level of both poetry and eroticism. The simplicity of the language also made me aware that Danticat is a writer who knows how to use understatement. I sometimes think that that is the hardest lesson for the young writer to learn, to stay away from purple prose. In writing, as in most areas of life, less is always more.

The scene is told in the present, but it is clearly a memory. Danticat ends Amabelle's love scene with: "At times Sebastien Onius guarded me from the shadows. At other times he was one of them." (p. 4)

And so we move into the novel's dramatic present. We have been offered a memory of love; now we are offered a scene of childbirth. The date, we learn later, is August 30, 1937. Amabelle is attending to her mistress, Señora Valencia, who is in premature labour. Amabelle hears screams:

> I ran through the house, to the señora's bedroom.
> Señora Valencia was lying on her bed, her skin raining sweat and the bottom part of her dress soaking in baby fluid.
> Her waters had broken. (p. 5)

I was struck by the emphasis on the breaking of water as a prelude to childbirth, especially when it is juxtaposed with the memory of the drowning of her parents. It seemed to me that, at the very beginning of the novel, Danticat is already using the traditional dual symbolism of water – water connected with life and water connected with death. Our poets have always loved the ambivalence of water imagery.

My suspicions were confirmed when the writer tells us that Señora Valencia is "drowning in the depths of the mattress." Water is going to play a major symbolic role in the novel. At the end of the story, the Señora will say to Amabelle, "'When we were children, you were always drawn to water, Amabelle, streams, lakes, rivers, waterfalls in all their power; do you remember?'" (p. 302)

Amabelle associates Sebastien with the waterfall at Alégria, an image of sexuality, of bounty, and of life.

And of course Amabelle is Haitian, and Haitian culture retains centuries-old memories of African religions. In many of those, water has the power of life and death and must be treated with respect, and is even seen as having its own identity.

We remember the drowning of Amabelle's parents:

> My father reaches into the current and sprinkles his face with the water, as if to salute the spirit of the river and request her permission to enter. My mother crosses herself three times and looks up at the sky before she climbs on my father's back. The water reaches up to Papa's waist as soon as he steps in. Once he is in the river, he flinches, realizing that he has made a grave mistake. (p. 51)

Remember, too, that the boundary between Haiti and the Dominican Republic is a river. When the massacre begins in the Dominican Republic, to cross the river back into Haiti will mean life for people like Amabelle.

Water and crossing rivers have immense symbolic significance, not just in the remembered African animism of Haiti but also in other religions, both ancient and modern. In Ancient Rome, death meant crossing the River Styx. In Christian tradition, the River Jordan is both a place of baptism and, especially in hymns, a boundary we must cross as we die and enter a better world.

But let us return to Señora Valencia, so superbly described as "drowning in the bed of childbirth," a perfect image of both life and death.

Not content with the duality of water imagery, Danticat gives us a second image of duality. Señora Valencia gives birth to twins. The first, the son, is the colour of blush pink, the colour of water lilies, the same colour as Señora Valencia. The second twin, the daughter, is much darker. Indeed her colour causes her mother to ask, "'Amabelle do you think my daughter will always be the color she is now?' . . . 'My poor love, what if she's mistaken for one of your people?'" (p. 12)

We flinch at the cruelty of her question. But it's a brilliant piece of writing by Danticat, who conjures up for us, first, the racism that permeates the whole of Dominican society, and, second, the incredible naiveté of Señora Valencia. This is a woman who goes through life totally unconscious of the sensibilities of other people. There is also a foreshadowing of danger to come for Dominicans who are "too black."

After establishing the imagery that will dominate the novel – the symbolism of the twins and the dual potential of water as healing or destructive – both dualities to remind us that the novel is about two nations sharing the same tiny space, Danticat begins an exciting narrative.

On his way back from Trujillo's headquarters to see his newborn twins, Señora Valencia's husband, Colonel Pico, kills a man with his automobile. Three Haitians – Sebastien, Amabelle's lover; Yves, who will become Amabelle's protector; and their friend Joel – are walking by the side of the road when Colonel Pico's car comes rushing up. Joel is killed and his body hurled into a ravine.

Typically, Colonel Pico does not want to stay and search for the body. What is the death of one Haitian compared to the birth of his two Dominican children?

In Colonel Pico, made in the image of his leader, we have racism gone mad. When his infant son Rafael dies, and Señora Valencia, without asking her husband, invites the Haitian workers to a little tea party to honour her son's memory, what is Pico's reaction when he finds out?

> He did not scold her, but once he discovered that she had used their imported orchid-patterned tea set, he took the set out to the yard and, launching them against the cement walls of the house latrines, he shattered the cups and saucers, one by one. (p. 116)

For Colonel Pico and General Trujillo, the Haitians have become untouchables; what the Haitian touches he defiles. The Dominican leaders have adopted the caste system and declared themselves the brahmins of Hispaniola.

It is at that tea party that we first hear major rumours of a massacre:

> A woman began telling stories that she'd heard. A week before, a pantry maid who had worked in the house of a colonel for thirty years was stabbed by him at the dinner table. Two brothers were dragged from a cane field and macheted to death by field guards – someone there had supposedly witnessed the event with his own eyes. (p. 114)

One of the rumours is particularly terrible:

Many had heard rumors of groups of Haitians being killed in the night because they could not manage to trill their "r" and utter a throaty "j" to ask for parsley, to say *péréjil*. Rumors don't start for nothing, someone insisted. (p. 114)

The truth of the rumour will soon be confirmed. That was the test. The Dominican mob would challenge a suspected Haitian with *"Qué diga péréjil!"* (Say "parsley!") No Haitian can roll the "r" or pronounce the *jota*. Failure to say *péréjil* correctly meant death. It wasn't the only criterion, however. Sometimes it was enough just to be black. Dark-skinned Dominicans died too, we are told.

Danticat also reminds us that ethnic cleansing is as old as history. She prefaces her novel by quoting from the Book of Judges, chapter 12, verses 4-6. You will remember that two tribes of the ancient Holy Land fought, and when the defeated Ephraimites tried to escape over the River Jordan, the victorious Gileadites, before they let the fugitives pass, would tell them to pronounce the word *shibboleth*. When the Ephraimites couldn't pronounce the "sh" and said *sibboleth*, they were executed. *shibboleth* and death at the River Jordan; *péréjil* and death at the Massacre River! How little ethnic cleansing has changed in three thousand years!

With a thrill of horror we learn that Colonel Pico is in charge of the massacre. In an apparently innocuous comment Colonel Pico makes to his wife, almost an aside, he tells her that he "would also be in charge of a new border operation . . . quick and precise . . . part of it had already started." (p. 42)

Danticat is not so foolish as to make all the Haitians noble and all the Dominicans vicious. Don Ignacio is both a Dominican and a decent man, and he and his neighbours try to help the endangered Haitians. The Dominican doctor, Dr. Javier, warns Amabelle and her friends and he pays with his life for the warning.

Initially, Amabelle pays little heed to Dr. Javier's advice to flee, partly because of her reluctance to believe her world is coming to an end, a common reaction among victims of a genocide, and partly because of her feeling of powerlessness, common to the poor of every culture. As Amabelle says of the rumours, "If they were true, it was something I could neither change nor control." (p. 147) And, finally, she has been a maid since she was eight; she can think only in terms of a little world centred on Señora Valencia: "The trucks speeding by worried me, but more worrisome somehow were the face-sized splotches of blood that I now saw on the back of the señora's dress." (p. 152)

After Sebastien, his sister, Dr. Javier, Father Romain and another priest, and all the Haitian immigrants are whipped onto an army truck, Amabelle and her protector, Sebastien's friend Yves, are left with no choice but to run, and a large part of the novel will be devoted to their flight to and across the Massacre River.

There will be a catalogue of atrocities: the *péréjil* test, bonfires of bodies, groups forced six at a time off cliffs, and women and babies hanged.

Danticat handles the tension brilliantly. At one point the fugitives are trapped in the Dominican border town of Dajabón, where a crowd stuffs Amabelle and Yves's mouths with parsley, but suddenly their tormentors turn away and they are left alone. Generalissimo Trujillo himself is visiting the city. He's about to leave the cathedral, and the crowd, mad with adoration, turn aside from Amabelle and Yves, who manage to escape.

I thought it such a clever touch for Danticat to put Trujillo in the cathedral. She has already reminded us of the ethnic cleansing in the Book of Judges, and now she is reminding us that in Biblical history God was invariably on the side of the ethnic cleansers.

When Amabelle and Yves, though not their friends and certainly not Sebastien, finally make it to refuge in Haiti, the scene is of desolation, one testimony to massacre after another. The Haitians cry out in their despair, not to the God who appears to have forsaken them – He was with Trujillo in the cathedral – but to the heroes of their early history:

"In those times we had respect. When Dessalines, Toussaint, Henri, when those men walked the earth, we were a strong nation. . . ."

"Papa Dessalines, where have you left us? Papa Toussaint, what have you left us to? Papa Henri, have you forsaken us?" (p. 212)

Only the Haitians who worked in the American-owned sugar mills have been spared. The United Fruit Company was apparently a better protector than the Almighty.

Yves's mother, Man Rapadou, receives them with rapture, but Amabelle and Yves are the walking dead, almost the zombies of Haitian folklore. They sleep together just once. Amabelle tells us why, and the answer in

Danticat's understated prose is like a blow in the face. "I'd wondered whether my flesh could feel anything but pain." (p. 250)

Both Yves and Amabelle want to bear witness. They shudder to hear a guide in Cap Haïtien tell the tourists, " 'Famous men never truly die. It is only those nameless and faceless who vanish like smoke into the early morning air.' " (p. 280)

They go to the courts to give depositions. Apparently Trujillo has offered President Vincent of Haiti some monetary compensation, as Trujillo put it, "to erase any bad feelings," but the money will never trickle down to the victims' families. As Yves points out, " 'The Generalissimo has found ways to buy and sell the ones here. Even this region has been corrupted with his money.' " (p. 246)

Sebastien's mother, Man Denise, has spoken to some who witnessed the murder of her son and her daughter, but Amabelle would be grateful for any more news of her lover, even the details of his death. She writes a letter to Dr. Javier, care of Father Romain, who she heard survived the massacre, but she knows Dr. Javier is dead and will never answer. The letter was just something to do. As Amabelle says, "I waited for Dr. Javier's reply by growing old." (p. 267)

The years pass. Twenty-four years after the massacre, in the thirty-first year of his reign, Trujillo is assassinated and in Haiti the people dance in the streets. Amabelle sees Father Romain and finds that the massacre had caused him to turn his face from his God. After torture and a mental collapse, he left the priesthood to marry and find some meaning in the creation of three sons.

But Amabelle has found no meaning. Haitian women in this novel are strong; they are what Danticat calls "the kitchen poets," the bearers of history and the oral tradition, but Amabelle has no strength left. In one of her dreams she conjures up Sebastien and tells him, " 'I chose a living death because I am not brave. . . . [P]erhaps you and I can meet again. I am coming to your waterfall.' " (p. 283) My breath was taken away by that last sentence. What could she mean?

Amabelle pays a smuggler to take her back across the border to Alégria for one day, to the house of Señora Valencia, to Sebastien's waterfall.

Señora Valencia will babble to her about forgiveness, about how the Señora could not defy her husband, about how she hid Haitians. Amabelle tells her, " 'Go in peace, Señora.' " She shows compassion for this weak woman just as she can show admiration for the strength of Yves's mother, Man Rapadou, who poisoned her husband for becoming a Yankee spy. By the end of the novel, Amabelle is an observer of, rather than a participant in, the life around her. She can note calmly that some of us are weak and some of us are strong. She can even make a bitter joke: "What could she have expected me to say? There were no medals to be given. If there were, I didn't know where to tell her to go to claim hers." (p. 299)

She can make a judgment, she can make a joke, but she no longer feels involved in the human comedy. She hasn't really been involved since she crossed the Massacre River into Haiti and safety twenty-four years ago.

It comes time in the late afternoon for the smuggler to take her back into Haiti, but she asks to be dropped by the Massacre River: "'My man is coming for me.'" How beautiful are the six words!

They lead us to the final paragraphs, a *tour de force* in which Danticat will effect a perfect reconciliation between the duality of water as both destructive and healing.

> I removed my dress, folding it piece by piece and laying it on a large boulder on the riverbank. Unclothed, I slipped into the current.
>
> The water was warm for October, warm and shallow, so shallow that I could lie on my back in it with my shoulders only half submerged, the current floating over me in a less than gentle caress, the pebbles in the riverbed scouring my back. (p. 310)

Although the text is not explicit, I am certain that Amabelle is scouring her back so that it will be scarred like Sebastien's. I am certain that she will let the current carry her to deeper water, where she will experience both death and rebirth with her beloved.

The water will carry her through the veil that separates her from Sebastien and his love, her father and his laughter and her mother and eternity.

CAPTAIN CORELLI'S MANDOLIN

Louis de Bernières
(Toronto: Minerva, 1995)

First let me point out that *Captain Corelli's Mandolin* is set in a real place, the Greek island of Cephallonia. Further, all the major historical events in the novel are true. Mussolini's Italy did attack Greece on October 27, 1940. In the face of fierce Greek resistance, the invaders failed to advance, many freezing to death in the Greek mountains. It was only when Hitler dispatched better-disciplined troops to help his fascist ally that Greece was forced to surrender and Italian soldiers were sent to occupy the Greek islands, including Cephallonia. The Italian occupation continued peacefully for three years until September 8, 1943, when Mussolini was ousted and Marshal Badoglio surrendered to the Allies. At that point the Germans turned on their former Italian friends and, as the novel indicates, there were massacres.

There are frequent references in the novel to the long friendship between England and Greece. The novel mentions a monument on the island "to the glory of the British people." It deserves an explanatory note.

Greece was under the domination of Turkey for five hundred years until it won its independence in 1830 with the help of the British government, anxious to limit the power of the Ottoman Empire. British-Greek friendship was further enhanced in 1864, when Britain returned to Greece a number of islands, including Cephallonia, which Britain had conquered fifty years earlier during the Napoleonic War.

As we enter the twentieth century, Greece is an independent monarchy with strong British ties. The Greeks begin a republican form of government in 1924, but they revert to the monarchy in 1935. Faced with the ever-possible threat of an Italian invasion – Mussolini is looking for living space – the Greek king appoints General Metaxas dictator of a government of national unity.

We see this Greek unity in the early pages of the novel. The Second World War is underway, but Italy has not yet attacked Greece. When Dr. Iannis, one of the major characters, meets his cronies at a café, they represent the whole of the Greek political spectrum. The doctor himself is a Republican, his friend Kokolios is a Communist, and another friend, Stamatis, is a diehard Royalist and supporter of Metaxas. But the three-way division is good-humoured; the argument is always theoretical on this little island paradise and the reader has the sense of little people going happily about their little lives.

The novel begins wonderfully well: "Dr. Iannis had enjoyed a satisfactory day in which none of his patients had died or got any worse."

Would that every doctor could say as much! And it continues with a delicious catalogue: "He had attended a surprisingly easy calving, lanced one abscess, extracted a molar, dosed one lady of easy virtue with Salvarsan, performed an unpleasant but spectacularly fruitful enema, and had produced a miracle."

In those few lines de Bernières has established both the doctor's position within the little island community and the character of a man willing to care for all the varied ills of humanity. A most un-doctorlike humility, I thought.

The miracle referred to, by the way, was the deft removal of a pea from the ear of his old friend Stamatis, thereby curing a long-standing deafness. Stamatis is of course not told it was only a pea; that would be to rob medicine of a little of its necessary mystery. In one of the novel's very many funny passages, Stamatis comes back later to demand the return of the impediment to his hearing. Stamatis's wife is a woman of loud and strong opinion, and Stamatis's cure is putting in peril the peace of his marriage.

As we meet the charming Dr. Iannis, we learn that he has decided to write the history of his island, beginning three thousand years earlier at the time of Homer. He never gets very far, because his daughter's goat usually gobbles up his daily output, but we are given fragments from time to time. Consider his first lines:

> "The half-forgotten island of Cephallonia rises improvidently and inadvisedly from the Ionian Sea; it is an island so immense in antiquity that the very rocks themselves exhale nostalgia and the red earth lies stupefied not only by the sun, but by the impossible weight of memory." (p. 5)

What a memorable phrase, "the impossible weight of memory"!

It has been put to me that Dr. Iannis is not a believable character. The argument usually runs that a self-taught ex-seaman who bought *The Complete Home Doctor* while his ship was docked in London, and who taught himself English so that he could read the two volumes, could not write so elegantly. A poor man, paid in chickens and eggplants for his services, could not be this wise, this perceptive, could not be so liberal and progressive with his daughter, could not know the history of Greece and the glory of Homer.

What nonsense! Words are free. Like Dr. Iannis, I was born in an area of material poverty, in my case the coal-mining area of South Wales, but my childhood was full of festivals of poetry and song, where coal miners, shop assistants, labourers, and clerks composed epic verse in both English and Welsh. For me, Dr. Iannis is an entirely realistic and plausible character and there is no false note as the novel sweeps me into its embrace.

As we enter the village on the island, we encounter a beautiful little world. We meet Alekos, the shepherd, and are told on page 16 that "his life was timeless." Each day is as peaceful and perfect as the one before. This is paradise, where time in the sense of measurement of change does not exist. We meet Velisarios, who puts on shows of strength – "a gentle giant who had never even become involved in a fight." We meet the priest, Father Arsenios, a Dickens-like figure, "a walking human globe, perpetually perspiring and groaning with the effort of movement . . . venial; a glutton, a would-be lecher, a relentless seeker of alms and offerings." (p. 18)

The novel is divided into seventy-three tiny segments. Some are hilarious set pieces, like the one where the strongman Velisarios lifts the immense priest off the ground to the applause of the crowd. Humiliated,

Father Arsenios hides behind the altar screen of his church, and in a typical act of kindness the villagers leave bottles of wine for him as a mark of contrition for their participation. Father Arsenios can't resist guzzling down the wine but has nothing to pee in except the emptied wine bottles. As his bladder fills, he must empty new bottles more and more quickly. Getting drunker and drunker, he is finally rescued and taken home by that ubiquitous solver of problems, Dr. Iannis.

We also meet one of the novel's two central characters, the beautiful, intelligent, wilful Pelagia, the doctor's daughter. She has inherited the doctor's strength and she is learning his knowledge. Pelagia is in love with a local fisherman. Mandras is beautiful, physically perfect, and when Pelagia spies on him swimming naked with the dolphins, she is overcome with physical desire. Indeed, when Mandras is wounded twice accidentally, once by the cannon of the strongman Velisarios and once by falling out of a tree onto a clay pot, de Bernières gets quite lyrical on the beauty of Mandras's wounded buttocks. But the early section of the novel is an interesting mix of innocence and practicality. Pelagia knows the fate of the unmarried mother, and the reciprocated physical attraction between her and Mandras is never consummated, although they do become engaged.

The idea of innocence in that little Garden of Eden is further embodied in the person of the little local girl Lemoni. She discovers "a funny kind of cat" – in fact a pine marten – trapped on barbed wire and drags Dr. Iannis, never one to worry about his personal dignity, through the undergrowth to rescue it. The pine marten becomes Pelagia's pet Psipsina, "pussycat" in Greek, and the centre of much humour later on.

We see the same innocence of the little girl in the innocence of Mandras, who swims with the dolphins. It is not a coincidence that he is imitating Tarzan to amuse Pelagia before he falls out of a tree and lacerates his buttocks. Like the original Tarzan, Mandras is meant to represent Rousseau's "noble savage." However, Mandras is illiterate and feels inferior to Pelagia and her father. Not all the horrors of the novel will come from outside; the canker is already within the community in the mind of Mandras, although it will take outside events to nurture it to its full, loathsome potential.

When I met de Bernières in 1996, he agreed with my observation that one of the themes in all his work is the heart of darkness within each of us, needing only the stimulus of a fanatic's ideology to bring it out into the open.

But for the moment Cephallonia is still a human, funny little world where the most important event of the year is the Feast of Saint Gerasimos, when faith can cure the insane and lovers slip off into the darkness to be together. This is the Garden of Eden with the addition of colour and humour.

Interspersed with the chapters on Cephallonia are scenes from Mussolini's headquarters in Rome. De Bernières wants to remind us that the outside world exists, that Mussolini is planning his attack, that external events may well intrude into the microcosm of the island.

The Mussolini scenes are hilarious, with the Bullfrog of the Pontine Marshes bellowing out a torrent of propaganda, non sequiturs, and outright nonsense. De Bernières assured me that every one of the sentences had been uttered by Mussolini, although de Bernières had taken some liberties with their arrangement. Among the dozens of orders Mussolini barks out to his aides is one to plant the mountaintops of Italy with trees in order to cause more snow and thus create a tougher breed of Italians. (p. 9) I thought de Bernières had gone too far in his ridicule of national leaders until I remembered President Ronald Reagan, on television, telling a group of reporters that most of the earth's pollution was caused by trees. I can see it now in my mind's eye. He ended his little lesson on ecology by saying, "I bet you didn't know that, did you?" and what I found incredible was that no one laughed. And what about Mackenzie King, who took advice from the spirits of his dead mother and his dog?

Twice in the novel we are taken by the author into the mind of the Greek dictator Metaxas. He is preoccupied by two events, the imminent Italian invasion of Greece and the notorious promiscuity of his daughter. He cannot control his daughter, but he can control the Greek nation, and so the order is given to resist to the death. De Bernières wondered aloud to me how often the decisions of national leaders are influenced by their own weaknesses, their personal humiliations, and their private defeats. He also lamented that these leaders use nationalism as a tool to inflame the worst instincts of their followers. The writer is preoccupied both by the dangers of jingoism and the terrible results the actions of powerful men can have on the lives of ordinary people. He put it succinctly to me: "Nationalism is something I despise more than anything else. How many millions of deaths has it caused? Nationalism – it just causes wars and prevents marriages."

I told him that I was surprised by his vehemence. I thought the aim of most novelists was to efface themselves, to let the work speak for itself. "Not me," he said, "I write passionately. I am not a cool, cynical, detached observer. I want the reader to be moved."

I felt that same rage in Dr. Iannis when he hears of Mussolini's attack on Greece. It is a rage we must all share from time to time as we witness the lunacy of leaders.

> The doctor put his hands to his face and felt his own tears fighting to appear. He was possessed by all the furious and impotent rage of the little man who has been bound and gagged, and forced to watch whilst his own wife is raped and mutilated. (p. 57)

Royalists, Republicans, and Communists will all unite behind the king and Metaxas, but they can fend off neither the Italian troops who arrive to garrison the island, nor the small German contingent sent to keep an eye on their notoriously inefficient allies, always believed by the Germans to have too little enthusiasm for the Axis cause.

So that we should not be overwhelmed by the power of de Bernières's hatred of nationalist ideology, the author cleverly plays the arrival of the Italian army as superb comedy.

They make their appearance as a group of soldiers marching deliberately out of step. (p. 157) One of them imitates Hitler, goose-stepping along with his finger under his nose. One group returns Kokolios's defiant clenched-fist salute with the same salute delivered *con brio*. Captain Corelli himself, carrying his mandolin, orders an "eyes left" for the beautiful Pelagia: "'*Bella bambina* at 9 o'clock.'"

Thus begins the Italian occupation and the billeting of Corelli and his mandolin at the household of Dr. Iannis and his daughter.

Meanwhile, the engagement between Mandras and Pelagia is over. No longer beautiful, Mandras returns from the front lice-ridden, with maggot-infested feet and a hundred unread letters from Pelagia. Nursed back to health by his mother, Drosoula, and a Pelagia motivated no longer by love but by a sense of medical vocation, Mandras will leave again to fight the Italians. He falls in with a Communist resistance group, who could have as easily been Royalist, since he doesn't understand their Marxist slogans. But he does understand the test of loyalty they give him. He is told to beat to death an old Greek peasant, suspected by the

Communists of giving British-dropped supplies to the Royalist resistance. At first Mandras is reluctant, but then gives in to the sense of power. It is a brilliant and terrible passage.

> It was easier at each stroke. In fact it became an exhilaration. It was as if every rage from the earliest year of childhood was welling up inside him, purging him, leaving him renewed and cleansed. The old man, who had been yelping and jumping sideways at every blow, spinning and cowering, finally threw himself to the ground, whining piteously, and Mandras suddenly knew that he could be a god. (p. 192)

De Bernières understands exactly what each ideology offers its bully boys: the chance to pay back a scapegoat for all they think they have endured. Ideology and war make it possible for Mandras to be overtaken by his darker side. Had it not been for Stalin and Mussolini, Mandras would have married Pelagia and they would have lived happily in their little paradise. Instead of Mandras learning to read Marxist claptrap from his sadistic mentors, Pelagia would have taught him to read Homer and the imperfection would have been corrected.

While Mandras is off to join the collective madness, Corelli enters the enchantment of Cephallonia.

> It was an island where it was physically impossible to be morose, where vicious emotions could not exist. By the time that I arrived the Acqui Division had already surrendered to its charms, had sunk back into its cushions, closed its eyes, and become enclosed in a gentle dream. We forgot to be soldiers. (p. 159)

If that passage reminds the reader of Homer's *Odyssey*, then de Bernières was successful. We are meant to think of Ulysses' sailors on the island of enchantment. Homer's epic is always just beneath the surface of the novel.

It is inevitable that Corelli should fall in love with Pelagia and she with him. His love of music and his goodness charm not only her but all the islanders. He is impossible not to love. When the Greek islanders refuse to surrender formally to the Italians, "a nation we have utterly routed," and a German officer has to be flown in, Corelli finds the situation hilarious.

When Dr. Iannis teaches him Greek obscenities as words of greeting, Corelli only laughs, albeit a little ruefully. This is a supremely civilized man, the yardstick in the novel by whom we must measure all others.

He organizes an operatic club, La Scala, at the Italian soldiers' latrine. The only order he ever gives is that "all aficionados of Wagner are to be shot peremptorily, without trial, and without leave of appeal." (p. 162) (I loved him especially for that; I am one with those who believe Wagner is much worse than he sounds.) To the German salute of "Heil Hitler" he responds with an enthusiastic "Hail Puccini." He manages to entice his German opposite number, Lieutenant Weber, into frolicking drunk and naked with ladies of easy virtue on the beach. He even persuades Weber to join La Scala. Since every member of the club must have a musical title, and since Weber cannot sing a note, he is given the honorary title of "dotted demi-semi quaver rest." (p. 203)

For a while we think that Weber, like the Italian soldiers, will succumb to love and to music and to the magic of the island, but of course when the Italian government surrenders to the Allies in 1943 and the Germans massacre their erstwhile allies on the island, Weber cannot find within himself the power to resist. Weber, like Mandras, is a man more good than bad who becomes corrupted because a weakness of character makes him so vulnerable to ideology. It is interesting that after the war Gunther Weber will spend the remainder of his life as a pastor, doing penance for his part in the horror of 1943. How wonderfully de Bernières captures the complexity of human character.

Over nearly three years spent in the same house, Corelli and Pelagia remain in love. They are bound by the power of music, the great harmonizer. When first Pelagia listens to Corelli's mandolin, Antonia, "she wanted to share the journey." (p. 186) Corelli will write a march for her, "Pelagia's March," which contains all her beauty and pride and strength.

These are healthy young people, and there is a strong sexual undercurrent. At one point Corelli, holding the wool for Pelagia to knit, is forced to fall to the ground and pretend to be a puppy to hide his erection. But generally it is a time of innocence, in great contrast to the brutality going on outside their little world.

They became lovers in the old-fashioned sense, and made love in the old-fashioned sense. Their idea of making love was to kiss in the dark under the olive tree after curfew, or sit on a rock watching for dolphins through his binoculars. He loved her too much to jeopardise her happiness. (p. 267)

And always there is music. Consider that great segment, No. 42, beginning on page 248, "How like a Woman is a Mandolin." It is not so much that Corelli's mandolin is shaped like Pelagia's breast, although that is true. More subtly, Corelli explains,

> I think of Pelagia in terms of chords . . . three chords . . . *doh*, *re*, and *sol*. . . . [She laughs] and it is *sol* . . . pretends to reproach me . . . and it is *doh*. She asks me a question . . . and it is like *re*, requiring resolution. I say, "Il Duce and I are conquering Serbia today," and she laughs. . . . She has returned to *sol*. (p. 249)

All is complete and Pelagia is a beautiful harmony in the key of G.

Corelli thinks of himself in terms of music. He is Italian and his nation has shamed him: "'I am a man who lacks the courage to take an evil by the throat and throttle it. . . . I play a diminished chord because I am diminished.'" (p. 251)

Pelagia and Corelli ride around the island in a cloud of love and music. They commit to each other and renounce all nationalism in the most beautiful hymn to love I can remember.

After the war, when we are married, shall we live in Italy? There are nice places. My father thinks I wouldn't like it, but I would. As long as I'm with you. After the war, if we have a girl, can we call her Lemoni? After the war, if we have a son, we've got to call him Iannis. After the war, I'll speak to the children in Greek, and you can speak to them in Italian, and that way they'll grow bilingual. After the war I'm going to write a concerto, and I'll dedicate it to you. After the war I'm going to train to be a doctor, and I don't care if they don't let women in, I'm still going to do it. After the war I'll get a job in a convent, like Vivaldi, teaching music, and all the little girls will fall in love with me, and you'll be jealous. After the war let's go to America, I've got relatives in Chicago. After the war we won't bring up our children with any religion, they can make their own minds up when they're older. After the war, we'll get our own motorbike, and we'll go all over Europe, and you can give concerts in hotels, and that's how we'll live, and I'll start writing poems. After the war I'll get a mandola so that I can play viola music. After the war I'll love you, after the war I'll love you, I'll love you forever, after the war. (p. 270)

Their declaration is a superb example of what a fine writer can do with the technique of incremental repetition. By the end of the passage, "after the war" is carrying more emotional weight than I would have thought possible. I would really put it at the same level as King David's repetition of "my son" in the Second Book of Samuel, chapter 18, verse 33.

De Bernières's control of language is masterly. When the British parachute in an officer, a former academic, who can speak Ancient, but not modern, Greek, in a stroke of genius de Bernières renders it as the fourteenth-century English of Geoffrey Chaucer. Alekos the shepherd can't understand a word and assumes that the British officer with his walkie-talkie is an angel. Innocent but not stupid, Alekos makes an interesting observation: "All the angels he had ever seen in pictures carried swords or spears, and it seemed odd that God had seen fit to modernise." (p. 273)

While we have followed the love of Antonio Corelli and Pelagia, a parallel love story has developed. Carlo Guercio, an Italian soldier, has been with us since the beginning of the novel in segments called "L'Omosessuale" ("The Homosexual"). We met him in 1940, tormented by his homosexuality. The literature of his own Italian culture condemns him. Dante, in his *Inferno*, placed homosexuals in the third ring of the Seventh Circle of Hell in the company of usurers. Desperate for validation, Carlo Guercio reads the literature of other cultures and finds solace in the writings of the ancient Greeks, who saw no sin in one man loving another. Most movingly, Carlo reflects,

Yes, I have read everything, looking for evidence that I exist, that I am a possibility. And do you know where I found myself? Do you know where I found out that I was, in another vanished world, beautiful and true? It was in the writings of a Greek. (pp. 23-24)

He joined the Italian army because there he could find the life promised by Aristophanes and Phaedrus, where lovers fought at each other's side: "I knew that in the Army there would be those I could love, albeit never touch. I would find someone to love and I would be ennobled by this love . . . [and] I would dare to die for him." (p. 24)

Carlo, advancing into Greece in Mussolini's army, is aware of the irony: "I am an Italian soldier oppressing the only people whose ancestors bestowed upon my kind the right to embody a most perfect form of love." (p. 24)

Carlo's first undeclared love is for a married corporal, Francisco. Together they will endure the icy agonies of the Greek mountains, where Carlo, a giant of a man, will repeatedly go out under Greek fire to carry back to safety wounded and frostbitten and gangrenous comrades.

After Francisco dies slowly and painfully in one of de Bernières's hellishly detailed scenes, Carlo, sick of the waste and the ideology that inspired the madness, shoots himself in the thigh and is declared fit only for garrison duty on the island of Cephallonia. For nearly three years he will be under the command of Antonio Corelli. The two men will become friends; despite the difference in their rank they are united by their hatred of war and nationalism.

The two narratives of the novel will become one as Carlo comes to love his captain secretly and completely. Corelli in turn sees the goodness of Carlo Guercio. He introduces him to Pelagia and her father as a man with "'a hundred medals for saving life, and none for taking it.'" (p. 168)

It is in the person of Carlo Guercio that we find the best evidence of de Bernières's profound compassion for his characters. In the first four segments in which Carlo appears, he is referred to as "l'omosessuale," but this is dropped in later segments as we begin to see him, not in terms of his sexual orientation, but of his infinite goodness and humanity.

When Italy surrenders to the Allies, the Germans line up the Italian soldiers on Cephallonia for execution. As the German murderers begin to fire, Carlo Guercio decides to save Corelli's life. Holding Corelli behind him in an iron grip, Carlo assumes the perfect tragic stance. He will die facing a hostile world, and in his death we see the greatness, the magnificence of which the human being is capable.

Carlo stood unbroken as one bullet after another burrowed like white-hot parasitic knives into the muscle of his chest. He felt blows like those of an axe splintering his bones and hacking at his veins.

He stood perfectly still, and when his lungs filled up with blood he held his breath and counted. "Uno, due, tre, quattro, cinque, sei, sette, otto, nove . . ." He decided in the arbitrariness of his valour to stand and count to thirty. At every even number he thought of Francisco dying in Albania, and at every odd number he tightened his grip on Corelli. He reached thirty just as he thought that he might be failing, and then he looked up at the sky, felt a bullet cave the jawbone of his face, and flung himself over backwards. Corelli lay beneath him, paralysed by his weight, drenched utterly in his blood, stupefied by an act of love so incomprehensible and ineffable, so filled with divine madness. (p. 325)

One British critic, Jasper Rees, said of the scene, "If it does not hold you in its thrall, it might be worth checking to see if your heart is made of stone." (*Daily Telegraph*, April 23, 1994)

The novel will move on. Corelli, wounded, will be rescued by Pelagia and will escape from the island. Mandras, coarsened, now literate and totally corrupted by politics, will return, only to be shot by Pelagia as he tries to rape her. He will stumble to the sea and die swimming with the dolphins in an innocence he would never have left had it not been for the evil teachings of wicked men.

Father Arsenios will die beating the Germans with his staff, a John the Baptist figure made mad by war. Dr. Iannis will die after enduring Communist brutality. ELAS, the Greek Communist organization, will kidnap thirty thousand Greek children for indoctrination in Yugoslavia. The mandolin Antonia and Carlo's unread love letters to Corelli will be buried in an earthquake under the ruins of Iannis's house. The Royalist Stamatis and the Communist Kokolios will die at German hands in each other's arms.

Pelagia, left alone as the war ends, will assemble a chosen family of herself, Mandras's mother, and a foundling child she calls Antonia. Together this little family will survive the Greek Civil War until a Royalist victory in 1949. The years will pass, tourists will come, and their tavern and souvenir shop will prosper. Antonia will grow up, marry a lawyer, and have a son, Iannis, who will dream of entertaining the female tourists who come "in search of true love and multiple orgasms." (p. 407)

There is much humour as the novel draws to a close, but there is also a terrible sadness. Pelagia has spent fifty years yearning for Corelli. In his memory, she speaks only Italian to her grandson.

Finally, in 1993, Corelli does return. He tells Pelagia, "'I didn't want to be Italian any more. . . . I've been living in Athens for about twenty-five years. I'm a Greek citizen.'" (p. 423) A successful musician, he has been playing his "Pelagia's March" all over the world.

Corelli had come back to Cephallonia in 1946 and for each of the ten years following, but he had always seen Pelagia with a child – we know it to have been Antonia – and kept his silence, assuming her to be married.

After some coquettish resistance by Pelagia, the aging couple, complete with false teeth, ride off on Corelli's motorcycle into the sunset.

Three thousand years ago, Homer kept Ulysses and Penelope apart for twenty years. I thought de Bernières was pushing it a little to make it fifty, but the parallel with Homer's epic still holds good. Love does triumph – dramatically in the heroic death of Carlo Guercio, quietly in a circular, satiric movement for Pelagia and Corelli.

Pelagia means "ocean," and a pelagic current is one that goes far out to sea before returning to its source. This circular movement is very much the underlying structure of the novel as far as it concerns Corelli and Pelagia. Consider too the return of Mandras to the sea after his disastrous foray into the outside world. The novel goes full circle; Mandras, Pelagia, and Corelli will all end where they began.

Before I end my review, a word on the author. Louis de Bernières was born in 1954, the scion of an old Huguenot family. Destined for the British army, he hated even then both regimentation and ideology and ran away to Colombia for a year as a cowboy and English teacher.

He saw first-hand the peculiar mix of wealth, poverty, drugs, super-stition, Catholicism, magic, and civil war that is South America. He came back to England to take a degree in philosophy and to write three novels in the South American tradition of magic realism. I love the titles: *The War of Don Emmanuel's Nether Parts*, *Señor Vivo and the Coca Lord*, and *The Troublesome Offspring of Cardinal Guzman*. Despite the South American setting and elements of fantasy in all three, very much in the style of Borges, I told de Bernières that I saw great similarities between the three earlier novels and *Captain Corelli's Mandolin*. Each of them contrasts brutality and tenderness, and there is in the first three an idyllic little town called Cochadebajo that seemed to me very like the paradise of Cephallonia before the invasion.

I asked him why, after the third novel, he had given up the South American setting and magic realism. He appeared to handle so well a world where the supernatural is routine, where magic and the old gods are everywhere.

De Bernières told me that his third novel was really the second half of his first novel and that he thought he was beginning to repeat himself. He said he had grown tired of magic realism: "It is the least attractive component of South American literature. It makes plotting too easy. It risks turning the plot into a series of marvellous and unlikely events." He had spent time on Cephallonia and had become interested in the island's history. He also wanted in this, his fourth novel, to make a more cogent exposition of brutality and the power of love and thought magic realism would get in the way.

I must admit that as we spoke, vulgar curiosity overcame me and I asked him about his personal life. Apparently his first three novels didn't provide him with enough money to support himself, so he has worked variously as a car mechanic, a landscape gardener, and a teacher of delinquent children. His hobby is repairing musical instruments with hand tools. He lives in an alley in South London over a junk shop behind a Chinese fish-and-chip restaurant. He told me that he had just ended a six-year relationship with "an Asian lady." Until recently he had a beloved cat called Nutkin and still has a sign over his door, "A very fine cat lives here."

Well, that cat's owner has written a very fine novel. He has contrasted brilliantly the lunacy of leaders and the beauty and variety of ordinary people. He has given us the ugliness of war and the glory of poetry, music, and love.

He has used two narrative courses: the linear, doomed heroic movement of Carlo Guercio, and the gentler, circular, satiric movement of Pelagia and Corelli. It is rare for a novel to contain two such different structures and rarer still for the two structures to mesh together so perfectly. I wept as Carlo Guercio died and I smiled sadly as Corelli and Pelagia rode off toothless into the sunset. I asked de Bernières if he was sure they would marry, and he said they would. I think he said it to comfort me.

Louis de Bernières has reaffirmed the power of love and of music. It is all there, you know, in Corelli's wonderful salutation to the human spirit, and I will end with that salutation, "Hail Puccini!"

PADDY CLARKE HA HA HA

Roddy Doyle

(Toronto: Minerva, 1994)

Before he wrote *Paddy Clarke Ha Ha Ha*, Roddy Doyle had already achieved international success with his first three novels, *The Commitments* (1987), *The Snapper* (1990), and *The Van* (1991), collectively known as the Barrytown Trilogy, all about one prolific family, aptly named the Rabbittes. In all three of the novels, Doyle wrote about the little world he knew best, working-class Dublin. It was the world in which he had grown up as the son of a printer and in which he had been a teacher for fourteen years, teaching ten-year-olds very much like his protagonist, Paddy Clarke.

Roddy Doyle is a modest man, and he found it hard to believe in the success of the Barrytown Trilogy. He never gave up his day job and continued teaching English and geography at Greendale Community School. It was only when his fourth novel, *Paddy Clarke*, began to win every major British literary prize and was hailed as a shoo-in for the Booker Prize that he found the courage to go into his principal's office at 12:30 on June 4, 1993, and give his notice.

Paddy Clarke, like the earlier novels, is situated in a Catholic working-class area of Dublin. Doyle calls it Barrytown, but it bears a close resemblance to his own native district of Kilbarrack.

The plot of the novel is simple. We are going to spend a year with ten-year-old Paddy Clarke. He is a mischievous little boy, exploring what for his young mind are the wonders of school, the drab streets around his house, and the fields not far from his home. We watch him play soccer with the other boys, fight with his best friend, Kevin, shoplift from the local stores for the bravado of it, and tease his little brother, Francis, mercilessly, refusing to call him anything but Sinbad.

At a darker level we note his childish concern for his father's black moods, his increasing fear as his parents bicker more and more, his attempts to restore peace between them, and his sense of loss when his father finally walks out.

Roddy Doyle made a brilliant decision to let the ten-year-old Paddy tell the whole story. The naive narrator, a writer's strategy that dates back to Chaucer's *Canterbury Tales*, forces the audience into a much greater involvement with the text. Paddy is a reliable witness, but his age prevents him from having a complete understanding of what he sees and hears. We, the readers, must intuit much of what is going on from Paddy's reported fragments, and so our attention is engaged even more closely. We also realize that like all naive narrators Paddy will never understand how much of himself he is revealing to us.

Roddy Doyle's choice of title is as masterly as his choice of narrator. When I first picked up the book, I thought the "Ha Ha Ha" of the title was an echo of a child's laughter, the laughter we would expect from a ten-year-old in an ideal world. But of course it's not. As we find out in the last pages of the novel, it comes from a little song the other children made up about Paddy – children are always so spiteful. (Remember that "da" is what a working-class Irish child calls his father.)

The four lines of the little song are:

Paddy Clarke
Paddy Clarke
Has no da.
Ha ha ha!

The two different interpretations of the title suggest the whole movement of the novel, from the joyful exuberance of the early pages, a ten-year-old discovering new marvels every day and laughing with the joy of being alive, to the heartbreaking loss of his father, a loss mocked so cruelly in the sneering "Ha ha ha."

I found the last lines of the novel exceptionally moving.

He came home the day before Christmas Eve, for a visit. I saw him through the glass door again. He was wearing his black coat. I remembered the smell of it when I saw it, when it was wet. I opened the door. Ma stayed in the kitchen; she was busy.

He saw me.

– Patrick, he said.

He moved the parcels he had with him under one arm and put his hand out.

– How are you? he said.

He put his hand out for me to shake it.

– How are you?

His hand felt cold and big, dry and hard.

– Very well, thank you.

The prose is deceptively simple; only one word has more than two syllables. It is indeed the language of a child. But consider how much hurt is communicated in those few simple words.

The formality of Paddy's last four words is worth our attention. The phrase is polite, even excessively courteous, spoken as if to a stranger. Those four words form the first piece of the hard shell Paddy Clarke is going to have to build around himself if he is to survive, fatherless at the age of ten, in what is a hard and very cruel world. We were prepared for that last cold, adult, formal "Very well thank you" some fifteen lines earlier when Paddy commented on the cruel song: "I didn't listen to them. They were only kids." Of course he listened to them; he is only ten years old. But he is no longer one of them; he is no longer a child. He has learned the first, great, adult lesson: Don't let other people see how easily you can be hurt.

Roddy Doyle has said in interview that the inspiration to write *Paddy Clarke* came when the first of his two sons was born to his wife, Belinda. He looked down at the baby boy and thought about the world his little son was about to enter, so magical, so real, so joyful, so cruel. (I should perhaps point out here that the novel is in no way an autobiography. Doyle's parents are still married, as he is. He is writing about the working-class Dublin in which he has spent his whole life, but his protagonist is wholly invented. As Roddy Doyle puts it, "It's not my life, but it's my geography.")

So far I have dealt only with the first and last pages of the novel. It is time now for us to step into the main body of the work, the little world of Paddy Clarke.

It is not an easy world for the North American reader to enter. Since the first English novel, *Pamela*, was written in 1740, the novel has been essentially a middle-class form, a mirror in which the middle-class reader may watch him- or herself move through a fallen world. *Paddy Clarke* is narrated by and is about a working-class child. And "class" has a totally different meaning for the Irish and the British – I group them together in this – than it does for North Americans.

The North American Dream holds that every person on the bottom rung of the economic ladder can and should move upwards. Anyone can become president. That is not the case in Ireland and England. There, there is such a thing as class loyalty. If you are born into the Irish or English working class, the chances are very great you will never move out of it. What is surprising to North Americans is that, in the great majority of cases, members of the British working class do not *want* to move out of it. They may want more money than they have, but that's not the same thing. A key to understanding Roddy Doyle's novel is the realization that the Rabbitte family in the Barrytown Trilogy and the Clarke family in *Paddy Clarke* accept their working-class lot in a way that few North American families would. There is, of course, some social mobility in Ireland and England, but those who do leave one class for another are never allowed to forget it. Take Margaret Thatcher, for instance, who dominated British politics for so long. I have never seen a piece about her in a British newspaper that fails to mention she was a shopkeeper's daughter who grew up living over the store. Her parents spent a fortune on elocution lessons for her so that she could speak Received English, but she still couldn't pass.

There have, of course, been English-language novels about the working class, but they have generally been by social reformers like Dickens, Dreiser, or Sinclair Lewis, attacking the socio-economic injustices that prevent the poor from lifting themselves up into middle-class happiness. A novel by and about a working-class member totally uninterested in upward social mobility seems a very strange phenomenon to the North American reader, particularly if the narrator is a ten-year-old with concerns more important to him than his poverty.

Many people have told me that they had difficulty entering both Paddy Clarke's world and the world of the Rabbitte family in the Barrytown Trilogy, and I think the different perceptions of class have a lot to do with it. But there are other obstacles to overcome for the North American reader, each obstacle providing what I like to call another degree of separation between the reader and the novel. The Irish Catholic background of the novel is one.

The Republic of Ireland doesn't just happen to be Catholic; Catholicism is at the centre of its being. More than 95 percent of Irish citizens are Catholic, and the power of the Church is written into the Irish constitution. While it may be true that fewer people attend Mass regularly than they did fifty years ago, traditional Catholic attitudes still prevail, particularly regarding the family and the male and female roles. Fewer Irish wives work outside the house than in any other European country, and families are still larger than in any other European country. I know new legislation is planned and attitudes are changing, but an ethos developed over centuries does not change overnight.

Paddy Clarke and his parents are hardly fanatical believers. Nevertheless, Catholic ritual and Catholic references permeate the novel. Paddy goes to a Catholic school, and the family still attends the odd Mass. Even while many of the Irish, including Paddy's father, criticize the Church, the fact is that the majority of the Irish still love it; it is not only the operator of many of their schools, social services, and hospitals, it is also their spiritual home, the provider of hope. A country with a population not much greater than that of Montreal has, even now, more than twenty thousand priests and nuns.

Another degree of separation between the reader and Doyle's work is the language of Doyle's novels. The Rabbitte family of the Barrytown Trilogy, even lower on the social scale than Paddy and his family, speak an English so impregnated with Irish dialect that it becomes almost impenetrable. The language of *Paddy Clarke Ha Ha Ha* is much less difficult, although it does help to know that a "mickey" is a penis, a "gee" is a vagina, and a "diddy" is a breast. Like all ten-year-olds, Paddy Clarke is intensely interested in the human body, both male and female, and in all human smells, liquids, and emissions.

Bearing in mind that we are entering a closed Irish Catholic working-class world, more traditional, more static, more accepting of its lot than

anything the ambitious North American is used to, let us get to know Paddy
Clarke a little better. We may find the terrain strange at first but we shall
persevere. I promise that the effort of the journey will be justified, once all
the obstacles are overcome.

Paddy is the oldest of four children; there had been a fifth, a little girl,
stillborn. Closest to Paddy in age is Francis, renamed Sinbad by his older
brother, a voracious reader.

Paddy's narrative, at least at first, is one of apparently unrelated incidents. Paddy finds it worthy of note that one of his friends, Liam, defe-
cated in his pants in the classroom, but Paddy's great interest is in what
Liam did with the shilling the principal gave him to stop his tears. We move
immediately to a local building site, where Paddy and his friends are stealing wood and nails to build a boat to sail to far-off lands. (I remember at
ten years old stealing wood in much the same way to build a helicopter.
Such was the imagination of childhood in the pre-computer age.) They
pretend to be chased by the watchman, but it's only to put the fear of God
into Paddy's little brother, Sinbad, whom they abandon, trapped and sniv-
elling, in a hedge.

Paddy tells us that his neighbour, Mr. Cornell, Liam's father, wails at
night in his garden for his dead wife. Paddy tells us, "We lit fires. We were
always lighting fires." Paddy tells us that during the Monday playground
recess, he and his friends conducted an experiment on Sinbad. Sinbad was
persuaded to hold a tube of lighter fluid between his teeth and allow the
other boys to light it. With enormous satisfaction Paddy assures us that "it
went like a dragon." Then we switch in the next sentence to the subject of
magnifying glasses. Paddy will devote a dozen lines to what you can do
with a magnifying glass and paper. He never mentions his little brother. It
isn't until six pages later that we learn Sinbad had burned his face so badly
that his mother had to tie his hands together to stop him from scratching
the scabs. In these six pages, Paddy has had a dozen more adventures. He
and his friends have cut great swaths in the stinging nettles in the field near
his home. Paddy's father has shown him, by pressing his finger on the win-
dowpane, that no two people have the same fingerprint. We have met the
local idiot, "Uncle Eddie" Donnelly, and heard his whole vocabulary of
two words. We've heard a fascinating but untrue rumour that Uncle Eddie
was trapped in a local barn that caught fire. We have jumped with Paddy
on and from piled bales of hay.

All that between Sinbad's mouth exploding and our being told the consequences of the prank.

It is an absolutely superb observation by Doyle that in a child's world there is no relation between cause and effect. If indeed there are consequences to any given action, they will be perceived by the child as a different experience, complete in itself.

I heard a very similar insight several years ago in a TV interview with Dennis Potter, the creator of *The Singing Detective* and *Pennies from Heaven*. He had full knowledge that he would die within weeks from cancer, and he spoke so succinctly, so truthfully, that I made many notes during the hour. On children he said, "Unlike adults, who are always planning and remembering, living in the future and in the past, children live in the present tense. The *now* is everything to a child."

That's what makes this novel so special. Roddy Doyle has recorded so perfectly the world view of a ten-year-old. Each of his experiences – the encounter with the stinging jellyfish, the mock fights, the real fights, the death of his grandfather, being beaten by his father for shoplifting – has about the same significance for Paddy.

The discovery that you can burn paper with a magnifying glass carries as much weight as his decision, temporary as are all the decisions of childhood, to become a missionary to the lepers.

We've all seen drawings and paintings by children; we've all put them up on our refrigerator doors. And we've all noticed that all the objects in those paintings are about the same size: the tree, the dog, the man, the house. We say that it's because the child has not learned perspective. That statement is surely far truer than we realize.

The point is not that a child has not yet learned a particular technique in drawing, it is that a child has not yet learned what an adult is forced to learn, how to arrange objects and experiences in their order of importance. As adults, we spend our whole life rearranging our memories into a hierarchy of significance. This remembering, classifying, ordering, is a purely adult activity. Children do not do this. This presents, I think, yet another degree of separation, another difficulty for the adult reader trying to engage the novel.

As adults, we all too often forget the pure joy of living, the pure joy of new, unrelated experiences that informed our childhood. We attempt to force an adult concept of hierarchical order onto a book that is largely a chronicle of a ten-year-old's experiences, and the book resists us. Paddy Clarke is a non-judgmental life force. He devours new facts and new experiences, he revels in them, he assimilates them, but he does not evaluate them. Further, Paddy and his friends are like machines of perpetual motion, unlimited energy. As adults we get tired just watching. Consider the following passage:

> We walked; we ran. We ran away. That was the best, running away. We shouted at watchmen, we threw stones at windows, we played knick-knack – and ran away. We owned Barrytown, the whole lot of it. It went on forever. It was a country. (p. 150)

At one level the passage contains the simple, joyful energy of what Wordsworth called "the glad animal movements of my boyhood days." But at another level the passage is an exquisitely constructed poem, built on the principle of incremental repetition, where an idea is repeated and repeated and repeated, carrying a little more weight each time. The Saint John who wrote "In the beginning was the Word and the Word was with God and the Word was God" understood the technique very well.

Roddy Doyle loves words, and so does Paddy Clarke. He is fascinated by polysyllables, and shouts them aloud in his joy: "ignoramus – ignoramus – ignoramus, hirsute – hirsute – hirsute, substandard – substandard – substandard." Sometimes his ear fails him and we get delightful unintentional errors: "The Israelis were always fighting the Arabs and the Americans were fighting the gorillas. It was nice that the gorillas had a country of their own, not like the zoo." (p. 227) There are many advantages to having a naive narrator!

In Doyle's work there is poetry, there is humour, and there are very many passages that are models of economy in writing. One such passage is about Paddy lying upstairs in bed, listening to his parents quarrelling below:

> For a while I thought it was only Da, shouting in the way people did when they were trying not to, but sometimes forgot; a bit like screamed whispers.
>
> My teeth chattered. I let them. I liked it when they did that.
>
> But Ma was shouting as well. I could feel Da's voice but I could only hear hers. They were having another of their fights.

> – What about you!?
> She said that, the only thing I could hear properly.
> I did it again.
> – Stop.
> There was a gap. It had worked; I'd forced them to stop. Da came out and went in to the television. I knew the weight of his steps and the time between them, then I saw him.
> They didn't slam any doors: it was over.
> I stayed there for ages.
> I heard Ma doing things in the kitchen. (p. 42)

In a very few words, Doyle succeeds in making a surprising number of points. We learn that Paddy feels a responsibility for his parents fighting. In some strange way it must be his fault. In a child's logic it would seem that if he caused it, he can stop it, if only he wants to hard enough. Night after night he forces himself to stay awake. If he relaxes for one moment, then the quarrel will have gone too far and there will be no going back. This belief in his own centrality to his parents' existence is just one of many manifestations of Paddy's self-involvement. There is another, more blatant example in the same passage. In the middle of his total focus on his parents fighting, Paddy can break off to note that his teeth are chattering and that he likes the feeling. Doyle is a master at recording the supreme consciousness of self of a ten-year-old.

Paddy is also much given, as all children are, to fantasizing about his own death, with a particular attention to the grief of the mourners. He even imagines the demise of his brother Sinbad and weeps at the sadness of the loss. The imagined emotion does not prevent him from watching his tearful face in the mirror and observing that "the tears on the left were going faster than the ones on the right." (p. 257)

When his parents' arguments become too painful, Paddy can always seek refuge in his beloved facts, chanted like a mantra:

> If your pony was healthy his skin was loose and flexible and if he was sick his skin was tight and hard. The television was invented by John Logie Baird in 1926. He was from Scotland. The clouds that had rain in them were usually called nimbo-stratus. The capital of San Marino was San Marino. Jesse Owens won four gold medals in the 1936

Olympics and Hitler hated black men and the Olympics were in Berlin
that year and Jesse Owens was a black man and Berlin was the capital
of Germany. I knew all these things. I read them all. (pp. 42-43)

Paddy is a fascinating child. He is still not quite sure about Santa Claus,
but likes to cover all his bases: "Putting two letters in one envelope was
stupid. Santy would think it was only one letter and he'd just bring Sinbad's
present and not mine. I didn't believe in him anyway." (p. 31)

He can be capable of terrifying logic, a logic that is absolutely fatiguing
to adults, including Paddy's father. We can sympathize with his putting an
abrupt end to his son's importunity when Paddy tells him what he has learned
at school about Father Damien and his lifelong devotion to the lepers:

> – Were there ever any lepers in Ireland?
> – I don't think so.
> – Why not?
> – It only happens in hot places. I think.
> – It's hot here sometimes, I said.
> – Not that hot.
> – Yes it is.
> – Not hot enough, said my da. – It has to be very very hot.
> – How much hotter than here?
> – Fifteen degrees, said my da. (p. 50)

To appreciate Doyle's mastery of prose technique, we have only to contrast that example of rapid exchange with the horror story Paddy tells his
mother about a man who went on holiday to Africa. It's the kind of horror
story that all children love to hear, believe, and repeat:

> When he was in Africa he had a salad for his tea and when he came
> back from his holidays he started getting pains in his stomach and
> they brought him into Jervis Street because he was screaming in
> agony – they brought him in a taxi – and the doctor couldn't tell what
> was wrong with him and the boy couldn't say anything because he
> couldn't stop screaming because of the pain, so they did an operation
> on him and they found lizards inside him, in his stomach, twenty of
> them; they'd made a nest. They were eating the stomach out of him.

– You're still to eat your lettuce, said my ma.
– He died, I told her. – The boy did.
– Eat it up; go on. It's washed.
– So was the stuff he ate. (p. 124)

In that passage there is a sentence of nine lines without a period. It conveys perfectly the anxiety, the breathlessness of a child desperate to pass on his new-found knowledge.

Paddy is an exceptionally creative child. No sooner do he and his friends kill and burn a rat but they stage an elaborate funeral, complete with clenched-fist muted trumpets. No sooner does Paddy hear the story of Father Damien but he recreates the martyrdom, naturally with his friends playing the lepers and he the saintly, adored missionary.

How accurately Doyle captures the world of an imaginative child! "I had a book on top of my head," Paddy tells us, "I had to get up the stairs without it falling off. If it fell off I would die." (p. 75) That is so authentic. Didn't we all set ourselves tests like that when we were young?

But the novel is more than a series of unrelated events, a chronicle of the *now* of a child. There are two narrative movements.

The first has to do with the relationship between Paddy and Sinbad. At the beginning of the novel, Paddy bullies his brother without mercy. Sinbad is the typical younger sibling, always wanting to tag along with the older children, however unwelcome they make him. (As the youngest of three sons I know the situation very well.) But during the novel Paddy's feelings towards him change. It begins when Paddy watches Sinbad play soccer: "He ran to get the ball. No one else did that. They all waited for it to come to them. He went through them all, no bother. He was brilliant. He wasn't selfish like most fellas who could dribble. It was weird, looking at him." (p. 167)

But the change doesn't come easily: "You couldn't be proud of your little brother."

Finally, Paddy accepts a startling discovery: "I realized something funny; I wanted to be with Sinbad." (p. 239) But it's too late. As his answer to the mounting domestic tension, Sinbad has retreated into silence, into some mysterious place of his own. As Paddy becomes increasingly aware of the conflict between his parents and his own resulting loneliness, he makes Sinbad an offer a younger brother can't refuse, a bribe brilliantly couched by Doyle in the language of a ten-year-old: "I won't hit you again, okay; ever!" (p. 241) But the answer is still silence.

And that leads me to the second narrative thrust of the novel, the growing rift between Paddy's mother and father. It is, I think, a master stroke of Roddy Doyle's that we never really know what is driving the couple apart. There is no omniscient third-person narrator, no adult editorializing. We know Paddy's parents and his brother only through Paddy's perception of them. We are forced to become one with a ten-year-old and be part of his struggle to make sense of a threatening situation. The technique is called *style direct libre*, where the environment is known only through the perception of the protagonist. It is the most dangerous of all techniques for a writer to use, since most readers demand some explanation of the action. We crave a Greek chorus. Doyle's triumph is that never once does he weaken and offer us a clue to help us solve the puzzle.

After all, Paddy's "da" is, at least at the beginning of the novel, a kind and sensitive man. When Paddy gives his father a clear and concise account of what he has learned at school about the Jews of the Ancient World, his father praises him, even quotes from Goldsmith's *Deserted Village*: "And still they gazed and still their wonder grew that one small head could carry all it knew." (p. 27)

Paddy knows his father works hard; so do all "das": "All das sat in a corner of a room and didn't want to be disturbed. They had to rest. They put the food on the table." (p. 203) In those three sentences we find a whole truth that Paddy has made up by analysis and synthesis of all the snippets of comments he has heard over the years in his own and his friends' houses. He honours his father and he loves him and he cannot bear the conflict: "I didn't understand. She was lovely. He was nice. They had four children." (p. 222)

He tries desperately to get to the heart of the matter:

> There must have been a reason why he hated Ma. There must have been something wrong with her, at least one thing. I couldn't see it. I wanted to. I wanted to understand. I wanted to be on both sides. He was my da. (pp. 258-59)

> Why didn't Da like Ma? She liked him; it was him didn't like her. What was wrong with her?
> Nothing. She was lovely looking, though it was hard to tell for sure. She made lovely dinners. The house was clean, the grass cut

and straight and she always left some daisies in the middle because Catherine liked them. She didn't shout like some of the other mas. She didn't wear trousers with no fly. She wasn't fat. She never lost her temper for long. I thought about it: she was the best ma around here. She really was; I didn't just reach that conclusion because she was mine. She was. (p. 257)

It would be hard to write a more moving statement of love.

It is a mystery to us, as it is to Paddy, why his father finally leaves the house. The difference of course is that we know the rupture has nothing to do with Paddy, and Paddy believes, as all ten-year-olds do, that it must somehow be his fault. As early as page 53 Paddy says, "I didn't know what I'd done!" He has tried so hard to keep his parents together with his concentration and his all-night vigils. He has even tried to be the model son. I was close to tears at one point when he said to his mother, "I appreciate this dinner very much." (p. 243)

Doyle writes from within the working class. His people are not failed would-be suburbanites but individuals who lead full and vibrant lives. There is no agitation for social reform in *Paddy Clarke*. When Paddy's teacher, Miss Watkins, tries to instill in her pupils a reverence for Ireland's fallen heroes, Paddy and his friends show no interest whatsoever. Politics in the world created by Roddy Doyle is purely a middle- and upper-class preoccupation. Political activity in *Paddy Clarke* and the Barrytown Trilogy consists in the main of shouting obscenities at any politician from any party who appears on the television screen. It's a surprisingly relaxing thing to do, I find much relief in it myself.

Doyle's novels are about working-class people trying to survive and trying to find a little pleasure in their lives. That is a fair comment on his first three novels. In this novel, *Paddy Clarke*, he has gone further. A novel that began with the joy of childhood, the joy of pure sensation, the joy of innocence, has become a novel about the loss of that innocence, all within the same closed little world that he created in the Barrytown Trilogy. Surely we can all identify with that loss, surely we can all remember that moment when the world outside ourselves robbed us of our innocence.

Do not let unfamiliar language or an unfamiliar culture keep you at a distance from this book. It is a masterpiece.

BIRDSONG

Sebastian Faulks
(London: Vintage, 1994)

Sebastian Faulks finished writing *Birdsong* in 1993 when he was forty. He had already written three novels that I liked very much, particularly the second, *The Girl at the Lion d'Or* (1989), a tragic love affair set in France in 1936. Nothing he had written previously, however, prepared me for the power of *Birdsong*. The story of how he came to write it is an interesting one.

Sebastian Faulks is an upper-class Englishman, the son of a judge, born with every possible advantage. He took a first-class degree in English and French Literature at Cambridge in 1974, spent a few years as a teacher, and then went into journalism. By 1991, when he gave up journalism to write full time, he had reached pretty well the top of his profession in England; he was the literary editor of the *Independent*, almost certainly the best-written British newspaper.

In 1988 he had an experience that had a profound effect on him. Because of his perfect French and his great knowledge of French literature and history, he was asked by the *Independent* to go to France in the company of a group of English veterans who were participating in the seventieth anniversary of the 1918 Armistice. They were old, old men who had fought in the great battles of the First World War: Ypres, Mons, and above all the great offensive on the Somme river in 1916. Sebastian Faulks talked to them, toured the battlefields with them, wrote about them, and became obsessed by the war.

He immersed himself in its history, and after five years of study and reflection felt able to write *Birdsong*.

Faulks demonstrates a total mastery of language in this marvellous novel, from the simplest and most affecting prose to great soaring passages of poetry. He touches on the profound truths of life and death and on every possible manifestation of human love. It is an exploration too of the complexity of human character. Who would have thought Michael Weir could suppress his terror for so long? Or that Stephen Wraysford would find a quiet kind of happiness with the person he did?

About the First World War, the setting of most of *Birdsong*, I am going to say very little. Unlike the Second World War, a righteous struggle against pure evil, the First World War was a conflict fought heroically by its participants for the most ignoble and unheroic motives of the governments involved. On one side were the Central Powers of Europe: Germany, Austro-Hungary, Bulgaria, and Turkey. On the other side, before America came so late into the fray, were Great Britain and its empire, France, Belgium, Serbia, and Russia. The rulers of those countries – all of them on both sides, except I suppose for little Belgium – were fighting for one or two of a variety of motives, including Serb nationalism, Russian pan-Slavism, French revenge, and British and German maritime and colonial jealousy. What all the governments had in common was a lack of any justifiable motive. The men on the ground, the men actually fighting, were different. They thought, or most of them thought, that they were fighting for justice and that God was with them. My own father went to fight in 1914, and he told me that it was not for years after the war ended in 1918 that he realized – he and those of his friends who had survived – how he and they had been used, how the genuine patriotism of those millions of men who served on both sides had been exploited by leaders so unworthy of the people they were supposed to serve.

Birdsong begins so quietly, so deceptively quietly. It is set in France in the year 1910, four years before the outbreak of war, in the peaceful town of Amiens on the Somme river in northern France.

The first thing I noticed in Sebastian Faulks's detailed description of this quiet town is that the word "garden" occurs five times in the first two paragraphs. A garden is the ultimate symbol of harmony; it has been so since the Garden of Eden in *Genesis*. A garden is the imposition of order upon nature, the perfect image of peace and balance, with everything in its allotted place. The mood continues with the introduction of another symbol of harmony, the family. There is nothing so ordered, so arranged, so balanced as the family of nineteenth-century French literature.

We meet the Azaire family, and they are like something out of the novels of Flaubert, or Zola in his happier moments. The family is composed of René Azaire, a middle-aged widower, his sixteen-year-old daughter, Lisette, his son, Grégoire, and his beautiful young wife, Isabelle, twenty-nine years old. The Azaires have dinner every night at the same time, and at exactly the same time after dinner every night they are joined by Azaire's friend M. Bérard, his wife, and on occasion his wife's mother. They will then settle down to hours of excruciating conversation, dominated by M. Bérard, a pontificating, pompous, self-satisfied fool, absolutely convinced, for example, that the English have rain five days out of six and that the English have only recently developed a railway system. He is the classic French bourgeois who believes that in France, and only in France, has civilization come to harmonious balance and ordered perfection.

Into the bosom of this family comes a twenty-year-old Englishman, Stephen Wraysford. Born out of wedlock and abandoned by his mother, he was brought up by his grandfather and later helped by a benefactor who treated him as a social experiment. In short, Stephen Wraysford has never known love. He has been sent by his English employer to study the French textile trade and in particular the prosperous business of René Azaire, with whom Stephen's employer is considering a partnership. Stephen is to stay in the Azaire household.

Inevitably, he will have an affair with Isabelle, Azaire's young wife. It begins delicately, with stolen glances and the brushing of one foot against the other, but it soon comes to full fruition in the forgotten spare room of the Azaire home, and we are treated to some of the most explicit and erotic passages I have come across in serious writing. Consider this, one of the milder passages: "His tongue, lambent, hot, flickering over and inside her, turning like a key in the split lock of her flesh." (p. 49)

Stephen is terribly aware of every detail of Isabelle's body, "the tiny white hairs on the skin of her bare arm . . . the blood he had seen rise beneath the light freckles of her cheekbones." (p. 19) What Faulks is doing is raising the reader to Stephen's level of visual and tactile awareness, an awareness the writer will exploit fully in the later battlefield scenes.

Like Stephen, Isabelle has led a life without love. The youngest of five daughters, close only to her sister Jeanne, she welcomed the marriage arranged by her father as an opportunity to be free of her loveless home. She is fond of her two stepchildren, but she has never experienced physical passion. Since her husband has taken to beating her as a kind of sexual fore-play, and since nothing much has happened for a year as a result of that foreplay, Stephen at twenty is irresistible. The affair is an earth-moving sexual awakening for both of them, but each finds a different meaning in it.

In her room Madame Azaire wept as she paced back from one side to the other. She was choking with passion for him, but he frightened her. She wanted to comfort him but also to be taken by him, to be used by him. Currents of desire and excitement that she had not known or thought about for years now flooded in her. She wanted him to bring alive what she had buried and to demean, destroy, her fabri-cated self. He was very young. She was unsure. She wanted the touch of his skin. (p. 48)

The passage is important for two reasons. First, it demonstrates that Faulks's prose often ascends into poetry. The parallelism is both antithetic and synthetic. "He was very young" is contrasted with "she was unsure," and both build into "she wanted the touch of his skin." The second point is that while Stephen feels love, Isabelle merely feels passion. The affair satisfies a need within herself; Stephen is no more than the instrument.

Eventually Stephen and Isabelle confess to Azaire and run away to Provence, but for Isabelle, "without the stimulus of fear and prohibition her desire had slackened." (p. 90) Pregnant by Stephen, yet without telling him of it, Isabelle leaves him, first to stay with her sister Jeanne and then, much later, to return to the harmony of her family and her garden: "She had gone home because she was frightened of the future and felt sure a natural order could yet be resumed." (p. 96)

For Stephen it is different. He had been abandoned once by his mother and now he feels abandoned again. He despairs of humanity and he despairs of himself. He doubts his own worth now that his one connection to self-awareness through love has been destroyed.

That ends the first section of the novel. It is so full of visual and tactile detail that I felt drained. I thought about what I had read, and it came to me, not after my first reading of the novel but after the second, that what Faulks had done in the first section was to introduce all the themes he would explore in the rest of the novel. The French family shattered in the first hundred pages is a microcosm of a world soon to be destroyed. The winding passages of the Azaire house through which Stephen had to make his way will have their counterpart in the complex trench systems of the battlefield. The conflict between the textile workers of Amiens and the factory owners, a part of the background to Stephen and Isabelle's affair, is a prelude to the greater conflict among nations. The owners' callousness about the welfare of the workers will be transmuted into the callousness of generals towards the cannon fodder they command.

Nowhere is the foreshadowing clearer than when Stephen looks at the tombs and memorial tablets of Amiens Cathedral. "So many dead, he thought, only waiting . . . before this generation joins them." (p. 59) What a marvellous line, both comment and prophecy!

We begin the second section of the novel *in medias res*, as befits an epic. We are in the middle of the First World War and its thirty million military casualties. The year is 1916 and Stephen Wraysford is now a British lieutenant in the trenches by the Somme river, not far from the town of Amiens.

Here I must step back from the novel for a moment and talk about the nature of trench warfare.

The initial German attack on France through Belgium had been halted with the aid of the British Expeditionary Force. Both sides began to dig in on two opposing fronts, separated by a no-man's-land of anything from two to three hundred yards. On a line from Flanders in Belgium to Picardy in France, a line six hundred miles long, each side established a staggeringly complex system of trenches. The men lived in holes, dugouts they carved out of the back wall of the trenches, and in those holes in the ground, full of water and rats and lice and mud, millions of men lived and died for years. The "front," as it was called, remained static until the very last months of the war.

The failure of either side to break through the enemy line is usually attributed to the stupidity of the generals. The only method of attack they knew was massive frontal assault, hurling hundreds of thousands of men and their rifles against enemy defences. While that is partially true, it is not the whole explanation. By 1914 the two best means of defence, barbed wire and the machine gun, had both been invented and perfected. Used in tandem, they guaranteed a defence that was virtually impregnable. On the other hand, the two best means of attack, the airplane and the tank, were still in their infancy even by the end of the war. Planes were used mainly for reconnaissance, and the early tanks were clumsy and ineffective.

And there you have the situation: both sides with perfect defences – for the time – but without the two attack weapons that could breach those defences.

It is an interesting historical footnote that no one realized the attack potential of the plane and the tank used together until years after the First War, when two men wrote on the subject. One was a German general, Heinz Guderian, and the other was a young French colonel, Charles de Gaulle. The problem was that, while Hitler listened to Guderian and acted accordingly in the production of tanks and planes, the French government didn't listen to de Gaulle. And that explains the rapidity of the early German victories in the Second World War.

By the time we meet Stephen Wraysford on the Somme in 1916, millions of men have died on both sides, rising up out of the trenches with rifles and revolvers to be machine-gunned while crossing no-man's-land before they can even reach the enemy's impenetrable barbed wire. The average life expectancy of a British junior officer who left the trenches to lead his men "over the top" towards the German lines was thirteen minutes.

There were also the tunnels, the terrible, terrible tunnels. Each side had had two years in which to dig tunnels from their own trench systems out towards the enemy lines. The object was to tunnel under the enemy trenches and lay huge mines. Sometimes the German and English tunnels would intersect and the tunnellers would fight each other in spaces three feet high and seventy feet below ground, with the danger of a cave-in and suffocation at any moment. I have a friend who was reading the tunnel scenes of this novel on a bus when claustrophobia overcame her and she had to get off and walk the rest of the journey in fresh air.

After two years of rats and lice and shells and attack and counter-attack and living one on top of the other in the trenches, Stephen has lost any belief in the purpose of the war. His friend Michael Weir, in charge of tunnelling, is half-mad with fear and the suppression of that fear.

Stephen Wraysford is sustained by only two things. He has sublimated his sense of loss and abandonment by Isabelle into hatred of the Germans, not because they are evil, but because they are there and they are killing his comrades. And together with the hatred comes a cold, intellectual curiosity. He says to Michael Weir:

> "I'm curious to see what's going to happen. There are your sewer rats in their holes three feet wide crawling underground. There are my men going mad under shells. . . . This is not a war, this is an exploration of how far men can be degraded." (p. 122)

To feed Stephen's curiosity – and our own – Faulks piles detail upon detail, with the same attention to flesh and touch that we saw in the early scenes of the novel. It is the perfect use of incremental repetition until we feel that we can bear no more, until each detail carries not only its own weight but the accrued weight of all the horror that has gone before. It is all the more terrible because Faulks charges his scenes with light, movement, sound, and colour – the dank air of the tunnel contrasted with the sudden bright shock of an exploding body.

If you have not yet read this book, please believe me that I cannot even begin to communicate the horror of the scenes of trench warfare. As they . bring back one body from no-man's-land, "Bright and sleek on liver, a rat emerged from the abdomen; it levered and flopped fatly over the ribs, glutted with pleasure." (p. 281) How rich the language, the alliteration, the assonance, how vile the image.

Next to the half-eaten corpse is a Private Brennan, "anxiously stripping a torso with no head. He clasped it with both hands, dragged legless up from the crater, his fingers vanishing into buttered green flesh. It was his brother." And then Private Brennan "sang all night for his brother, whom he had brought home in his hands." (pp. 281-82)

The horror takes many forms. Sometimes it lies not in the detail of tormented flesh but in the helplessness of the onlooker. Stephen, shot by a German tunneller deep, deep underground, is rescued and taken to a field hospital. There he watches a young man

> trying to scream with the top layer of skin gone from his body. . . . He begged to die. . . . The nurse had left the screens slightly apart and Stephen saw her lift the tent away with great care, holding it high above the scorched body before she turned and laid it on the floor. She looked down at the flesh no one was allowed to touch, from

the discharging eyes, down over the face and neck, the raw chest, the
groin and throbbing legs. Impotently, she held both her arms wide in
a gesture of motherly love, as though this would comfort him.

He made no response. She took a bottle of oil from the side of the
bed and leaned over him. Gently she poured some on to his chest and
the boy let out a high animal shriek. She stood back and turned her
face to the heavens. (pp. 150-51)

Heaven does not answer and the scene presages a later one when a chap-
lain, faced with the unspeakable all around him, rips the cross off his chest
and denies the existence of his God. (p. 381)

(I was not surprised when Louis de Bernières, the author of the deeply
moving *Captain Corelli's Mandolin*, told me he was so overwhelmed by
the war scenes of *Birdsong* that he sat down and wrote Sebastian Faulks to
tell him how much he admired his work.)

As the generals call for more and more millions of men, each soldier
reacts in his own way to the carnage. Some, like Stephen, retreat into their
intellect. Others, like Stephen's company commander, Captain Gray,
retreat behind a facade of weary cynicism and black humour.

On July 1, 1916, comes the great British offensive on the Somme that
the generals are sure will break the German line. Over the top the British
pour in their hundreds of thousands towards the German guns and wire.
Two hours later there are sixty thousand British dead with not a yard of
new ground taken.

Bloodied beyond caring, Stephen watched the packets of lives with
their memories and loves go spinning and vomiting into the ground.
Death had no meaning, but still the numbers of them went on and on
and in that new infinity there was still horror. (p. 186)

Almost as terrible is the roll call next day:

. . . Llewellyn, Francis, Arkwright, Duncan, Shea, Simons, Anderson,
Blum, Fairbrother. Names came pattering into the dusk, bodying out
the places of their forbears, the villages and towns where the telegram
would be delivered, the houses where the blinds would be drawn,

where low moans would come in the afternoon behind closed doors; and the places that had borne them, which would be like nunneries, like dead towns without their life or purpose, without the sound of fathers and their children, without young men at the factories or in the fields, with no husbands for the women, no deep sound of voices in the inns, with the children who would have been born. (p. 190)

This novel is like a handbook for the would-be writer in the use of language. Compare the sonorous poetry of the roll call with the unbearable simplicity of a letter written by a private soldier on the eve of the great Somme push:

"Well, my dear Mum and Dad, that's all I've got to say to you. Tomorrow we will know if we will be seeing each other again one day. Don't worry about me. I am not frightened of what is waiting for me. When I was a little lad you were very good to me and I won't let you down. Please write to me again, I do like so much to hear the news from home. . . . You have been the dearest Mum and Dad to me. From your Son, John." (p. 178)

As the war approaches the eleventh hour of the eleventh day of the eleventh month of 1918, the ordinary soldier does not know that an Armistice has been signed and that peace is only minutes away. Stephen and Private Firebrace are caught in a tunnel explosion. Firebrace dies, but his body, and the living Stephen, are both dragged to the surface by Lieutenant Levi, a German officer. In the explosion, Stephen has lost his friend, and Levi has lost his brother. The German and the Englishman stare at each other and then, slowly, slowly, each opens his arms and they embrace, "weeping at the bitter strangeness of their human lives." (p. 390) The war is over, the horror is ended, and they bury their dead.

Let us look for a moment at the soldier crushed at Stephen's side in the last moments of the war.

Jack Firebrace was a simple man; he loved his country, his God, his wife, Margaret, and, most of all, his eight-year-old son. And then comes the letter to Jack in the trenches – his little boy has died in the great diphtheria epidemic of 1916.

Jack put the letter down on the ground and stared in front of him. He thought: I will not let this shake my faith. His life was a beautiful thing, it was filled with joy. I will thank God for it.

He put his head in his hands to pray but was overpowered by the grief of his loss. No polite words of gratitude came, but only the bellowing darkness of desolation. "My boy," he sobbed, "my darling boy." (p. 168)

In that one repetition, "my boy . . . my darling boy," we are raised to Biblical heights of intensity. In that moment of Firebrace's grief I heard the voice of King David weeping for the dead Absalom:

And the king was much moved, and went up to the chamber over the gate, and wept: and as he went, thus he said, O my son Absalom, my son, my son Absalom! would God I had died for thee, O Absalom, my son, my son! (The Second Book of Samuel, chapter 18, verse 33)

For a time Jack Firebrace is sustained by his love of God and the memory of his son, but as he writes so simply to his wife, "I am finding it difficult to keep bright." Dear heavens, in the horror of the trenches and faced with the death of his beloved, he "finds it difficult to keep bright"! Finally, crushed and dying, he confides to Stephen that he has lost all faith in God and humanity: "'What I've seen . . . I don't want to live any more. . . . My boy, gone. What a world we made for him, I'm glad he's dead. I'm *glad*.'" (p. 381)

The story of Jack Firebrace is the story of the whole novel writ small. This is not a novel primarily about war and death, it is above all a novel about love and the loss of love and the consequences of that loss.

Consider the character of Stephen's friend Michael Weir, a fascinating, complex man of tormented sexuality. At twenty-two, Michael Weir has known neither the love of a woman nor love from his parents. After one brief leave in London he comes back filled with rage. He says, "'I wish a great bombardment would . . . kill the whole lot of them. . . . Particularly my family.'" (p. 235) He hates them because they do not try to understand his fear of the trenches and the tunnels, and because they have always denied him the love that is a child's due from his parents. Until he meets Stephen, his one link to sanity has been the Army Officers'

Manual, but Stephen takes its place as Michael's guide. Michael Weir comes to love Stephen with the most complete of loves: he says that, if Stephen were gone, he'd open his mouth to the next cloud of gas. During the Battle of the Somme, when the earth itself is groaning with the explosions, Faulks brings Michael and Stephen together in the most delicate of scenes:

> "Oh God, oh God." Weir began to cry. "What have we done, what have we done? Listen to it. We've done something terrible, we'll never get back to how it was before."
>
> Stephen laid his hand on Weir's arm. "Be quiet," he said. "You must hold on."
>
> But he knew what Weir was feeling because he had felt it himself. As he listened to the soil protesting, he heard the sound of a new world. If he did not fight to control himself, he might never return to the reality in which he had lived. . . . "Hold me," said Weir. "Please hold me."
>
> He crawled over the soil and laid his head against Stephen's chest. He said, "Call me by my name."
>
> Stephen wrapped his arm round him and held him. "It's all right, Michael. It's all right, Michael. Hold on, don't let go. Hold on, hold on." (p. 192)

Paradoxically, the horror of war has imbued Stephen with enormous understanding and compassion. He can return Michael's most tender feelings without sharing Michael's sexuality and he can see to the heart of Michael's fear. As Stephen explains to another officer, Weir is "'frightened that it doesn't make sense, that there is no purpose.'" (p. 247) Weir dies of a sniper's bullet without finding any purpose but at least sustained by Stephen's compassion.

It is Stephen, abandoned first by his mother and then by Isabelle, who must find a reason to go on living. As a boy he had created a make-believe world for himself into which he could retreat when reality became too harsh, but that escape is no longer available to him. And then, on leave in the English countryside during the last year of the war, he finds love and forgiveness for himself and for others in a sudden, mystical revelation that he is at one with the world around him.

He wanted to stretch out his arms and enfold in them the fields, the sky, the elms with their sounding birds; he wanted to hold them with the unending forgiveness of a father to his prodigal, errant but beloved son. Isabelle and the cruel dead of the war; his lost mother, his friend Weir: nothing was immoral or beyond redemption, all could be brought together, understood in the long perspective of forgiveness. . . . His body shook with the passion of the love that had found him, from which he had been exiled in the blood and the flesh of long killing. (p. 291)

It is this realization that will make it possible later for him to embrace the German enemy, Levi. It is this realization that will permit him to find love again in the arms of Isabelle's sister Jeanne. They meet by chance in Amiens, where Jeanne has come to look after her sister, who is disfigured by bomb fragments. Stephen sees Isabelle, but she doesn't tell him that she has had his child, or that she has found love with a German officer, and she and Stephen go their separate ways.

In the third, brief section of the novel, all the loose ends are tied up. It is set in England in 1978, sixty years after the end of the First World War. The central character is Stephen's granddaughter, Elizabeth Benson, a young unmarried woman – pregnant by her married lover – who has not yet made sense of her life. She finds the diaries of Stephen, and becomes convinced that if she can break the Greek code in which Stephen wrote she will find a great truth. If she can understand his life, she will in some way understand her own. Through extensive inquiries of those of her grandfather's contemporaries still living, through extensive travels to France and Belgium, through extensive questioning of her mother, and through a partial decoding of the diaries, Elizabeth finds out a great deal about herself, but no great illuminating truth. I suppose the moral is that each of us must find our own meaning within our own experience. Elizabeth learns that her mother, Françoise, was not, as she had always supposed, the daughter of Stephen and Jeanne but the daughter of Stephen and Isabelle, adopted by Stephen and Jeanne after Isabelle's early death.

There are those who feel that the introduction of Elizabeth Benson into the novel sixty-two years after the Somme was a mistake by Faulks, that her modern identity crisis spoils the momentum of the narrative. I understand the point of view, but I do not subscribe to it. I needed desperately an end to the horror, a return to the life I understand, however mundane. I could not bear any more the detail of the trenches; I needed the emotional relief of a nice little piece of detective work, and Elizabeth Benson gave me that relief.

At the very end of the novel, Elizabeth leaves for the country to give birth to her child. Her lover arranges to be with her, and with the doctor out on call has to deliver the baby himself. When the doctor finally arrives, the lover goes out into the garden and throws chestnuts at a tree, disturbing the crows and provoking a "harsh, ambiguous call . . . to be heard by those still living." That is the birdsong of the title. We have heard the sound of birds throughout the novel. Sometimes they are the echo of man's love, sometimes they are the echo of his folly, but high above man's foolishness they represent the continuity of existence.

Thus the novel has come full circle. It began and it ends in a garden. The story also began when an unmarried woman gave birth to Stephen Wraysford, and it ends with an unmarried woman of Stephen's blood giving birth to another child. No great truth has been revealed and nothing has been resolved. It is the perfect circular movement of satire.

As we reflect on the novel, we realize that we have witnessed every manifestation of love: Stephen's passion for Isabelle; his quieter, more resigned love for Jeanne as they both try to create something good out of all the horror; Isabelle's love for her German officer; the love of poor, mad Michael Weir for Stephen Wraysford; the compassionate love of an unnamed nurse for her dying patient; Stephen's love of his broken men, a love that leads him to his epiphany; and Jack Firebrace's total love of his little son. We have even seen commercial love in a brothel when Stephen strokes a whore with a bayonet and realizes how close are the twin mysteries of love and death.

It's a remarkable catalogue, but when I think about the novel I remember, not the love nor the consequences of its loss, but the horror of the Somme.

My father was at the Somme on July 1, 1916. He often told me about how he joined up in 1914 when he was twenty-five. He spoke to me about the campaign in Salonika in the last years of the war, against an enemy my father called "Johnny Turk." But he would never talk to me or my brothers about the trenches and especially not about the Somme. Sebastian Faulks explains why in an entry from Stephen's diary:

"No child or future generation will ever know what this was like. They will never understand.

"When it is over we will go quietly among the living and we will not tell them.

"We will talk and sleep and go about our business like human beings.

"We will seal what we have seen in the silence of our hearts and no words will reach us." (p. 340)

And with that I will end. There is no more to say.

THE POISONWOOD BIBLE

Barbara Kingsolver
(Toronto: Harper Perennial, 1999)

Before I begin to talk about *The Poisonwood Bible* by Barbara Kingsolver, set in what is now the Democratic Republic of Congo, I want to indicate the direction my discussion is going to take. In my view, this novel is not primarily about an obsessed man who abuses and nearly destroys his family. In my view, this novel is not primarily about American consumerism, or driver ants devastating a Congolese village, or how a mute, crippled, American girl grows up to become a doctor. This novel is mainly about three crimes – three terrible, terrible crimes. Two of these crimes were committed before I was born, but the third was committed during my lifetime. As I examine the novel, I trust that what I believe was the intention of the author will become clear: to expose three appalling crimes committed by people very like us against millions of innocent victims.

To understand the nature of the three crimes, indeed to understand fully the events of the novel, it is necessary for us to begin with a broad overview of the whole of African history.

The northern coast of Africa was known to Europeans since the days of the Roman Empire two thousand years ago. From what we now call Morocco all the way east to Egypt, North Africa belonged to Rome. After the fall of Rome and the later foundation of the religion of Islam by the Prophet Mohammed in the seventh century, all of North Africa fell to the invading Arabs and the Moslem faith, and for the last thirteen hundred

years, North Africa has been mainly Arab and Moslem in its racial and
religious character.

Below Arab North Africa we have the Sahara Desert, and below the
Sahara Desert is the rest of Africa, what we call sub-Saharan Africa, what
was even called a generation ago, when we were less sensitive to other
people's feelings, "black" Africa. This is the area of interest to us today, an
area almost unknown to Europeans until the last two centuries.

Before the nineteenth century, there were only two areas of Africa
below the Sahara in which the European powers had shown any interest.
On the southern tip of South Africa the Dutch had established a small settlement in 1652, which we now call Cape Town. It wasn't really a colony,
it was just a stopping-off place for European ships on their way to the Spice
Islands in the Far East.

The other area of interest was on the west coast of Africa. After
Columbus discovered the West Indies and the Americas in 1492, and after
the Spanish, French, and British colonists had killed off the original inhabitants by overwork and disease, they needed slaves, and they came back
across the Atlantic to find those slaves in West Africa. They didn't colonize
West Africa, they simply established settlements along the coast – they
called them factories – where they bought slaves from the local African
kings and chiefs. Every major European nation was involved in the slave
trade. Often they would use Arabs as middlemen, Arabs who had come
down from North Africa for profit. When the African chiefs couldn't supply
enough defeated enemies, the Arabs would organize expeditions into the
interior and just round up whole villages for export from the factories on
the coast. I repeat, everyone was involved: the African kings and chiefs,
the Arab middlemen, and the Europeans who bought the slaves and
shipped them back to the West Indies and North America.

The Portuguese and the French started claiming some of the coastal
areas as colonies, but there was no major European move into the interior
of Africa. The Europeans were content to let the African chiefs and the
Arab traders do the difficult work for them.

All that changed with the Industrial Revolution. By 1800, Western
Europe had begun to industrialize, and it had a huge need for more and
more raw materials: timber, minerals, industrial diamonds, rubber, and so
on. The enormous continent of Africa below the Sahara was there for the
taking. And so, in the nineteenth century, we have what the history books

call the Scramble for Africa. Between 1800 and 1900 the European nations divided Africa up among them. By 1900 there were only two independent African nations, Ethiopia up in the northeast – and Italy would take that over in 1935 – and the tiny country of Liberia on the west coast, founded by American abolitionists in 1847 as a haven for freed American slaves. The rest of Africa now belonged to Europeans. The French had grabbed most of North Africa and much of West Africa, but Britain had taken the lion's share, from Egypt in the north, down through the Sudan, through Kenya and Uganda and Rhodesia, all the way to the colonies of South Africa at the southern tip. Everyone else had a piece or pieces – Germany, Italy, Spain, and Portugal. Everyone! The small European country of Belgium left it a little late in the day to seize its share, but its chance came in 1885.

Now we are getting closer to the novel. The great British-born American explorer Henry Morton Stanley had recently traced the Congo River to its source and had mapped much of the area we now call the Congo. Since the area hadn't been claimed by any other nation, King Leopold II of Belgium decided to step in. He told the other European leaders at the Berlin Conference of 1885 that he would administer the area of the Congo as his own property and make it his own personal crusade to stamp out the slave trade. By now, the European nations had decided to mask their greed for Africa's raw materials under a facade of "civilizing" Africa. Christian missionaries flooded into Africa, and Britain led the way for the new morality by abolishing slavery throughout the British Empire in 1833. Abraham Lincoln, of course, ended slavery in the United States during the Civil War in 1863, but there was still a healthy African slave trade when Leopold claimed the Congo in 1885. Slavery still existed in much of the Arab world and in parts of South America, particularly Brazil. When Leopold II promised to stamp out the slave trade in the Congo in 1885, it is estimated that one hundred and fifty thousand slaves were still being taken every year out of the Congo alone. And so, with general European consent, the Congo Free State was created in 1885 as the personal fiefdom of King Leopold II of Belgium.

King Leopold did exactly what he said he'd do. After 1885 no more slaves were exported from the Congo. But there was a downside. Leopold enslaved the whole population for his own purposes. They were put to work on the Belgian-owned rubber plantations. Anyone who failed to produce his daily quota of rubber had one hand amputated. A second failure to produce the daily quota meant amputation of the other hand or a foot. It came to much the same thing. This went on for more than two decades. Finally even the European nations were too disgusted for the practice to continue, and in 1908 Leopold turned over the Congo Free State, including the capital Leopoldville, to the Belgian government. It became the Belgian Congo. The last population figure I saw for the Congo was thirty million in the census of 1984 – it must be much greater now. What I do know is that while he owned the Congo Free State in the twenty-three years from 1885 to 1908, Leopold of Belgium caused the death of ten million Congolese. It is one of the great forgotten genocides of modern history.

I think one reason the world forgot so quickly what the Belgians had done was that, so soon afterwards, in 1914, Germany attacked France by marching through neutral Belgium and suddenly Belgium was seen as a victim of German brutality. It is just one more example of how rapidly we readjust our political memories.

I have so far indicated two of the three crimes I mentioned at the beginning. The first crime was the enslavement and kidnapping of millions of Africans from the sixteenth until well into the nineteenth century. The second crime was the murder of ten million Congolese by Leopold II of Belgium. So what about the third crime, the one that took place during my lifetime?

After the Belgian government took over in 1908, the amputations and executions diminished, but the exploitation of the Congo continued. And that brings us right up to modern times and the background of today's novel.

After the end of the Second World War in 1945, it became clear that the European nations could no longer hold on to their colonies, including their colonies in Africa. When India got its independence from Britain in 1947, the movement for independence everywhere became unstoppable. In the 1950s, both Britain and France dismantled their African empires. In the Belgian Congo, the population had been so bullied, so downtrodden, so browbeaten, that the movement for independence came later than elsewhere. It wasn't until 1958 that there was any civil unrest, any real public call for independence.

The Belgian government thought they could have it both ways. Following the example of the French and the British in their African colonies, Belgium gave the Congo independence on June 30, 1960, but retained control of the Congolese Army and, Belgium hoped, control of the copper and diamond mines concentrated in the south in the province of Katanga. Within weeks the Congolese army mutinied, and the new Congolese leader, a declared Marxist, made it clear that he wanted an end to Belgian control of the copper and diamond mines of the south. At that time, in 1960, the Congo was producing three-quarters of the world's industrial-quality diamonds.

The Belgians were horrified by the independent spirit of Patrice Lumumba, the newly elected prime minister of the Congo. They denounced him to the Americans as a Russian agent, ready to create a Soviet beach-head in Central Africa. The Belgians also encouraged the southern provinces of the Congo to secede, notably the diamond- and cobalt-rich province of Katanga.

Katanga accordingly declared itself a separate nation under the leader-ship of Moïse Tshombe, a Belgian puppet. Supported by Belgian para-troopers and enough CIA money to pay for white mercenaries, Tshombe's Katanga defied the central Congolese government. The result was civil war.

The Belgians and the Americans arranged for the Katangese to capture and murder Patrice Lumumba, but the president of the Congo, Joseph Kasavubu, continued the fight against Katanga's secession. The United Nations sent its secretary-general, Dag Hammarskjöld, to try to mediate an end to the conflict, but he was killed in a mysterious plane crash.

With the final collapse of Moïse Tshombe's rebel government in 1963, the Congo seemed reunited, but the country lay in ruins. The United States made one last abortive attempt to save their friend Tshombe by installing him as the president of the whole Congo, but he lacked countrywide support and was seen universally as a lackey of the Western imperialists.

To restore peace and order, the CIA-backed chief of staff of the Congolese Army, Joseph Mobutu, staged a military coup and declared himself presi-dent on November 25, 1965. Until the Belgians and Americans had begun to groom him as a less visibly tarnished candidate for power, Mobutu had been an army sergeant.

You have to understand how totally unprepared the Congo was for independence. When the Belgians left in June of 1960, out of tens of millions of Congolese, there were not twenty people who had had a uni-versity education. None of the imperial European powers had anything to be proud of, but Belgium was far and away the worst. The Congo never had a chance.

Within a few years, Mobutu changed the name of the country from the Congo to Zaire and the name of the capital from Leopoldville to Kinshasa. His own name he changed from Joseph Desiré Mobutu to Mobutu Sese Seko Koko Ngbendu Wa Za Banga, which translates as "the all-powerful warrior who, because of his endurance and inflexible will to win, will go from conquest to conquest leaving fire in his wake." The world knew him as just Mobutu Sese Seko.

During the next thirty-two years, from 1965 to 1997, the World Bank estimates that Mobutu creamed off 65 percent of Zaire's wealth. But he was a staunch anti-communist and thus enjoyed the ongoing support of the American government.

In 1996 conditions were so nightmarish in the Congo that rebellion broke out against Mobutu and he was forced to flee the country. Since May of 1997, Zaire, now renamed the Democratic Republic of Congo, has been led by the self-declared president Laurent Kabila. The consensus is that he is no better than Mobutu, perhaps even worse, and civil war and corruption still rage in the country.

I don't know if you watched Oprah Winfrey's hour-long NBC program on *The Poisonwood Bible* in the summer of 2000. It included several meetings between Barbara Kingsolver, her admiring readers, and Oprah herself. Ms. Kingsolver explained that one of her intentions in writing the novel was "to lay open the thing our government did to the Congo . . . the U.S. usurped the independence of the Congo . . . it was done in our names." Ms. Kingsolver continued, "How do I live in a world where there is such evil? How do I raise my kids?"

What I found remarkable is that at no time did Oprah or anyone else specify exactly what it was that the American government had done. I don't know if Barbara Kingsolver made any precise accusations – her contributions were, I noticed, all pre-recorded – but if she did they were edited out. Let me hasten to offer the missing details.

The United States government arranged for a province of a sovereign nation to rebel against the central government. It arranged for the murder of an elected prime minister. It installed a vicious, greedy tyrant who bled the country dry, and the United States government must be held ultimately responsible for the present terrible civil war that is ravaging an already ruined country. That is the political message of *The Poisonwood Bible*. That is what Barbara Kingsolver wanted to "lay open" to the world. And that is the third of the three terrible crimes I have already referred to.

What do we know about Barbara Kingsolver? She was born in Maryland in 1955 but grew up in Kentucky. She took her Master's in Biology at the University of Arizona at Tucson, and after two years of odd jobs in France and Greece, she settled down to a career in journalism and scientific writing. In 1988 she produced her first novel, *The Bean Trees*, which I reviewed, I remember, with great enthusiasm. Like the two novels that followed, *The Bean Trees* was set in the American South and South-west, dealing mainly with the problems of single women trying to sort out their lives against a background of social injustice.

When Kingsolver left the America of her first three novels and wrote *The Poisonwood Bible*, it came as a surprise to her readers, including me. What I didn't know at the time was that she had spent a year in the Congo when she was eight years old – her father was a doctor with a social conscience, not a missionary – and that she had prepared for this novel over the last eighteen years. She had returned repeatedly to Central and West Africa, although not to the Congo itself – it was a very dangerous place under Mobutu Sese Seko – and had read in depth on African history. While she was writing this novel, she studied a French-Kikongo dictionary every day and re-examined her parents' journals and photographs of their stay in 1963.

Barbara Kingsolver lives now with her husband, a chemist, and their two children in the mountains outside Tucson, Arizona. Her husband is extremely supportive both of her writing and of her interest in political and social issues.

Finally we come to the novel itself. The year is 1959 and the Price family is arriving in the Congo. It's a patriarchal American family, led by the evangelical Baptist missionary Nathan Price. With him is his wife, Orleanna, and his four daughters: Rachel, fifteen, the twins Leah and Adah, fourteen, and five-year-old Ruth May. That's a total of six people. One of them Africa will drive insane, one of them Africa will kill, one of them will not let Africa touch her, and one of them will just let Africa happen. Of the remaining two, the twins, one will embrace Africa and the other will grow to her full intellectual potential because of the African experience. By giving all the female characters a narrative voice in alternating chapters, Kingsolver allows us, the readers, to understand what is happening within each of the characters as a result of the collision between Congolese and American cultures.

The Price family is being sent to a remote Congolese village, Kilanga, by a reluctant Mission League – reluctant because political upheaval is already beginning as Congolese independence draws nearer. Nathan Price insisted on coming, although the mission at Kilanga had already been abandoned and the family is allowed only a one-year contract at a minimum stipend. The one year will become seventeen months.

Let us begin with the patriarch, Nathan Price. He is a driven man, full of guilt at being the only member of his unit to survive the Bataan Death March in the Second World War. Orleanna, his wife, remembers how he condemned even her joy in her first pregnancy: "'Not a one of those men will ever see a son born to carry on his name. And you dare to gloat before Christ himself about your undeserved blessing.'" (p. 198)

Orleanna knows exactly what lies at the root of Nathan's character: "[H]is guilt had made him a tyrant before men, it made him like a child before his God." (p. 198) I found a strange thing when I began to write about Nathan. Barbara Kingsolver gave him no narrative voice of his own; my notes on Nathan are, in fact, all about the brilliant insights of Orleanna. And she can be very funny. One of her comments I thought summed up Nathan Price beautifully: "[H]ell hath no fury like a Baptist preacher." (p. 8)

Nathan Price is a single-minded, elemental force. More than one person has told me he reminds them of Captain Ahab in his dedication to the one goal he has set himself, to convert to Christ more souls than had perished on the road from Bataan. The problem of course is that Nathan Price's version of Christianity has very little to do with the gentle message of Christ. Consider what happens when the Price family arrives in the mud-hut village of Kilanga. The villagers, with very limited resources, have prepared a feast, and the bare-breasted women welcome the American newcomers. Nathan's greeting is not of the good news of the risen Christ, it is the promise of the terrible punishment that God will mete out to sinners. He quotes from chapter 19 of the Book of Genesis:

"The *emissaries* of the Lord *smote* the sinners, who had come *heedless* to the sight of God, *heedless in their nakedness.*" . . . "*Nakedness,*" . . . "and *darkness* of the *soul! For we shall *destroy* this place where the *loud clamor* of the *sinners* is waxen *great* before the *face* of the Lord." (p. 27)

Nathan Price has come to save a people he sees as childlike, innately inferior to the white race, and his arrogance never diminishes. After a year in the village of Kilanga, he says to his Anglican counterpart, who has flown in to the village to urge him to leave,

> "Frank, this is not a *nation*, it is the *Tower of Babel* and it *cannot* hold an election. If these people are to be united at all, they will come together as God's lambs in their simple love for Christ. Nothing else will move them forward. Not politics, not a desire for freedom – they don't have the temperament or the intellect for such things." (p. 168)

He is as misogynist as he is racist. He is a tyrant not only to his wife but to his daughters. He has them copy out a hundred verses of the Bible for any transgression, with the hundredth verse the one relevant to their sin. He has an encyclopedic Biblical knowledge without any understanding of the message the book contains. Nathan Price considers himself a witty man, but it is always at the expense of other people. His twin daughters were diagnosed early as "gifted," but in his patriarchal faith there is no room for further education for women: "'Sending a girl to college is like pouring water in your shoes. . . . It's hard to say which is worse, seeing it run out and waste the water, or seeing it hold in and wreck the shoes.'" (p. 56)

Only once in the novel did Nathan Price make me laugh, and I'm not sure he meant to. It's when the parrot Methuselah, bequeathed by the Prices' predecessor, Brother Fowles, comes out with "'Piss off, Methuselah!'" and the Reverend Nathan Price declares, "'That is a Catholic bird.'" (p. 59)

Usually, of course, Nathan Price doesn't amuse me, he appalls me. Nowhere in the novel are his attitudes made clearer than in the argument he has with a doctor in Stanleyville, where he has flown with Ruth May to get attention to her broken arm. As Ruth May reports the conversation:

> Without looking up from my arm, the doctor said, "We Belgians made slaves of them and cut off their hands in the rubber plantations.

Now you Americans have them for a slave wage in the mines and let them cut off their own hands. And you, my friend, are stuck with the job of trying to make amens." . . .

But Father wasn't done with the doctor yet. He was hopping from one foot to the other and cried, "Up to *me* to make amens? I see no amens to make! The Belgians and American business brought civilization to the Congo!" (p. 121)

I think too much is made by some readers of the fact that the Price family came from Georgia – Bethlehem, Georgia, to be precise, a subtle reminder by the author of how far Nathan Price has travelled from the original message of Christianity. I have both read and heard that the Price family brought Southern racial attitudes with them and that is what creates the conflict. I cannot agree. While the children may still hold some racial stereotypes from their early years in the American South, Nathan Price embodies far more than just the racial prejudice common in certain American states. He is the embodiment of the whole American belief that the United States has a divinely appointed status. Barbara Kingsolver has often written about it, and she even repeated it to Oprah Winfrey: "Historically, the attitude of the U.S. is that we know better . . . in 1960 the religion of the U.S. was Christianity and shiny modern technology."

The first of Nathan Price's many defeats comes when he plants an American-style garden, against the advice of the Prices' housekeeper, Mama Tataba. First, it is washed away, because Nathan Price did not make little hills to protect the seeds against the African rains, and when it does grow the plants run wild. The garden image really is a most brilliant metaphor for the impossibility of attempting to impose one culture upon another. Before the Europeans came, before the missionaries came, before the Prices came, the people of the Congo had evolved a way of life exactly suited to their needs. They did not need Americans to tell them to get out of the path of killer ants, they got out of the way of killer ants and allowed them to act as scavengers, cleaning away all organic matter. What all the women of the Price family discover, with one exception, is that the Congolese have adapted perfectly to the harshness of their life. As Leah Price observes much later, when the Congolese are suffering under Mobutu, "the Congolese are skilled at survival and perceptive beyond belief, or else dead at an early age." (p. 453)

The people of Kilanga, of the Congo, did not need missionaries. They already had an abundance of God's grace. Nathan Price's predecessor, Brother Fowles, understood that. He accepted the Congo as he found it, and in his Christlike humility respected the traditions. As he says to the Prices, "'You'll have to forgive me. I've been here so long, I've come to love the people here and their ways of thinking.'" (p. 248)

Brother Fowles is as American as Nathan Price, but unlike Nathan Price he does not believe that American religion and technology have a monopoly on truth, or that he has a divine mission to "civilize" the natives. His life and his goals are touchingly modest: "'I rejoice in the work of the Lord,' said Brother Fowles. 'I was just telling your wife, I do a little ministering. I study and classify the fauna. I observe a great deal, and probably offer very little salvation in the long run.'" (p. 250)

And yet he has achieved much. By respecting the village headman, Tata Ndu, and noting that for the most part he ran his village well, Brother Fowles has been able to persuade Tata Ndu and his people to abandon the practice of wife-beating. Brother Fowles knows, as we do, that the villagers need no thundering diatribes from Nathan Price on charity. They already have an ample supply of it. Mama Mwanza is a villager who lost her legs in a fire, but she makes her way over to the Prices on the palms of her hands to give them oranges and promise them fish. As Mama Mwanza puts it, "'Whenever you have plenty of something, you have to share it.'" (p. 206)

But Nathan Price blunders on with no idea that the Congolese already have religious beliefs that suit them perfectly. Anatole, the village teacher, tries to explain the situation to the American as tactfully as possible.

Anatole sighed. "I understand your difficulty, Reverend. Tata Ndu has asked me to explain this. His concern is with the important gods and ancestors of this village, who have always been honored in certain sacred ways. Tata Ndu worries that the people who go to your church are neglecting their duties." (p. 128)

Nothing will stop Nathan Price. He demands, in the full Baptist tradition, that converts immerse themselves and their children in the local river, refusing to be told that they are terrified of the crocodiles, which have already taken children. He continues to thunder at the villagers in his American

English with the occasional Kikongo phrase, Anatole the teacher providing a simultaneous translation for the congregation. It is in Nathan's sermons that I think Barbara Kingsolver shows her genius, particularly in Nathan Price's exhortation, "'Tata Jesus is bangala!'" What he intends to say is, "Father Jesus is beloved," or, more freely translated, "The Word of Christ is precious!" What Nathan Price does not know is that Kikongo is a language where the meaning of a word depends on the speaker's intonation. As Nathan Price pronounces the words, he is saying, "Jesus is the poisonwood tree!" What Mama Tataba explains to Orleanna Price, and to us, is that the tree is so poisonous that even the fumes of a *bängala* stick in a fire can kill. (p. 93) "Tata Jesus is bangala" is emblematic of the theme of the novel – that Christianity, and the Western culture with which it is identified, really are toxic when transplanted into an alien, African culture, especially by carriers as unprepared and ignorant as the Reverend Nathan Price.

The novel is certainly to a large degree a political allegory, with Nathan Price cast as the very Ugly American, but there is also much humour, at least until the ant attack and the proclamation of independence.

The humour begins even before the Prices arrive in Kilanga. They are carrying possessions far in excess of the airline's baggage allowance, including an ample supply of Betty Crocker cake mix for the girls' birthdays in the year to come. There seems no solution to the problem until the Southern Baptist Mission League gives them the hint, "'They don't weigh the passengers.'" (p. 15) The result is very funny, especially when we remember they are flying to a very hot place. As Leah reports,

> We struck out for Africa carrying all our excess baggage on our bodies, under our clothes. Also, we had *clothes* under our clothes. My sisters and I left home wearing six pairs of underdrawers, two half-slips and camisoles; several dresses one on top of the other, with pedal pushers underneath; and outside of everything an all-weather coat. (The encyclopedia advised us to count on rain.) The other goods, tools, cake-mix boxes and so forth were tucked out of sight in our pockets and under our waist-bands, surrounding us in a clanking armor. (p. 15)

The novel is also full of the fascinating detail of everyday life in a Congolese village. Let me cite one of many such scenes, as recorded by the perceptive fourteen-year-old Adah:

Clumps of children stonethrowing outflowing rush upon terrified small goats, scattering them across the road so that the goats may tiptoe back and be chased again. Men sit on buckets and stare at whatsoever passes by. The usual bypasser is a woman sauntering slowly down the road with bundles upon bundles balanced on her head. These women are pillars of wonder, defying gravity while wearing the hohum aspect of perfect tedium. They can sit, stand, talk, shake a stick at a drunk man, reach around their backs to fetch forth a baby to nurse, all without dropping their piled-high bundles upon bundles. They are like ballet dancers entirely unaware they are on stage. I cannot take my eyes from them. (p. 31)

We learn that the villagers of Kilanga observe no calendar. Every fifth day is market day, and then the five-finger week starts again. It makes life very difficult for missionaries who want to celebrate the Christian festivals. In his arrogance, Nathan Price of course finds a solution. He declares Easter on the Fourth of July and starts his calendar from there. (p. 45) I thought it a lovely manifestation of the American habit of equating religious practice and American patriotism.

Kingsolver is just as able to describe natural wonders as she is the customs of the village. In her old age, back in Georgia, Orleanna Price remembers the overwhelming beauty of the jungle outside the village. It has remained so vivid in her mind that she thinks of it in the present tense.

Every space is filled with life: delicate, poisonous frogs war-painted like skeletons, clutched in copulation, secreting their precious eggs onto dripping leaves. Vines strangling their own kin in the everlasting wrestle for sunlight. The breathing of monkeys. A glide of snake belly on branch. A single-file army of ants biting a mammoth tree into uniform grains and hauling it down to the dark for their ravenous queen. And, in reply, a choir of seedlings arching their necks out of rotted tree stumps, sucking life out of death. This forest eats itself and lives forever. (p. 2)

As the year of their mission to Kilanga comes to an end, and the threat of violent political unrest becomes very real, one might wonder why Orleanna does not insist upon leaving with her children. The answer is clear. She has come to believe that God is on Nathan's side. No matter that his congregation is pitifully small, comprising the families of lepers, the families of outcasts, and the families of twins, thought unlucky by the villagers. No matter that Nathan and Jesus both lost an election called by Tata Ndu. This election is one of Barbara Kingsolver's most accomplished set pieces. The villagers believe, wrongly, that Nathan's daughter Adah was saved from a lion by her Christian God. Fair-minded as ever, Tata Ndu decides to give this powerful god a chance, "'*Ici, maintenant,* we are making a vote for Jesus Christ in the office of personal God, Kilanga village.'" (p. 330)

To Nathan Price's expostulations, Tata Ndu replies, "'The program of Jesus and the program of elections. You say these things are good. You cannot say now they are *not* good.'" (p. 331)

The result of the vote? Jesus Christ lost, eleven to fifty-six.

But even this humiliation of her husband does not deter Orleanna. She has been her husband's creature since she bore him their last child: "By the time Ruth May was born . . . Nathan was in full possession of the country once known as Orleanna Wharton." (p. 200) Nathan has crushed the spirit out of her. Even when he breaks a plate, one of her few pretty possessions, she can make no response to his jibe "'I had hoped you might know better than to waste your devotion on things of this world.'" (p. 134) She does dream of the freedom of her youth, but Nathan is too strong.

Orleanna will not leave him until her five-year-old dies from the bite of a green mamba, planted in their henhouse by the Nathan-provoked witch doctor, and even then, "I didn't set out to leave my husband." (p. 383) Orleanna was fleeing from her grief. Kingsolver describes the flight with an exquisitely delicate simile. "As long as I kept moving, my grief streamed out behind me like a swimmer's long hair in water. I knew the weight was there but it didn't touch me." (p. 381) As Leah later remembers,

We only took what we could carry on our backs.

Mother never once turned around to look over her shoulder. I don't know what would have become of us if it hadn't been for Mama Mwanza's daughters, who came running after us, bringing oranges and a demijohn of water. (p. 389)

What do we know of the three remaining girls who follow their mother?

Rachel, the oldest, is by now nearly eighteen. After seventeen months in the Congo, she is the same shallow, appearance-obsessed teenager that she was when she came. Her first reaction when the family arrived in Kilanga was typical: "Already I was heavy-hearted in my soul for the flush commodes and machine-washed clothes and other simple things in life I have took for granite." (p. 23)

Barbara Kingsolver tries to flesh her out a little, to add a little texture to her character, by giving her the mildly amusing habit of creating malapropisms like the one above, but her contempt for Africa is odious and it is hard to excuse her outburst to Leah: "'Shut *up*, damn it! I wish you'd just shut up forever like your Goddamn deaf-mute genius twin!'" (p. 242) I know that it is possible to see her as a typical teenager, but she is a particularly repulsive example of the species, and unlike most adolescents she will never get better. Rachel describes herself as "a girl whose only hopes for the year were a sweet-sixteen party and a pink mohair twin set." (p. 28) In the case of the pale blonde Rachel, beauty really is only skin deep.

Rachel will make her escape from the Congo by flying out as the common-law wife of Eeben Axelroot, the diamond smuggler and shady pilot involved in the Eisenhower plot to murder Lumumba. They will establish themselves in pre-Mandela South Africa, and Rachel will feel perfectly at home.

> I've always made sure I go to church with the very best people, and we get invited to their parties. I insist on that. I have even learned to play bridge! It is my girlfriends here in Joburg that have taught me how to give parties, keep a close eye on the help, and just overall make the graceful transition to wifehood and adulteration. (p. 405)

At least, in white South Africa, Rachel is with her own: "Oh, I thought I'd died and gone to heaven. Just to be back with people who spoke the good old American language and understood the principle of a flush toilet." (p. 404)

She sees the black South Africans of the townships with the same understanding that she had of the villagers in Kilanga: "They will make their houses out of a piece of rusted tin or the side of a crate – and leave the writing part on the outside for all to see! But you just have to try and understand, they don't have the same ethics as us." (p. 424)

Rachel will leave Axelroot and marry further and further upmarket until finally she becomes both a wealthy widow and the owner of a fine hotel. When she and her sisters attempt a reunion in 1984, Rachel has a problem because of Leah's African husband, the teacher Anatole. "We have a strict policy about who is allowed upstairs, and if you change it for one person then where does it end?" (p. 477)

Rachel stays in Africa because as a wealthy white businesswoman she enjoys a standard of living not available to her in North America. Let us leave Rachel Axelroot DuPrée Fairley as she argues with her sisters at that dreadful reunion.

> "You two can just go ahead and laugh," I said. "But I read the papers. Ronald Reagan is keeping us safe from the socialistic dictators, and you should be grateful for it."
>
> "Socialistic dictators such as?"
>
> "I don't know. Karl Marx! Isn't he still in charge of Russia?" (p. 478)

Rachel is as ethnocentric as her father, without the religion but with just as self-centred a view of the world. How different she is from her youngest sister, Ruth May, the dear little girl who died at five from snakebite.

Ruth May came to Africa with a memory of half-understood racist slurs she'd heard in Georgia, but they fall away as she alone among the sisters learns to play with the village children. Ruth May is the naïve narrator, repeating overheard but not understood conversations – revealing to us, for instance, the diamond-smuggling operation of Eeben Axelroot and his involvement in Eisenhower's plot to kill Lumumba – all the while trying to make sense of the exotic new world in which she finds herself.

Let us consider now the twins, fourteen years old as we meet them on their arrival in the Congo. Each has been declared "gifted," but they are very different, both physically and emotionally.

Adah was born hemiplegic, with a right side that drags. As she puts it, "In the Eden of our mother's womb, I was cannibalized by my sister." (p. 34) Adah has also decided not to speak. The doctor at her birth mistakenly pronounced her mute, and the very perceptive Adah sees many advantages in the condition: "When you do not speak, other people presume you to be deaf or feeble-minded and promptly make a show of their own limitations. . . . I write and draw in my notebook and read anything I please." (p. 34)

At fourteen, Adah has already made some astute judgments on the people around her: "It is true I do not speak as well as I can think. But that is true of most people, as nearly as I can tell." (p. 34)

She has also taken a very accurate measure of her father's megalomania – "Our Father speaks for all of us, as far as I can see." (p. 32)

Adah leads a rich interior life, full of verbal gymnastics. She adores palindromes, and "When I finish reading a book from front to back, I read it back to front. It is a different book, back to front, and you can learn new things from it." (p. 57)

There is very little that escapes Adah's attention and her logic is inexorable. At the age of five, back in Georgia, she used "a month's ration of words" to ask her Sunday-school teacher why a child would be "denied entrance to heaven merely for being born in the Congo rather than, say, north Georgia, where she could attend church regularly." (p. 171)

The teacher's answer was swift.

Miss Betty sent me to the corner for the rest of the hour to pray for my own soul while kneeling on grains of uncooked rice. When I finally got up with sharp grains imbedded in my knees I found, to my surprise, that I no longer believed in God. . . .

From that day I stopped parroting the words of *Oh, God! God's love!* And began to cant in my own backward tongue: *Evol's dog! Dog ho!* (p. 171)

Adah finds an acceptance in Kilanga that she had never known before. The villagers accept her without judgment; she is part of an imperfect world they have learned marvellously well to live with.

Adah is as well-informed as she is wise. When she sees Axelroot stuffing village goods and diamonds into his sacks while everyone except the Prices are preparing to evacuate during the post-independence violence, Adah reflects, "The Belgians and the Americans who run the rubber plantations and copper mines, I imagine, are using larger sacks." (p. 174)

It is Adah's cold intelligence that saves her on the terrible night when the driver ants come to eat everything in their path. Adah sees her mother staring at her "out in the moonlight where the ground boiled," Orleanna holding Ruth May in her arms and "weighing the two of us against one another." Orleanna chooses to take the "sweet intact child with golden ringlets" and to seek refuge with her and her alone from the ants. Adah does not collapse in a heap of self-pity; she merely notes drily, "After hesitating only a second, she chose to save perfection and leave the damaged. Everyone must choose." (pp. 412-13)

With Anatole's help, Adah will survive the ants, and later, as Orleanna and the twins flee from the violence, Orleanna will chose Adah over Leah to carry to safety. Without rancour, many years later, Adah will accept her mother's explanation of both incidents with the same passionless, scientific objectivity: "'After Ruth May you were my youngest, Adah. When push comes to shove, a mother takes care of her children from the bottom up.'" (p. 444)

I know that Adah's calm reason was what sustained her all those years, but I confess that there is something in her cold lack of emotion that I find very frightening.

Once safe in America, Adah will make the decision to speak as a necessary step to obtaining a university education. She will be told that her hemiplegia is psychosomatic, and she will relive the crawling of her infancy in order to relearn how to walk. Adah will become a doctor and do research on viruses, and her life will have purpose. As she says, "In organic chemistry, invertebrate zoology, and the inspired symmetry of Mendelian genetics, I have found a religion that serves." (p. 409)

Sometimes she will regret losing the self she had in Africa, as *benduka* the crooked walker, as *bënduka* the sleek bird, and as she tells her mother, "'I will always be Adah inside. A crooked little person trying to tell the truth.'" (p. 496)

She will never marry, because no one who would choose her after she has become straight would have chosen her when she was mute and crooked.

I have already said that Adah's coldness frightened me. I only warmed to her when as a mature woman she confesses to her mother how much she had hated her father.

"Do you know when I hated him the most? When he used to make fun of my books. My writing and reading. And when he hit any of us. You especially. I imagined getting the kerosene and burning him up in his bed. I only didn't because you were in it too." (p. 496)

But my warm feelings didn't last long. Four lines later we have this terrible exchange between mother and daughter, when Orleanna asks, *"'Then why didn't you? Both of us together. You might as well have.'"* Adah replies, *"'Because then you would be free too. And I didn't want that. I wanted you to remember what he did to us.'"*

That was when my blood ran really cold, as I realized that Adah blamed her mother just as much as she hated her father, for permitting the abuse to go on. For all her appearance of intelligent, scientific objectivity, there is a maelstrom of consuming, unresolved hatred at the well-hidden heart of Adah Price.

Last of all the daughters, we have the other twin, Leah. She does not become as close to the village children as her innocent little sister Ruth May, but she makes friends like Pascal and Nelson from whom she learns much. Her father takes her to see the Independence celebrations in Leopoldville, and she loses the last of the prejudices she brought with her from Georgia.

> I wish the people back home reading magazine stories about dancing cannibals could see something as ordinary as Anatole's clean white shirt and kind eyes, or Mama Mwanza with her children. If the word "Congo" makes people think of that big-lipped cannibal man in the cartoon, why, they're just wrong about everything here from top to bottom. (p. 235)

Initially, Leah loves her father, but as it becomes clearer and clearer that the Prices should leave with the other missionaries, she begins to waver: "If his decision to keep us here in the Congo wasn't right, then what else might he be wrong about? It has opened up in my heart a sickening world of doubts and possibilities, where before I had only faith in my father and love for the Lord." (p. 244)

She transfers all the loyalty she had felt towards her father to Anatole, he of "the kind eyes." Rapidly approaching sixteen, she studies French and Kikongo with Anatole, helps him to teach his younger students, and gradually falls in love. She becomes defiant of her father – her favourite expression when they argue is, "'Is that your point of view, Father? How interesting that you think so.'" (p. 356) Leah is too strong, both physically and in her spirit, for Nathan Price to abuse.

When the violence finally erupts, and Orleanna saves Adah as a penance for her earlier abandoning of her lame daughter, it is Anatole who saves Leah. At first refusing her advances because of her youth, Anatole finally accepts her as his partner in the struggle against the American-imposed government. He has always been a secret supporter of Lumumba, and now his friends will hide Leah in a Catholic convent as Anatole is taken into custody.

When he is released after three years, they marry, and Leah becomes Mrs. Ngemba, although the gentle, loving Anatole will call her what he has always called her, *Béene-béene*, "as true as the truth can be." Leah embraces Africa both metaphorically and literally.

With Anatole, Leah will bear four sons, Africa's future, and they will have many friends, among them American missionaries like Brother Fowles. Leah loves it when they stay, "these soft-spoken men who organize hospitals under thatched-roofs." She loves "to hear the kindness in their stories. They're so unlike Father." (p. 435) Anatole becomes principal of a regional *école secondaire*, and Leah will teach at an American school, where the students, as ignorant as her sister Rachel, will call her "Mrs. Gumbo." (p. 457)

Leah and Anatole will visit the United States with their son, Pascal, to see Adah and to study agronomics, and Pascal will be open-mouthed at the rampant consumerism of America. His aunt Adah will try to explain that the stores are full of things people don't really need, but Pascal persists: "'But, Aunt Adah, how can there be so many *kinds* of things a person doesn't really need?'" (p. 441)

Eventually, Leah and Anatole will have to send their boys to safety in America. Mobutu's Zaire has become a hell where no public servant outside the army has been paid for two years and where eleven-year-olds like Anatole's cousin Christiane must prostitute themselves for food. By 1986 the Ngembas, Anatole and Leah, are forced out of Zaire over the border into Angola, the former Portuguese colony where the United States has also fomented a country-destroying civil war. There Anatole directs a farmers' cooperative and Leah teaches survival skills to women ravaged by war, and there we will leave them in the wedded bliss they call "The New Republic of Conubia." Leah lives in a dimension beyond happiness:

I wake up in love, and work my skin to darkness under the equatorial sun. I look at my four boys, who are the colors of silt, loam, dust, and clay, an infinite palette for children of their own, and I understand that time erases whiteness altogether. (p. 526)

There are those who would agree with Leah's sister Adah that Leah has gone too far, that she can see no fault in Africa, that she denies not only her own whiteness but her own selfhood in her total dedication to Anatole and to Africa. Perhaps the African experience was too great even for Leah. Perhaps Leah too, in a sense, was as much a victim of Africa as was little Ruth May. I don't insist upon the point. Perhaps total love, whether it be of a person or a country or, as in this case, both, is always destructive of the individual's sense of self. In any event, I leave you to decide whether or not Leah Ngemba finds a happy ending. What is certain is that each of the daughters was damaged by their monomaniacal father.

As we leave the novel we know that Nathan Price disappeared after Orleanna took the children out of the Congo and reappeared in a hut in the jungle as the leader of a new faith, The New Church of Eternal Life, Jesus is Bangala. We know that he was blamed and burned to death when a boatload of children was overturned and the children killed or maimed by crocodiles. We cannot grieve at the death of Nathan Price, because he was never really a person. Barbara Kingsolver never even gave him his own narrative voice. Nathan Price was no more than a symbol, the embodiment of certain American colonial attitudes. Nobody can weep when an allegorical figure is killed off.

We know from her own words that Orleanna Price ended up on Sanderling Island off the Georgia coast in a little house bought with an inheritance from her grandfather. There she is visited by Leah and Adah, but not by Rachel, and spends her time selling flowers by the roadside and begging forgiveness from the five-year-old she did not save in time. Orleanna and her twin daughters will make a last visit back to the Congo, but Kilanga has been swallowed up by the jungle. The spirit of little Ruth May hovers over the end of the novel as she proclaims herself part of the African earth, a child of Africa, *muntu* Africa, and as she proclaims that Africa is eternal: "The forest eats itself and lives forever." (p. 537)

What do we remember from the novel? The details of Mobutu's corruption in Zaire in the last chapters of the novel, when he brings two boxers together for the "Rumble in the Jungle" at a cost of twenty million dollars, the fight to be held in a stadium in the cellars of which hundreds of political prisoners are being tortured to death? The revelation that Americans have too many useless possessions? (Although that can't be much of a revelation.) The terrible night when the driver ants attack Kilanga, or the two occasions when Orleanna has to choose between one of her children and another? The grace and the charity of the Kilanga villagers?

I remember all those things. And I remember Barbara Kingsolver's perfect prose and the individuality of the four daughters and the passive victimhood of the mother and the zealot father and his terrible God.

But most of all I remember one sentence of the novel. It is such a quiet sentence. It is a sentence in which Orleanna Price reveals something she found out years after she had left the Congo.

This is it:

On a day late in August, 1960, a Mr. Allen Dulles, who was in charge of the CIA, sent a telegram to his Congolese station chief suggesting that he replace the Congolese government at his earliest convenience. (p. 319)

If there is a heart of darkness in this novel, it is not an African heart of darkness, it is an American heart of darkness. And that American heart of darkness is what caused the third crime, the third genocide, and *that* is what the novel is about.

PALACE WALK

Naguib Mahfouz

(New York: Anchor Books, 1991)

Palace Walk by Naguib Mahfouz is the first of three novels that make up the Cairo Trilogy. Collectively they form a fifteen-hundred-page saga of the life of a Cairo family between the years 1917 and 1944. This first novel deals only with the years 1917 to 1919.

Like all the novels of the first half of Mahfouz's writing career, *Palace Walk* and the other two novels of the Cairo Trilogy are written in the style of social realism, a style very accessible to the Western reader. Although the background is Egypt's struggle for independence, the novels are full of family detail in a precisely described local setting, each member of the family made vivid by Mahfouz's record of his or her idiosyncrasies and deepest longings. The little stories he makes up about each of his characters, familiar stories told from new perspectives, go a long way towards explaining his popularity among his Arab readers in a land that loves the storyteller.

The Cairo Trilogy, including *Palace Walk*, is the best work of his early writing period from 1945 to 1961 before he left realism to turn inward and write more than a dozen novels using modern techniques like fragmented narrative, stream of consciousness, and a disdain for traditional chronology. I have read only a little of that later work, much of it not yet translated into English, and my belief in his greatness as a writer is founded mainly on the evidence of the Cairo Trilogy. Mahfouz says that he wrote all three novels of the trilogy before 1952, although they were not published until 1956 and 1957. The delay was caused by the chaos after the revolution of

1952, the abdication of King Farouk, and the accession to power of Gamal Abdel Nasser.

Strangely enough, the translation into English of the Cairo Trilogy was not begun until 1990, and if Mahfouz had not won the Nobel Prize for Literature in 1988, I do not think it would have been translated even then. I know that before 1990 all I had read of Mahfouz's work was one small collection of short stories published in 1973. I remember liking the realism of some, the lyricism of others, and having trouble with the later work because of its experimental style.

Mahfouz has long been hailed as the finest novelist of the Arab world, and yet his best work, the trilogy, was not available to the English-speaking world for more than thirty years after it was written. There has never been much interest by the West in Arab literature, or indeed Arab culture or Arab history. It is true that one tiny corner of the Arab world, that of the nomadic Bedouin, has been glamorized through the writings of T.E. Lawrence and the explorer Sir Richard Burton, but for most of us our knowledge is limited to *Lawrence of Arabia* with Peter O'Toole, and perhaps vague childhood memories of the stories of the *Arabian Nights*.

I have never noticed any Western interest in the Arab masses, in the bustling streets of Cairo for example. Most of us would do badly on the most elementary quiz on Arab history or Arab culture.

Naguib Mahfouz has opened a window on that world for us, and his achievement is as remarkable as the man is modest. He was born in Cairo in 1911, taught at Cairo University from 1936 to 1939, and then left to become a civil servant at the Ministry of Culture. He wrote short stories and novels and newspaper articles for *Al Ahram*, but in a largely illiterate Egypt no writer can live on his writing alone, and Mahfouz was compelled to follow a civil service career until his retirement in 1971. Now he lives quietly in a Cairo apartment with his wife and two daughters, spending most of his time in his beloved cafés, exchanging gossip and watching the passing parade of humanity. In recent years he has listened rather than watched, because he has lost his sight. I find it endearing that he failed to show up in Stockholm to accept his Nobel Prize in person, not for any political reason, but because he is absolutely terrified of flying.

I said a moment ago that Mahfouz's achievement is remarkable. *Palace Walk* would be a great book in any company, but it is all the more exceptional when we remember how recently the novel became a genre in Arabic.

The first novel in Arabic, *Zainab* by Mohammed Husayn Haykal, was written as late as 1911, and even then it was written in Paris by an Egyptian in exile.

Yet how could it have been otherwise?

Literacy, an industrial revolution, and a *substantial* middle class came late to the Arab world, including Egypt. In 1911 only 8 percent of Egyptians could read and write. Even today, 70 percent of Egyptians are still cut off from reading.

Arab literature, apart from some religious drama, always took the form of poetry, usually in easy-to-remember couplets. It was the means by which an intelligent illiterate could receive and pass on learning. It is how the Prophet Mohammed himself, who could neither read nor write, received the Koran from the Angel Gabriel.

But there is another reason why the novel appeared as late as it did in the Arab countries.

All literature, especially the novel, is about identity, our need to know who we are. In the Islamic monolith of belief that existed before this century, why would anyone have asked the ultimate question that literature poses, "Who am I?" The question would have been meaningless to a true believer. He knew who he was: the child and servant of the one all-powerful and all-merciful God. The novel, like any other literary genre that asks questions, was irrelevant.

Only when the Islamic structure began to crack with the twentieth-century failure of Turkey, the leader of the Islamic world, did the appearance of an Arab novel become both possible and inevitable.

I would like, now, to approach the novel *Palace Walk*, but there is a problem. What is the Western reader to make of the repeated lament for the lost caliphate? What are we to make of Egyptian adoration for the exiled Khedive Abbas II, so often referred to as "our *effendi*"? Why is Sultan Husayn Kamil so hated? Why do the Egyptians so love Sa'd Pasha, leader of the *wafd*? What is the *wafd*? Why are there British and Australian soldiers on the streets of Cairo in 1917? Why do the Egyptians use so many Turkish words, especially as honorifics?

None of these questions can be answered, none of the novel's references can be understood, without a fair knowledge of Egypt's past.

Let us begin at the beginning. The Prophet Mohammed, founder of the religion of Islam, died more than thirteen hundred years ago in 632. Within eight years of his death, Egypt was conquered by Moslem forces and became part of an immense Islamic empire that stretched from Morocco in the west to Persia in the east. Henceforth, Egypt, like all the other Islamic countries, would be governed by a viceroy appointed by the *caliph*, a pope-like figure, both the spiritual and temporal leader of Islam. Over the generations, the caliphs would have their capital sometimes in Damascus and sometimes in Baghdad, until the Sultan of Turkey assumed the caliphate into his own person in the sixteenth century and the centre of Islamic authority became Constantinople. There was not always agreement in Islam about who was the rightful caliph, and sometimes, just as on occasion there were two popes, there were competing caliphs. Indeed the great schism in Islam, between Shi'ite and Sunni Moslems, rested on exactly that point: whether the caliphate belonged in perpetuity to the family of Mohammed's son-in-law, Ali, or not. The followers of Ali we know as Shi'ites.

The important thing is that Egypt would always owe its allegiance to a caliph who was not Egyptian and who appointed non-Egyptian viceroys. Sometimes there were whole dynasties of viceroys of Syrian or Tunisian or Kurdish blood, but never, never Egyptian.

After the great Turkish expansion of 1517 and the establishment of the Ottoman Empire, the sultans of Turkey would always choose for Egypt a Turkish viceroy, usually from the same family. Some of them, like Mohammed Ali from 1805 to 1848, ruled Egypt almost like an independent kingdom, but the ultimate authority was always the caliph, the Sultan of Turkey. All the titles of rank in *Palace Walk*, like *effendi* or *pasha* (both meaning "lord"), are always Turkish and not Egyptian. The one exception is *Al-Sayid*, accorded to the patriarch in the novel, but although it translates as "master" it is more commonly used as "mister." Any elevation above the usual in the Egypt of 1917 would result in a Turkish, not an Egyptian honorific.

When the First World War broke out in 1914, the Khedive of Egypt was Abbas II. (The Sultan of Turkey had changed the title from Viceroy to Khedive some fifty years earlier, but the position was the same.) Since Abbas II was of Turkish descent and naturally pro-Turkish and pro-German, the British simply exiled him to Constantinople as the guest of his master, the Sultan of Turkey. He was too dangerous for the British to leave in place, since Egypt and the Suez Canal were of such vital strategic importance.

The British were in a position to do this because they exercised massive control over Egyptian affairs. Even before they bought the Suez Canal in 1875, they owned the whole of the Egyptian railway system and had such a stranglehold on Egyptian business that they were able to demand that the Egyptian minister of finance be an Englishman, Sir Evelyn Baring.

Once the Khedive Abbas II, known and loved by the Egyptians as "our *effendi*," was deposed in 1914, the British installed a puppet, Abbas's uncle, Husayn Kamil. They called him not Khedive but Sultan and declared Egypt independent of Turkey and a British protectorate. Already at war with Great Britain, the Sultan of Turkey could do nothing about it. He was already losing control of his country to Mustafa Kemal and the Young Turk movement. (In 1922 Kemal would proclaim Turkey a republic and both the sultanate and caliphate would disappear forever. In 1926 a pan-Arab conference tried to find a new caliph, but it was unsuccessful, and Islam has not had a supreme leader since 1922.)

In 1917, the pro-British sultan died. His son, Kamal al-Din, won the respect of all Egyptians by refusing the succession. He became the hero of the *wafd*, the pro-independence lobby led by Sa'd Pasha.

However, the British had no trouble in finding another quisling. Fuad, the brother of the late Husayn Kamil, accepted the position of Sultan of Egypt. The title would be changed to King of Egypt in 1922. (Fuad would be succeeded by his son Farouk in 1936, who would reign until the Neguib-Nasser Revolution of 1952.)

Permit me to summarize my remarks. The action of *Palace Walk* is set in Cairo in the years 1917 to 1919. For the previous thirteen hundred years Egyptians had owed their allegiance to a viceroy of foreign blood and to a Moslem caliphate in a foreign country. For nearly three hundred years, beginning in the thirteenth century, they had even been governed by their own slaves! The Mameluke period is a fascinating one. The Mamelukes were well-educated slaves, usually Greek, employed as tutors just as they had been in Ancient Rome. Until the Ottoman Empire came into being in the sixteenth century, it was the Mamelukes who ran Egypt after seizing control of the country from their incompetent and incapable masters. However, even during the Mameluke period, titular authority remained with the viceroy and the Moslem caliphate.

As the novel begins we meet a people with no sense of themselves, a people who see those of Turkish descent as a natural-born elite and the British and their Commonwealth allies as a superior race.

Yasin, the oldest son of the novel's patriarch, Ahmad Abd al-Jawad, is in rapture when an English soldier thanks him for a box of matches.

> An Englishman – in other words, the kind of man he imagined to embody all the perfections of the human race. Yasin probably detested the English as all Egyptians did, but deep inside he respected and venerated them so much that he frequently imagined they were made from a different stuff than the rest of mankind. (p. 395)

I studied at the London School of Economics in the middle fifties with many Arabs among my fellow students. I could never understand their adoration of President Nasser until I did a little research and realized that, whatever else Nasser was, he was the first Egyptian to rule Egypt. The three novels of the Cairo Trilogy will have as their background the emergence of a people from a long, dark night of denial of self.

Let us now finally meet the family of Ahmad Abd al-Jawad, respectfully referred to by his friends as *Al-Sayid* Ahmad, "Mr. Ahmad."

In November 1917, Ahmad is a prosperous merchant living on Palace Walk, one of the three Cairo streets after which the three novels of Mahfouz's trilogy are named. Ahmad has a son, Yasin, by his first marriage, a twenty-one-year-old school secretary who lives at home. By his second wife, Amina, Ahmad has four younger children. The two sons are Fahmy, eighteen and a potential law student, and Kamal, ten years old and the baby of the family. The two daughters, Khadija, twenty, and Aisha, sixteen, named after the first and last of the Prophet's twelve wives, naturally live at home, have never been to school, and know of the world outside their house only what their father tells them. Like their mother, Amina, their whole education has been limited to the rote learning of the *suras* of the Koran, verses they do not begin to understand and which they use as incantations to ward off the powers of darkness in every household crisis or as they hurry past a dark alley. Khadija is described as having a disfiguringly large nose, and Aisha, the sixteen-year-old beauty, is described as unpleasantly thin. We are reassured by the omniscient third-person narrator that there will be time to fatten her up to a pleasing corpulence.

Outside the house, the streets are full of British and Australian soldiers, and Ahmad, his family, and friends pray regularly for their downfall. When Ahmad opens his shop every day, an old blind shaykh comes in to lead the morning prayers, ending always with "'And that He afflict the English and their allies with a shocking defeat, leaving them without a leg to stand on.'" (p. 39)

Ahmad, the protagonist of our story, leads two lives. To his family he is a stern patriarch, enforcing the traditional seclusion of his women from all males other than blood relatives. He observes the custom so strictly that Amina has rarely left the house in their twenty years of marriage, even to go to the nearby al-Husayn mosque.

To his friends outside the family he shows his other face. In their company – and he loves friendship above all else – he frequents nightly the salons of famous female singers and courtesans, taking as a mistress the magnificently fat Madam Zubayda after he tires of the wonderfully obese Jalila. He is a famous *bon vivant*, enjoys wine, and is frequently drunk.

There are two passages involving Ahmad's lechery and drunkenness that I found both amusing and insightful. The first is when the old, blind shaykh reproaches Ahmad for his two vices, both specifically forbidden by the Koran. Ahmad excuses the first by citing the Prophet, who loved both perfume and women. (p. 40) He does not even offer an excuse for the second but pleads that he overlooks only one rule, "harming no one," and besides, "God is merciful." (p. 43) It seems to me Mahfouz is making Ahmad the personification of the Egypt the author describes as containing "mutually contradictory elements, wavering between piety and depravity." (p. 41)

There is a much later lyric passage that confirms this view of Ahmad and his family as a microcosm of the whole of Cairo. Speaking of the family, the narrator Mahfouz says,

Some of them had a capacity for anger like that of alcohol for combustion, but their anger would be quickly extinguished. Then their souls would be tranquil and their hearts full of forgiveness. Similarly in Cairo, during the winter, the sky can be gloomy with clouds and it even drizzles, but in an hour or less the clouds will have scattered to reveal a pure blue sky and a laughing sun. (p. 239)

The other passage touching on Ahmad's vices occurs when he is beginning the seduction of Madam Zubayda. She teases him with, "'They told me you're a womanizer and heavy drinker.'" Ahmad sighs audibly in relief, "'I thought it would be criticism of some fault, thank God.'" (p. 94)

Ahmad and his oldest son, Yasin, share the same view of women. We are told that Ahmad's conjugal love was "based on bodily desire. . . . No woman was anything more than a body to him," (p. 99) while Yasin says of his own biological mother, Ahmad's first wife,

> "A woman. Yes, she's nothing but a woman. Every woman is a filthy curse. A woman doesn't know what virtue is, unless she's denied all opportunities for adultery. Even my stepmother, who's a fine woman – God only knows what she would be like if it weren't for my father." (p. 81)

When Yasin begins his seduction of the lute-player Zanuba, he sees his father in the company of Zanuba's aunt, Madam Zubayda, flushed with drink, beating a tambourine and obviously ready for sex, and his reaction is to feel new love and admiration for his father. "He was near at hand, a bit of his own soul and heart. Father and son were a single spirit." (p. 251) After Yasin marries, he confides to his brother Fahmy, "'I've come to understand my father's position perfectly. . . . How could he have put up with a single dish for a quarter century when I'm dying of boredom after five months?'" (p. 337)

(By the way, Mahfouz's sharp depiction of hypocrisy in an Islamic society, together with his support of Anwar Sadat's 1977 peace initiative, made him the target of many sermons in the mosques and caused a ban on Mahfouz's work in many Arab countries for a number of years.)

Every night, Ahmad, the master of the double standard, is out carousing with his friends, and every night his wife, Amina, waits for him into the small hours. She is the prisoner of tradition, superstition, and the house itself.

Mahfouz begins the novel brilliantly with a claustrophobic description of Amina waiting. The house is her whole world, so she is acutely aware through all her senses of every tiny detail around her.

> She woke at midnight. She always woke up then without having to rely on an alarm clock. A wish that had taken root in her awoke her

with great accuracy. For a few moments she was not sure she was awake. Images from her dreams and perceptions mixed together in her mind. She was troubled by anxiety before opening her eyes, afraid sleep had deceived her. Shaking her head gently, she gazed at the total darkness of the room. There was no clue by which to judge the time. The street noise outside her room would continue until dawn. She could hear the babble of voices from the coffee-houses and bars, whether it was early evening, midnight, or just before daybreak. She had no evidence to rely on except her intu-ition, like a conscious clock hand, and the silence encompassing the house, which revealed that her husband had not yet rapped at the door and that the tip of his stick had not yet struck against the steps of the staircase.

Habit woke her at this hour. It was an old habit she had devel-oped when young and it had stayed with her as she matured. She had learned it along with the other rules of married life. She woke up at midnight to await her husband's return from his evening's entertainment. Then she would serve him until he went to sleep. She sat up in bed resolutely to overcome the temptation posed by sleep. After invoking the name of God, she slipped out from under the covers and onto the floor. Groping her way to the door, she guided herself by the bedpost and a panel of the window. As she opened the door, faint rays of light filtered in from a lamp set on a bracketed shelf in the sitting room. She went to fetch it, and the glass projected onto the ceiling a trembling circle of pale light hemmed in by darkness.

This, and what she can glimpse of the street outside through her latticed windows, is her world. Later in the novel, when she ventures out to a mosque with her son, other men will see her. Mahfouz tells us that in spite of her heavy veil, "She trembled from the impact of these looks." (p. 172)

The world of Amina's daughters is not significantly different. Aisha, her sixteen-year-old, sees a handsome Egyptian officer from her window. He cannot of course raise his head, that would be to violate the honour of the house, but she feels his glance. She is caught out even in this innocent transgression by her older sister, Khadija, whom she has to bribe to silence with candy. Nothing of course comes of the incident and both sisters will accept arranged marriages to the sons of the widow Shawkat, much admired both for her wealth and for her Turkish ancestry.

We have no reason to doubt that Aisha and her sister are both perfectly happy with the arrangements. They accept their father's dictum that "no woman has a fully developed mind," (p. 156) and we are told about Aisha that "it would have been inconceivable for her to express a desire for some specific man. . . . [She] was happy [with her arranged marriage] beyond words." (pp. 236-37)

Yasin also marries during the novel. He is assigned Zaynab, the daughter of Ahmad's old friend, Muhammad Iffat, also honoured for his Turkish ancestry. Poor Yasin by the way has a hard time of it before his marriage. Until he begins to have regular sex with Zanuba the entertainer, he lives in an absolute sweat of physical desire. When he sees Zanuba's buttocks "compressed and ballooned out to the right and left" as she sits in a wagon, he follows the wagon down the street, watching the sway of Zanuba's magnificent arse:

"O God, may this street never end. May this dancing movement never cease. What a royal rump combining both arrogance and graciousness. A wretch like me can almost feel its softness and its firmness both, merely by looking. This wonderful crack separating the two halves – you can almost hear the cloth covering it talk about it." (p. 74)

Mahfouz is equally effective when he conjures up the affinity between politics, sex, and religion in the mind of the Cairo male. At one particularly stimulating evening at Madam Zubayda's, she reveals a strong, fleshy leg and one of her clients is moved to shout in a voice like thunder, " 'The Ottoman caliphate forever!' " (p. 102)

The younger brother Fahmy is going through his own sexual crisis. He has long been attracted to the neighbour's daughter Marryam, but he is far too young to marry, and anyway his little brother, Kamal, brings him the distressing news that Marryam and a young British soldier have been ogling each other. Fahmy sublimates his pent-up sexual longings into political activity and embraces the nationalist cause. He realizes that Turkey is losing the war and there is no longer any hope that Khedive Abbas will return to Egypt or that the Moslem caliphate can be saved. He pins all his hopes on Sa'd Pasha, the leader of the *wafd*, the delegation of Egyptians who ask Fuad and the British for independence. (The term *wafd* will come to be used for the whole independence movement.) But Sa'd Pasha is refused by the British and their puppet and is exiled to Malta. The Egyptian masses take to the streets and there are pro-*wafd* riots, and Fahmy continues to believe in the cause. "Talk of national liberation excited great dreams in him. In that magical universe he could visualize a new world, a new nation, a new home, a new people." (p. 326)

Against the backdrop of political unrest, there is domestic calamity in Ahmad's household. While he is away on a business trip to Port Said, his wife, Amina, dares to fulfill her long-time dream of visiting the al-Husayn mosque only a few streets away. Urged on by her stepson, Yasin, and escorted by ten-year-old Kamal, she makes her visit but is grazed by a car on the way home. Because of her injury her disobedience is discovered and she is expelled to her mother's house.

Divorce seems imminent – Amina would not be the first wife Ahmad has cast out for disobedience – but the children intervene with their father and he relents, not out of love, but out of pride that his children can show such affection for their mother.

Meanwhile Yasin, bored in marriage and unable to get out of the house because of the British-imposed curfew, assaults his wife's maid, Nur. She is at the bottom of the social ladder not only because she is a maid but because she is black. She knows she has no recourse against Yasin; all she can do during the rape, over and over again, is to say, "'Shame on you, master.'" Yasin's wife discovers them together and wakes the household with her screams. (p. 384)

After Ahmad's initial anger at his son, he rages even more against the screaming wife. As Ahmad says, "Yasin had made a mistake but she had made an even greater one." What counts in the Cairo of Mahfouz's description is not virtue but the appearance of virtue. It was Zaynab's screaming and not Yasin's assault that had caused the uproar. As a matter of fact, Ahmad is rather proud of Yasin's virility. "With inner joy he thought about the temperament they both shared." (p. 389)

Yasin does rebel against his father's code once, when he takes his wife to see the great comedian Kishkish Bey in vaudeville, but he accepts the subsequent admonishment of his whole family, including his sisters, that he has violated "common decency and tradition," and there is no reason to believe that he will ever sin again.

The cause of feminism advances not one iota in this novel, so entrenched in all the characters, both male and female, are the attitudes that Ahmad embodies.

But what of political progress, the movement to Egyptian independence? The novel will end with the death of Fahmy, killed by the British in the pro-*wafd* riots. As the news is broken to his father, we remember that Ahmad himself had signed the pro-*wafd* petition. He will certainly hold himself at least partly to blame for encouraging the nationalist aspirations that caused his son's death. (That is a topic Mahfouz will explore in the second novel of the trilogy, *Palace of Desire Alley*.)

The only possible agent of change to come is the young Kamal, inquisitive, alive, seemingly less accepting of the past than his elders, but with a direction and a future not yet spelled out. Kamal is the Egypt yet to come.

As we reach the end of the novel, we realize how great is Mahfouz's achievement. He has created a Cairo with a real physical presence, as memorable as Dickens's London or Zola's Paris. He has peopled the city with unforgettable characters, full of complexity and contradictions, people like Khadija, whose "heart had no equal both in coldness and in compassion." (p. 29) Even when Mahfouz brings on a character only peripherally important to the narrative, like Yasin's mother, Ahmad's first wife, the author fleshes her out completely. I would know her if I met her, not as easily as I would know Ahmad, but I would know her.

But of all the characters Mahfouz has created, none lingers in my thoughts more than Amina, waiting nightly for her husband in the stultifying boredom of her prison on Palace Walk.

My wife, Pearl, and I visited Cairo briefly several years ago. We saw the Sphinx and the pyramids, and I think we understood what we saw. But we also saw shuttered windows and veiled women, and we did not know what reality existed behind the facade. I know that Mahfouz is writing about Amina and her daughters *then*, and not the fate of Egyptian women *now* – or at least I hope so – but his trilogy has shown me where modern Cairo came from. He has allowed me a glimpse behind the shutters and the veil, and I am very grateful.

ASYLUM

Patrick McGrath

(Toronto: Vintage, 1998)

A friend of mine recently sent me a review of Patrick McGrath's novel he had clipped out of a Florida newspaper. Although it was a very short review it used the word *Gothic* eleven times. It is certainly true that *Asylum* is a Gothic novel, but the term is much misused. I thought I might begin by discussing the expression so that we are agreed on its definition.

About eight hundred years ago, the commonest feature of all larger structures in the Western world was the round arch, called the Romanesque arch after the Ancient Rome where it originated. Gradually however, architects began to use a higher, pointed arch. As time passed by, some remembered that among the barbarians who had destroyed Rome in the fifth century were the Goths. What better name for an arch that replaced the Romanesque arch than "Gothic" arch? The choice was ironic really, because the Goths, at least in the fifth century, were doing very little building. The medieval period of European architecture became characterized by castles and cathedrals using a high vault and the pointed arch, the Gothic arch. So important was the arch that we call the whole period until the Renaissance the Gothic period.

Now we come to the literary use of the term. In 1740 came the first novel in the English language, *Pamela* by Samuel Richardson. It was a complex psychological portrait of a person moving through a believable, contemporary setting. But writers began very soon to experiment with this new genre, and in 1764 Horace Walpole wrote a novel set in the past, in a medieval castle with high vaults and Gothic arches. He called his work *The Castle of Otranto, a Gothic Story*. Other similar novels followed – readers enjoyed the medieval setting, castles with dungeons and hiding places and torture chambers and sometimes even a hint of the supernatural. Thus the term *Gothic*, used originally to describe the setting, came to be used for any novel whose purpose was to evoke horror or terror. Writers began to explore physical and psychological abnormality. If they could situate the stories in a medieval castle, so much the better. But even in popular nineteenth-century Gothic novels like *Dracula* or *Frankenstein*, we can already see a movement away from the haunted castle into the haunted mind.

Now we have the wonderful neo-Gothic writer Patrick McGrath. His primary interest is in the labyrinth of the human mind, but he always gives a nod to the Gothic settings of the past. The asylum of our novel's title is a gloomy, Victorian maximum-security building, and the building in Southwark, South London, where our two lovers hide is old, abandoned, and crumbling.

The plot of *Asylum* is very simple. Permit me to recapitulate.

The year is 1959 and we are in an English prison-hospital for the criminally insane. One of the many inmates is Edgar Stark, who has been an inmate for the five years since he murdered his wife. A sculptor on the outside, he had come to believe that his wife was betraying him. His reaction was to cut off her head and sculpt it, trying to get down to the truth of her. He was imitating that African form of sculpture that had so inspired Picasso and others, that sculpture which reduces a shape, a figure, a person, to its few basic elements, stripping away the external details to see the essence of it. His crime is described in detail:

> He had cut Ruth Stark's head off and stuck it on his sculpture stand. Then he'd worked it with his tools as though it were a lump of damp clay. The eyes went first. One of the policemen told me it was like something out of a butcher's shop. You wouldn't know what it was, but for the teeth, and a few lumps of matted hair. (p. 241)

Now that is Gothic!

The deputy-superintendent of the hospital is Dr. Max Raphael, a psychiatrist newly arrived from London who is being groomed to take over when the present superintendent retires. He has with him his ten-year-old son, Charlie, a little overweight with rabbit teeth and freckles (a fair description of McGrath when he was ten years old).

Dr. Raphael also has with him his beautiful, bored wife, Stella, who misses the excitement of London terribly. She begins a mad, passionate affair with Edgar Stark, follows him to London when he escapes, and lives with him in an abandoned building until she is caught and brought back to her husband. He loses his job and is obliged to take a much inferior position at a mental hospital in North Wales, where he and his wife live in a state of unresolved tension.

Stella's son, Charlie, dies in an accident that is seen to be Stella's fault, and she is convicted of manslaughter "while the balance of her mind was disturbed." She is sent as a patient to the same prison-hospital where she had lived with her husband and where she had met Edgar Stark. Stark too is caught and returned to the same hospital. Both she and Stark will be under the care of Dr. Peter Cleave, a one-time colleague of Stella's husband. After the dismissal of Dr. Raphael and the retirement of Dr. Straffen, it is Dr. Peter Cleave who now runs the institution.

This is the story of the novel up until the last few pages – which I will discuss later – as narrated by Dr. Peter Cleave. Now you have almost the whole plot. But our interest must be in the complexity of character, the labyrinths of the mind, particularly of the disordered mind.

It is certain that some of the characters are abnormal. Edgar Stark the murderer? Of course! Stella Raphael, who runs off with a murderer and later allows her child to die? Abnormal? I suppose so. But perhaps Edgar and Stella are not the only "abnormals." After all, what is normal? That is one of the themes of the novel and we will return to it.

What are Patrick McGrath's qualifications to write a novel about abnormal behaviour?

He was born in 1950 in London, England, to parents of Irish descent. His father was the chief psychiatrist at Broadmoor, the prison-hospital where the British send the most dangerous of the criminally insane. It was where Patrick McGrath grew up, living *inside* the grounds. McGrath has often talked to the media about his childhood, about his friends among the trusties, those prisoners allowed to move freely about the grounds and help his mother in the garden. He says, "It was like having a lot of uncles for my personal enjoyment. There was no sense that they were criminal lunatics because I'd been carefully taught that these were men who had suffered mental illness, under the influence of which they might well have murdered, but it was illness nonetheless." (from an interview with Judy Stoffman, *Toronto Star*, October 29, 1997)

As a matter of fact, McGrath says in the same interview that the homicidal sculptor Edgar Stark is based on McGrath's particular childhood friend, a murderer named Dennis. "He was a thirtyish, handsome man with a very jovial, warm spirit. He could build things. I looked up to him. It was a splendid place to grow up in."

You may well wonder why Patrick McGrath in real life and Charlie in our novel were allowed to play with murderers. It was because, in both cases, the murderers were paranoid but not psychotic. The difference is vital. A person with a psychosis is one whose *whole* personality is disordered. They are in every asylum and they lead very restricted lives. Someone who is paranoid, on the other hand, is often completely healthy except for one *idée fixe*. That one fixed idea is the paranoia; it may be an illusion, that he is Napoleon, or it may be a delusion, that he is being persecuted or betrayed.

In the case of Edgar Stark, the delusion takes the form of believing that any woman with whom he is intimately involved, his wife for example, will inevitably be promiscuously unfaithful to him. Therefore, any woman in an emotionally charged relationship with him is in great danger. But no one else is, and that is why Patrick McGrath and Charlie could play with murderers – they were not the focus of the murderers' paranoia.

After what seems to me to be a unique childhood, Patrick McGrath went to university, graduated, and began to travel. He came to Canada and spent two years as a social worker's assistant at the Penetang Mental Health Centre near Toronto, playing chess with and writing letters for the criminally insane. He spent the next ten years wandering across Canada, teaching and writing. He wrote thrillers and science fiction, but nothing was published because he hadn't yet found his true voice.

In 1982 he ended up in New York as editor of the magazine *Speech Technology*. He also met and married the actress Maria Aitken (John Cleese's wife in *A Fish Called Wanda*) and kept on writing.

Finally, in 1988, he published a collection of short stories about mental illness, sex, guilt, violence, death, and horror. He had found his writing voice and it was Gothic! *Asylum* is the fourth of his neo-Gothic works, and I believe his best.

He now spends six months a year in North America – he loves the space – and six months in London, which he describes as "damp, rainy, grey, and dull," but stimulating to his writing. He told the *Toronto Star*, "England is a repressed society with a rigid class system. The tension of a repressed, rigid society is an attractive tension to work with. And, besides, I grew up there. I know the rules."

Let us now spend a little more time with Stella, the wife of the ambitious Max Raphael, who is described by his fellow psychiatrist, the narrator Dr. Peter Cleave, as "a reserved, rather melancholy man, a competent administrator but weak; and he lacked imagination." (p. 4)

Their marriage was in trouble even before Max took up his appointment at the asylum:

> [S]he'd told Max that she was not prepared to be buried alive in a cold
> marriage, a white marriage, because his own sexual drive was weak,
> or because he lacked the moral or physical imagination to continue to
> find her attractive, or because he channeled all his libido into his work,
> or because of whatever explanation he cared to offer. (p. 74)

The problem is a serious one, because Stella Raphael is a beautiful, passionate woman. The sixty-three-year-old Dr. Peter Cleave appreciates her very much. He waxes lyrical about Stella Raphael on the night of the hospital dance:

> Oh, I have known many elegant and lovely women, but none matched
> Stella that night. She was in a low-cut black evening dress of coarse
> ribbed silk, an exquisite grosgrain I had never seen before. The neck-
> line was square and showed the curve of her breasts. It clung to her
> body then belled from the waist, scooped in a fold over each knee
> like a tulip, with a split between. She was wearing very high heels
> and a wrap thrown loosely about her shoulders. (p. 7)

The marriage isn't helped by the visits of Max's mother, Brenda, a wealthy, bitchy member of London's smart set whose visits are designed, in part, to make her daughter-in-law's life miserable.

Edgar Stark is assigned to work on renovating the Raphaels' conservatory. (Patrick McGrath makes what I thought was a very clever little joke in that the conservatory has Romanesque arches, hardly appropriate to a Gothic novel.) We are not surprised when Stella and Edgar feel an immediate physical attraction. Edgar manipulates her brilliantly. He is helpful when Charlie falls out of a tree, and he tells Stella of the difficulties of asylum life, the old plumbing, the overcrowding. He seems so sane. She knows he killed his wife – although she doesn't know the details – and convinces herself that it must have been a crime of passion. Edgar plays his hand superbly. He tells her about the *other* patients, about a bridge game that turned into a fight where someone nearly lost an eye. Edgar: "'We are all mad.'" Stella: "'I don't think you're mad.'" Edgar: "'Neither do I.'" (p. 18)

At that moment Edgar knows he's got her, and he plans to make his move at the hospital's annual dance.

Edgar invites Stella onto the dance floor and holds her tightly so that she can feel his erection. Then McGrath is inspired to let Stella herself analyze her feelings. She does it just like a mental-health professional, detailing the split-second stages of her reaction: first, incomprehension; second, outrage; third, pity, as she sees the apparent helplessness in his face and that he can't control his desire; and fourth, acceptance, and she returns the pressure. (pp. 18-19)

Next day Edgar, a gifted strategist, phones her to apologize for his behaviour. How could Stella find the phone call anything but normal, even endearing, heightening her desire? "[T]he violence of feeling he had aroused in her would shatter the constraints of caution and common sense, and overwhelm their fragile status quo." (p. 24)

Sex between them is inevitable, and although it is Edgar who invites Stella into the conservatory, it is she who actually pulls him in, who spreads her fingers across his cheeks to kiss him fiercely on the lips, and who lowers herself to the ground to receive him. (p. 25)

There is no nonsense about spiritual union or shared intellectual interest or finding God together, this is pure physical passion and Stella is helpless to resist it. She can no more fight it than Edgar could have fought the paranoia centred on his wife. Stella can and does consider the implications of the affair.

She was moved suddenly by the idea of the security of her family life, its comfort and meaning and order, all of which rested squarely on Charlie and his welfare.

. . . [She felt] horror at the very thought of endangering not only her own security but Charlie's too. (pp. 33-34)

But it's not enough; in any struggle between reason and passion, passion always stands a very good chance.

Stella is not a cardboard character – bored housewife has it off with handsome lunatic. That is a part of it, but there is much more. There is her understandable hostility towards a mother-in-law who has never forgiven Stella for marrying her darling, dependent son. There is her understandable resentment of the way Max punishes her with monstrous silences "that filled the room with hurt and anger." (p. 51) There is her growing suspicion that her husband's calling, the whole profession of psychiatry, is built on less than solid foundations. Stella gets confirmation of her doubts when Dr. Straffen makes a very frank admission at a dinner party:

"A man like Edgar Stark," . . . He sighed. "We have a number of patients diagnosed as paranoids. Now, these patients, Stella. . . . We don't medicate them. We try and treat them, but not I'm afraid with any great success. We can manage them, we can contain them, but we don't really know how to treat them. Because we don't really understand what they are." (p. 72)

(Dr. Straffen's view, by the way, is a restatement of the opinion held by McGrath's father, himself the director of an asylum. Apart from providing a supportive and controlled environment, he didn't think there was much society could do for the paranoid.)

Stella is a thoughtful, insightful woman when not in the throes of passion. When at the same dinner party Dr. Straffen makes a casual comment that illicit alcohol has been found in the hospital, that Stark *might* be the culprit, and that action might have to be taken, Stella is horrified to realize how totalitarian is the structure of the asylum. "Their power is absolute, and suspicion alone is quite enough to seal a man's fate. . . . It was the raw bare face of institutional power she was seeing . . . she was hearing the voice of the master." (pp. 49-50)

Stella is rapidly switching sides; she will dismiss as unfounded any details of Edgar's crimes given by doctors she now regards as fascist charlatans.

We are not surprised when Edgar absconds to London with Stella's money and, ironically, her husband's clothes, nor are we surprised that Stella meets him almost daily on spurious shopping trips up to the West End. Her physical passion has expanded to fill her universe, and there is no room for secondary characters like a husband or a son. Nothing can keep Stella from Edgar and the stinking, filthy, abandoned building where he hides in Southwark. McGrath gives two more nods to the tradition of the Gothic novel, one in the decay of the hiding place and the other in providing Edgar with an acolyte, a young, admiring, non-judgmental would-be artist. Frankenstein had Igor, Svengali had Gecko, and Edgar has Nick.

Edgar is becoming increasingly jealous that Stella still shares a bed with Max. "'Don't let him touch you,'" says Edgar, and Stella lies with, "'Not for years.'" (p. 94)

Finally, absolutely overcome by passion, Stella clears her bank account and leaves for London to share Edgar's little world. What Stella has done is to create a perfect little world of "us," rather like John Donne's lovers for whom "nothing else is." She has not forgotten that she has a son, but "she had tried to blur him into Max . . . to make him part of the man she was leaving." (p. 104)

Her first complete night with Edgar is full of sex, "primitive, urgent – and loud," (p. 87) and for Stella it is the happiest night of her life.

And who can say it was not worth it? Who can say that a few hours of passion, of experiencing life with every fibre of being, do not have more value than a well-ordered lifetime of little feeling?

I remember that when I left South Wales to study in London, the British government made the cardinal error of sending me my scholarship money in one lump sum at the beginning of the academic year. It was meant to sustain me for twelve months. I received it on a Friday. On the following Tuesday I had to borrow bus fare to get back to my rented room. I have only confused memories of the few days: in one I am in a Piccadilly nightclub, calling the orchestra to my table to play "Begin the Beguine" one more time and announcing drinks "for all my friends." My profligacy meant that in addition to my studies I had to work full time at night in factories and hospitals for the rest of the year. Strangely enough, I didn't mind. I had travelled Blake's road of excess; I had known the madness of which the poets wrote. And I did exactly the same thing with the government cheque at the beginning of the following year. One of McGrath's achievements in the novel is to make Stella's passion for Edgar so understandable, even palpable, that I cannot imagine her not going to him any more than she can.

Edgar will have Stella model for him, and knowing what he did to his wife we feel a cold *frisson* of foreboding. Our fear grows as he becomes erratic and abusive, sometimes slapping, sometimes clinging. He sculpts her head in clay, then scars the bust. He even begins to insist that she taste his food before he eats. He starts to imagine her unfaithful with every man. Even Stella, with all her distrust of psychiatric diagnosis, is frightened. I was terrified.

She runs from Edgar, hiding out in Nick's Soho flat. On the third night, she gives way to Nick's urging and lets him copulate with her, but it's a poor performance and Stella tells him so. Nothing could compare to the physical ecstasy she shared with Edgar.

Unbelievably – or almost so – Stella returns to the South London slum and finds, to her horror, the police. They take the view that she is a victim and not an accomplice and return her to her husband. The marriage will continue, not because Max loves her, but because Brenda, his mother, makes a very stupid error. She threatens her son with an ultimatum: either he gets rid of Stella or she stops his allowance. Brenda has miscalculated – even a gutless wonder of a mama's boy like Max could not give in to such a threat. Besides, Max will now have the upper hand: "[H]e would never let her forget that she had hurt him, or rather that she had humiliated him publicly; the needle would be inserted whenever he chose." (p. 150)

With Max wallowing in self-pity and Stella sinking ever deeper into lethargy, they move to bleak Cledwyn and the misery of unending Welsh rain. It is a place of great natural beauty, but the weather is abominable and the asylum Max now works at is drab and depressing. The locals are unprepossessing and hostile, "suspicious, watchful men, dour and sly. They didn't like the Raphaels because they were English. They bore old grudges. The women were hard-worked and bitter." (p. 166)

Living in the other half of the Raphaels' grey semi-detached are Trevor and Mair Williams and their rotten, ever-barking dog. The husband, Trevor, is particularly unpleasant. McGrath describes him as having a "weaselly" smile (p. 172) and the local schoolteacher as having a "wheedly Welsh voice." (p. 177) A touch prejudiced, I thought, on McGrath's part, but fair enough. If the psychiatric profession can take criticism, then so can we Welsh. I wish, though, that McGrath had made it just a little clearer that Cledwyn is in *North* Wales. The climate of the South is just as awful as that of the North, but to the discerning, we of the South have an accent far more pleasing to the ear. We – and I include Dylan Thomas, Richard Burton, and Anthony Hopkins – may well be both introspective and self-destructive, but any fair-minded person will readily concede that we are also full of fun and the life and soul of any party.

Stella doesn't like the look of Trevor Williams, or anything else in Cledwyn, but when he tries to seduce her she acquiesces, ". . . it would be so much trouble to try and stop him." (p. 172) Sometimes Trevor's wife, Mair, silent and miserable, comes in for a cup of tea, so when the doorbell rings Stella never knows if it is Trevor for sex or Mair for tea. The situation gives McGrath the opportunity for the sparest and saddest of sentences: "[I]t didn't really matter to Stella which one of them came to see her, it relieved at least for a little while the numbness." (p. 174)

And what of her son, Charlie? For a while after her return to her husband, Stella associates Charlie in her mind with Edgar. At night, she is flooded with memories of sex with Edgar, and the daily sight of Charlie provokes even more memories of Edgar: "She thought it was because Charlie was back, and loving Charlie roused her to the other, greater love, and so the loss and longing came." (p. 154)

But in North Wales, when the whole world seems malevolent, Charlie begins again to blur into Max, the way he had when she first ran away to Edgar.

> She knew what was happening, she was starting to see Charlie as an extension of his father, and so a part of the conspiracy against her. She didn't want to feel this way about the boy, she knew it was unfair, but she couldn't seem to help herself. (pp. 177-78)

One of the delicious complexities of the novel is that the besotted Stella sometimes sees her son as Edgar, sometimes as Max, but rarely as himself.

Because she knows she is being unfair to her son, she agrees to chaperone one of his school's field trips; it would mean so much to him and his teacher has told her that Charlie is desperately unhappy at school. But, before they set off, Stella hears devastating news. Edgar has been arrested in Chester, twelve miles away, presumably on his way to see her. He will be incarcerated for the rest of his life.

McGrath handles the pathos of the scene superbly. Stella's world has just collapsed around her while just ahead of her is her little boy, so pleased that his mother has taken the trouble to come.

> Charlie marched on ahead of Stella, his satchel bumping up and down on his back and his head moving from side to side so as to miss nothing, turning now and then to make sure his mother was keeping up, eager pleasure in his lonely little face. (p. 199)

It would not be too hard to cry for that poor neglected little boy.

Charlie leaves the other children and goes off alone to look for newts in the pond. He gets into difficulty in the water. Enjoying a cigarette, Stella "dimly saw a head break the surface, and an arm claw the air, then go under again, and she turned aside and again brought the cigarette to her lips." (p. 200)

The teacher comes running, but it's too late. In the reaction of the police, I hear the sing-song of the Welsh voice. McGrath has a perfect ear: "[S]he was a mother who watched her child drown and done nothing to save him. It was unnatural, they said. It was evil. They couldn't understand it; she has no feelings, they said, she isn't human, she's a monster. Or perhaps she's mad." (p. 202)

In a private interview with Max before she is taken to the asylum, Stella tells him, "It was Edgar in the water." (p. 205) But I didn't trust her explanation. Why would she let her beloved Edgar drown? And is she telling Max the truth? She's lied to him before.

I was so troubled by the drowning that I wanted to talk to Patrick McGrath about it. Our timetables didn't coincide when he came to Toronto, so I asked my friend Judy Stoffman, who I knew was going to interview him, to put a question to him for me and to send me his exact answer. She was kind enough to do just that.

Question: Why did Stella let Charlie drown?

McGrath: Stella is profoundly depressed and deeply alienated from her surroundings, frozen out by this cold, punitive husband – she has identified her son as somehow on his side – her family is very hostile to her – so she is as alone as anybody could be, and also she is not thinking right – her disturbance is deep enough that she is perceptually disordered. What she sees out there on the pond is not her son but her lover.

By this point her obsession with her lover is so deep that she sees him only in a hallucinatory way: for her to see Edgar drown would be liberation, release from this compulsive attachment, so she can only stand there and smoke. In her mind the unbearably heavy burden is sinking and she doesn't want to pull him back – she has pulled him back too many times already, as when she returns to him in London after three days, and so she lets him go.

She is in a trance. Only a little later does she waken and understand that it wasn't her lover but her son in the water.

I had been wrong not to trust Stella's explanation. The drowning was her second chance to free herself from the burden of her passion. Except, of course, she does not free herself from Edgar but from poor little Charlie. She will never be free of her obsession with Edgar for the rest of her days.

In the last pages of the novel, Stella is back at the asylum where her husband once worked, but this time as a patient. So is Edgar Stark, in isolation. Both are being treated by Dr. Peter Cleave, once Max's colleague and now the superintendent after the disgrace of the Raphaels and the retirement of Dr. Straffen. Cleave tells Stella that he took on the post reluctantly, and that struck a chord in my memory. Without reading any further I turned back to the first page and began to reread the novel, bearing in mind that the whole novel is Dr. Peter Cleave's version of events, compiled from interviews with his patients Stella and Edgar, reports from his spy, the orderly Archer, and his own witness to much of the action. The sophisticated sixty-three-year-old is hardly a naive narrator, but he is a human, not an omniscient, narrator, and I wondered what, in a careful rereading, he might reveal about himself.

I found the point early in the novel, where Stella's mother-in-law asked Peter Cleave if he had any ambition to become superintendent. He'd laughed it off: "'Oh no,' I said, 'not me. No, it's a young man's game running the big bins. I'm much too long in the tooth.'" (p. 47)

And then I came to his answer to the same question put to him by Stella. He'd replied, "'I wonder sometimes. But no, I think not. It's a young man's game, and I should have to work much too hard. And all so political nowadays.'" (p. 98)

Political? As I read on, I realized that no one in this novel had played politics as well as Dr. Peter Cleave.

Consider the scene where Cleave and Dr. Straffen and his wife are discussing Edgar's escape and the likelihood that despite her denials Stella has helped her lover. Bear in mind that the "I" is Peter Cleave:

> "Max doesn't see she's lying?" said Bridie.
> Jack opened his hands. He said nothing.
> "I suspect," I said, "that he does. But he would rather *not* see it. Which is why he let him get away." (p. 65)

Cleave's brilliance took away my breath. Without any proof that Max had participated in the escape, Cleave offers a very persuasive reason as to why he had done so. It is that last sentence of Cleave's, in my opinion, that decided Max Raphael's professional fate and left the way clear for Peter Cleave.

I became even more interested in our narrator the good doctor, and I went back to the beginning again. He tells us in the first pages that "The catastrophic love affair characterized by sexual obsession has been a professional interest of mine for many years now." (p. 3) But what has he revealed of his own sexuality? Edgar Stark calls him "an old queen," (p. 241) but there's no evidence of that. And then I thought about that first hospital dance and Cleave's attention to what Stella wore, to the texture and material of her dress and how it hung on her. (p. 7)

Dr. Peter Cleave sees Stella as an art object, just as he sees Edgar Stark as an object for scientific study. I remembered how many times he refers to his "handsome house, a few miles away with its fine paintings, its fine furniture, and its fine library." (p. 98) After Stella becomes his patient, he confesses, "In recent days I had more than once imagined her in my house, as she once so frequently had been, among my furniture, my books, my art. Oh, she had a place there, among my fine *objets*." (p. 222)

Peter Cleave is a profoundly disturbed man: he is capable of only two feelings, the aesthetic appreciation of beauty and a scientific interest in the object under scrutiny. His cold-bloodedness is clear when his spy, Archer, lets him know of the developing relationship between Stella and Edgar: "I decided to do nothing about it. I was curious. Edgar had had no contact with a woman for five years." (p. 32)

Cleave sees himself as a man of infinite taste, one of nature's aristocrats. The only person in the novel he can possibly receive as an equal is Max's mother, a woman as unprincipled as he is: "We understood each other. She relied on me for reports about her son." (p. 39)

Now I could continue reading the last pages of the novel with a better understanding of the narrator who had unwittingly revealed so much in spite of his sophistication.

Now I understood that this man thinks he's God, if we can imagine God as an asexual, manipulative, beauty-obsessed mad scientist. Cleave also has a touch of sadism; he lets Edgar and Stella each know that the other is in the building but never allows a meeting. Further, after he proposes marriage to Stella, he hurries to tell Edgar of the development.

The marriage proposal is incredible; it reveals much of Cleave's megalomania. To a woman who gave up everything, everything, for physical passion he proposes

a life of civilized companionship. I told her one afternoon that marriage was held to be the answer to the problem of sex, but that I rather thought that marriage, at least as we conceived it, would instead be the answer to the problem of conversation. (p. 238)

In his arrogance, he believes that he can read Stella's mind: "She pictured my house and my garden and I think that even without intending to she began to yearn for it, for it meant peace and sophistication and comfort, and what else did she want? Suddenly she wanted the life I was offering her." (p. 236)

He offers her "Safety. Asylum." (p. 232) We remember that "asylum" has two very different meanings in English. But then so does "cleave": it can mean to join together or to cut apart. Opposites – like our perceptions of Dr. Peter Cleave at the beginning and at the end of the novel.

Just as the seemingly gifted Dr. Cleave reveals himself as stupid because of his arrogance, so does Stella, once the bored housewife, reveal a brilliance the reader could hardly have expected. She begins a fantastic masquerade.

She accepts the doctor's proposal and begins to play him like a fish. The manipulated has become the manipulator. She pretends to Peter Cleave that her dreams are less and less about Edgar and more and more about Charlie. Cleave is thrilled: "I knew then that her recovery was properly beginning, that she had let go of Edgar and allowed herself to start dealing with the death of Charlie." (p. 226)

He anticipates his own success. If she is dreaming of Charlie, she is exhibiting the classic Medea complex – and that is treatable. He can persuade her that she had projected her hatred of Max onto her son, persuade her to face it and come to terms with it, and thus she will be cured. He can then recommend her release – Max will certainly let her go – and they will be married. How neatly he can solve life's problems!

Not once does Stella let the mask slip. At the annual dance she behaves superbly. Cleave goes back to his own quarters to reflect happily on the beauty of the evening and the beauty of the married life to come. And then he realizes that Stella has worn the same black dress that she had worn a year earlier when she had danced with a tumescent Edgar. The truth comes crashing in on him:

> [I]t was not her child who disturbed her nights, it was him, it was Edgar! And her engagement to me, that too a masquerade, the desperate duplicity of a woman still passionately in love with another man and frantic to conceal it. . . . If she couldn't have Edgar then she might as well be dead. Life was no longer tolerable without him. (p. 252)

Cleave races back to the hospital but it is too late, Stella has already swallowed her carefully accumulated hoard of sedatives. She has made the perfect gesture of tragic defiance. In her mind, the sexual passion she shared with Edgar had made them gods among mortals and she will settle for nothing less. Unwilling to accept the world on the terms on which it is offered to her, she has chosen to leave it, affirming, at least in my view, the greatness of the human spirit.

Dr. Peter Cleave has no time to grieve for his dead fiancée; he will be too busy studying Edgar Stark: "I am all he has now. I have not told him that Stella is dead, for I am eager to hear his side of the story first." (p. 253)

I hear the relish in his voice when he makes his pious declaration, "I feel for those two poor disordered souls, trapped here these last weeks, twisting in their private hells, each aching for the other," (pp. 253-54) and I do not believe that this lying psychotic is capable of feeling one iota of compassion.

We find that Dr. Cleave has taken into his possession all of Edgar's sketches of Stella, together with the bust that Edgar had gouged in his jealous rage. Cleave reminds me of the Duke in Browning's "My Last Duchess," who can look upon the portrait of the wife he murdered and say, "That's my last Duchess painted on the wall." As the Duke transmuted his wife into an *objet d'art*, so can Dr. Cleave, the owner of many of Stella's likenesses, claim, in the penultimate sentence of the novel, "So you see, I do have my Stella after all."

I loathe Dr. Peter Cleave, but he is totally believable. Nothing in this fine novel strikes me as false. There is none of the element of exaggeration I detected in McGrath's first three novels. (I thought for example that when the butler fed the prospective son-in-law to the pigs in *The Grotesque*, 1989, McGrath had really gone too far.) In *Asylum*, McGrath has gone to the extremes of abnormal human behaviour but he has not gone beyond the limits.

In the last sentence of the novel, Dr. Peter Cleave is planning his dissection of the psyche of Edgar Stark – "I still, of course, have him" – and we leave the true lunatic in complete charge of the asylum.

A FINE BALANCE

Rohinton Mistry

(Toronto: McClelland & Stewart, 1997)

A Fine Balance by Rohinton Mistry is set in India in the year 1975. Most of the action takes place in what Mistry calls "The City by the Sea," which we can take to be the great crowded metropolis of Bombay.

There are four major characters, two of whom are Hindu and two Parsi. At one point the four will come to live together in a small apartment.

But there is a fifth character in the novel, one whose presence is felt on almost every page although she is rarely physically present. That fifth character is Indira Gandhi, the prime minister of India in 1975, and her importance in the novel cannot be overstated. To understand why she should be so important, we must return to earlier events in which Indira Gandhi's father played so great a part.

The first event was the independence of India, declared at midnight on August 15, 1947. The two leaders of the struggle against British rule had been Mohandas Karamchand Gandhi, better known as the Mahatma ("great soul") or even as *Bapu* ("father"), and Jawaharlal Nehru, known everywhere as Pandit Nehru. (The third leader of the independence struggle, Mohammed Ali Jinna, led Moslem India into a separate independent existence as Pakistan.)

While Gandhi was the spiritual leader of the movement, it had always been Nehru who arranged the practical politics. He did this through a political organization he dominated, the Indian National Congress. Nehru *was* the Indian National Congress, called the Congress Party after independence.

The party had but one objective, to get the British out of India. Other than that there was no unifying ideology. The Mahatma, in his wisdom, often said that once independence had been achieved the Indian National Congress would have to be dissolved to allow the formation of new parties to represent the political spectrum from left to right. The Mahatma saw the danger of a one-purpose party – that it would seek to cling to power, once its objective was achieved, with no purpose other than to stay in power. (Those of us who live in Quebec would do well to reflect on the Mahatma's observation.)

After independence and the secession of Pakistan with the attendant Partition Massacres, and after the assassination of Gandhi by a Hindu fundamentalist, Nehru was left as the undisputed ruler of India for seventeen years until his death in 1964. He governed a country of eight hundred million Hindus with a 10 percent Moslem minority, those who had been unwilling or unable to flee to Pakistan. Two percent of the population were Sikh, 2 percent were Christian, and there was a tiny sprinkling of other minorities: Jainists, Jews, and Buddhists. There was also a tiny Parsi community, fewer than sixty thousand, most of whom lived in Bombay. They were the followers of the pre-Christian prophet Zoroaster, who taught the oneness of the Supreme Being, Ahura Mazda, and the ongoing struggle in the universe between Good and Evil. As a soldier on the side of Good, the Parsi must devote himself to education, moral living, good deeds, and justice. Fire and light figure so prominently in Parsi ritual that there is a common misconception that the Parsis worship fire. In fact, the fire is merely a symbol, not only of Ahura Mazda, but of the divine fire, the movement to Good that burns within each of us. Apart from its monotheism, Zoroastrianism differs sharply from Hinduism in that Parsis observe no social division, no caste system, within their community. Two of our novel's main characters are Parsi, as is the author, Rohinton Mistry.

As the ruler of an India mainly Hindu in character, although secular in law, Nehru had a very different vision of the future from that of the late Mahatma. Gandhi had dreamed of an India centred on village life, where people lived simple, frugal, happy lives. But Nehru looked forward to an age of technology and great industry, and all his policies were designed to bring that about. India was no more ready for the change, however, than Britain had been for its own Industrial Revolution. The rapid growth of industry in cities like Bombay meant the hundredfold multiplication of social problems like slums, homelessness, sweated labour, and over-crowding. But Nehru was not deterred. He thought that India's best hope for the future lay in cooperation with India's great northern neighbour China. What could they not achieve together in industrial progress?

His heart was broken in 1962 when he was left with no choice but to go to war with China over Tibet. He gave up all his dreams and any real effort for social reform. Only one thing remained important to him: ensuring that his only child, his beloved daughter, Indira, would succeed him in political power.

Against her father's wishes, Indira had married outside the Hindu faith. Her husband was a Parsi lawyer, Feroz Gandhi (no relation to the Mahatma), but after a few years Nehru compelled his daughter to choose between a life with her husband and a life as Nehru's second-in-command and political hostess. Indira chose power, and her marriage continued in name only until Feroz Gandhi died in 1960.

After Nehru's death in 1964 and a brief interregnum under the weak leader Lal Bahadur Shastri, Indira Gandhi succeeded her father as supreme leader of the Congress Party and prime minister of India.

Although she was elected in 1967 on a platform of "Eradicate Poverty," Indira Gandhi never had any objective but to hold on to power, and under her the Congress Party became even more hideously corrupt. The Mahatma's worst fears about a one-purpose party had been realized.

In 1975 a surprisingly courageous Indian Supreme Court convicted Indira Gandhi and the Congress Party of massive electoral fraud. Her reaction was immediate. The student leader Avinash summarizes it for a friend in Mistry's novel:

> "Three weeks ago the High Court found the Prime Minister guilty of cheating in the last elections. Which meant she had to step down. But she began stalling. So the opposition parties, student organizations, trade unions – they started mass demonstrations across the country. All calling for her resignation. Then, to hold on to power, she claimed that the country's security was threatened by internal disturbances, and declared a State of Emergency. . . . Under the pretext of Emergency, fundamental rights have been suspended, most of the opposition is under arrest, union leaders are in jail, and even some student leaders." (p. 285)

The Emergency would last twenty months, and those twenty months provide the background to Mistry's novel. It was a dreadful period during which the individual lost all safeguards under the law. Salman Rushdie deals with it extensively in *Midnight's Children*, as does V.S. Naipaul in *Area of Darkness*.

You may be interested in what happened to Indira Gandhi after our novel ends. After twenty months of dictatorship she called new elections. As Nehru's daughter she was convinced she could not lose. But she did. To embarrass the new government, she began to promote civil unrest, particularly by encouraging Sikh nationalism in the Punjab. It is ironic that after she returned to power in 1979, when the ruling coalition collapsed, the Sikh nationalist movement she had encouraged became a monster out of control. She would be assassinated by her own Sikh bodyguards.

Now I am close to approaching the novel, but before we meet our four protagonists I must comment on the Hindu faith of two of them, Ishvar and his nephew Omprakash. Their Hindu religion is polytheistic and goes back into the mists of time, but the tenet that is most relevant to our novel is that of caste, a kind of rigid class system. The highest caste are the *brahmins*, the caste of Nehru and the Mahatma. The lowest castes are the *chamars*, the leatherworkers, who handle the skins of dead animals, and the *bunghi*, the night-soil collectors. They and their like constitute the Untouchables, those whose voice, presence, even shadow, can defile their social superiors. Caste is decided by birth and can never be changed. Your occupation and your place in society is entirely decided by what family you are born into. You may pray to be reincarnated into a higher caste in your next life as a result of virtuous living, but any change you try to make within your own lifetime would be seen by your fellow Hindus as an insult to the gods. In the great cities like Delhi or Bombay, the system has become less rigid under the demands of modernization, but in the villages, where 76 percent of Indians still live, caste is still absolute. The Indian Constitution of 1950 prohibits discrimination because of caste, but the injunction is in practice meaningless.

Gandhi had wanted to get rid of the concept of untouchability. He called the Untouchables *harijan*, "the children of God," and he wished to relieve their misery, but even he did not want to give up the caste system. He believed that it gave order and structure to the vastness of

India. Without caste, a system unique to Hinduism, the Mahatma believed there would be chaos.

Now we can enter the novel in which Mistry is going to examine three societies: life in a Hindu village, life in the tiny Parsi community of Bombay (Mistry's birthplace), and, most dramatically, the life of the poor in the great city.

We will visit first the Hindu village and meet the Mochi family. Mistry is going to give a voice and a face to the rural poor, as he will later do for the urban dispossessed.

Like all their neighbours, the Mochis are leatherworkers, *chamars*, and therefore Untouchables. As part of a wonderfully detailed portrait of village life, Mistry tells us of what happened to some of the friends of the Mochi family for violating the strictures of caste:

> For walking on the upper-caste side of the street, Sita was stoned, though not to death – the stones had ceased at first blood. Gambhir was less fortunate; he had molten lead poured into his ears because he ventured within hearing range of the temple while prayers were in progress. Dayaram, reneging on an agreement to plough a land-lord's field, had been forced to eat the landlord's excrement in the village square. Dhiraj tried to negotiate in advance with Pandit Ghanshyam the wages for chopping wood, instead of settling for the few sticks he could expect at the end of the day; the Pandit got upset, accused Dhiraj of poisoning his cows, and had him hanged. (p. 125)

What I found remarkable is that Mistry shows how these people can still lead lives filled with love and family and the familiar rituals of birth and marriage. The Indian critic A.G. Mojtabai compared Mistry to the painter Bruegel in the way he is filled with wonder and sorrow at the means by which poor people manage to endure. (*New York Times*, June 23, 1996)

The father of the Mochi family has ill-advised ambitions for his sons, Ishvar and Narayan. He sends them to the nearest small town as apprentices to his friend, the Moslem tailor Ashraf. Moslems do not observe caste.

Ashraf and his wife are good and decent people, and they are not alone. During the Partition riots of 1947 they were saved from murderous Hindu extremists by their apprentices and neighbours, all of them Hindu. When I discussed his novel with him, Rohinton Mistry spoke about his Parsi faith and his conviction that each of us must be a soldier in the struggle for Good. It was a delight to talk with him, as it was a delight to have found that he peopled his novel with soldiers for Good from faiths other than his own.

At the end of their apprenticeship, Ishvar stays with Ashraf while Narayan returns to the village, where he defies the caste system by sewing for clients of all castes. He prospers, builds a house, marries, and has children, two daughters and a son, Omprakash, whom Narayan sends back to town to work with his brother, Ishvar, and the Moslem Ashraf. The success of the Untouchable Narayan provokes the enmity of the local *thakur*, "headman," Dharamsi, who is also the local Congress Party leader. His power is absolute over the law, the police, and every detail of village life. The crisis comes when Narayan and a few friends decide to challenge the usual electoral practice that voters register at the polling booth and Dharamsi's men fill out the blank ballots later. The protesters decide to record a genuine vote.

All this is described by Mistry with a quiet objectivity that serves only to heighten the horror of what is to come.

Narayan and his two friends are flogged while hanging upside down. Their genitals are burned with hot coals, which are then forced into their mouths. Then they are hanged, and Narayan's mutilated body is shown to his wife, daughters, and parents. The last action of Dharamsi's men is to tie up the whole family in their house and set it on fire.

The police, servants of the Congress Party, conduct an investigation, but in spite of the burned house and the bodies they find no evidence of arson or murder.

Narayan's brother, Ishvar, and his son, Omprakash, are safe in the nearby town, but they are still too close to Dharamsi and they too have violated caste. It seems a good time to leave for Bombay, especially since the new factories in the city are putting small tailors like Ashraf out of business.

They are so poor that the journey to Bombay will be very harsh. They are always hungry, but when they do manage to buy a little food the uncle, Ishvar, always gives the greater portion to his nephew. When Omprakash protests, Ishvar says, "'What will they think in our village when we return? That I starved my nephew in the city and ate all the food myself? Eat, eat!'" (p. 4)

In those few lines, and in the many similar lines in the novel, we see the greatness of Rohinton Mistry. How can we account for the success of his novels in North America, novels about a culture so alien to most of us? There is only one possible explanation, that the North American reader sees in Mistry's Indian characters the humanity we all share. And that's the point. Rohinton Mistry has achieved the novelist's dream, of touching both the particular and the universal. While we see the uniqueness of the Indian society he describes, we can still relate it to our own experience. We have all heard the love in the voice of someone who has said to us, "Eat, eat!" We have all felt the love of someone who would put himself last so that we might be first. With what delicate strokes does Mistry create two complete human beings, the quiet, stoic, loving Ishvar and the more rebellious Omprakash. When we look at their village, where simple people like them struggle to survive and find a measure of love and dignity among dreadful hardships, the *shtetlakh* of Sholem Aleichem do not seem so very far away.

Ishvar and Omprakash are on their way to Bombay. Let us go there ahead of them and visit a Parsi family, the Shroffs. We come to know the family history intimately and to witness so many details of Parsi ritual, especially when we visit the fire temple and the Parsi priest Dustoor Framji, who is rather too fond of holding little girls very close. We are told of the late Dr. Shroff, who died of snakebite after he went into the interior to treat typhoid and cholera, one of the many altruistic acts of kindness in the novel.

We are treated to the complexity of a sibling relationship as his children grow up and his son, Nusswan, bullies his little sister, Dina – a bullying with strong incestuous undertones. We see the adults the two children have grown into, and we see signs of a real affection behind Nusswan's domineering facade. We sense that he is not a bad person, just a weak one who has accepted the role a patriarchal society has given him to play. It would not be difficult to find his counterpart very close to home.

A grown-up Dina Shroff marries very happily after we enjoy all the delicate details of her courtship, but her young chemist husband is killed in a traffic accident and Dina Dalal becomes a widow at twenty-six.

As Ishvar and Omprakash arrive in Bombay, Dina has completed her sixteenth year of widowhood. Life has been very difficult since the death of her husband. Her brother, who has become a successful businessman, helps, but his charity is reluctant and all of Dina's enterprises over the years, from baking to hairdressing, have failed.

In a last effort not to lose her minuscule apartment, Dina resorts to two measures: she will take in a paying guest and she will set up a little tailoring business in the apartment.

The paying guest comes easily. He is Maneck Kohlah, the seventeen-year-old son of old Parsi friends from a hill station up on the northern frontier. Once affluent, the Kohlahs lost much land during the 1947 Partition of India and were reduced to running a little general store. Torn between their desires to keep their boy at home and to get him an education – Maneck and his family have sacrificed, as parents do, to send Maneck to college in Bombay. Desperately unhappy at the students' hostel, with its minimal food and non-existent hygiene – all because of the corruption of the contractor – Maneck and his family have decided he would be happier as a boarder with "Dina Aunty" (the title, according to Parsi custom, follows the name). It is important to note that although they are now in straitened circumstances, both Dina and Maneck have led relatively sheltered lives – relative, that is, to the homeless on the street outside Dina's home.

Dina does not find it as easy to find tailors, but she finally chooses two new arrivals from the country, Ishvar and his nephew, Omprakash. They have a brand-new family name, Dharji instead of Mochi, to disguise their *chamar* status.

Thus, after two hundred and fifty pages on rural and Parsi India, Mistry has finally brought together his four main characters: the Parsi widow Dina Dalal, the Parsi student Maneck Kohlah, and the two Hindu Untouchables. It is through the experiences of the two Hindus in the city that Dina and Maneck, and the reader, will be exposed to an urban poverty of which they had been only dimly aware.

I protested the point when I talked about the novel with Mr. Mistry. I argued that as Indians, surely Dina and Maneck must have been aware of what life was like on the city streets. I even cited to him his own description of Dina's apartment when Maneck first saw it.

Everywhere there was evidence of her struggle to stay ahead of squalor, to mitigate with neatness and order the shabbiness of poverty. He saw it in the chicken wire on the broken windowpanes, in the blackened kitchen wall and ceiling, in the flaking plaster, in the repairs on her blouse collar and sleeves. (p. 230)

I pointed out too the run-down nature of the Kohlahs' little store. "Surely, both Dina and Maneck are poor," I said.

Mr. Mistry replied, "Dina is the daughter of a doctor and she is educated. Maneck's family have a business, however small, and they live on a hill station in the coolest, most beautiful part of India. There is as great a gulf between them and the world of the Bombay gutters as there is between you and me and a billionaire, and they are just about as aware of each other."

Ishvar and Omprakash work long hours under sweatshop conditions. Dina keeps aloof and enjoins Maneck to do the same. The Hindus are from a different world. Above all, she cannot let them stay the night, even on her balcony. She is in an ongoing war with her landlord, who would use the presence of a business on the premises as a pretext to evict her. Also, if she did let them stay on the balcony, it might give them squatters' rights and she'd never be able to get them out.

Paid minimum wages, the two tailors join the millions of Bombay homeless, bribing watchmen and porters, who in turn must bribe the police, to let them sleep in doorways and railway stations. For a while, Ishvar and Omprakash move one step up on the housing scale and rent a hovel in a *jhopadpatti*, a shantytown, one of many built on empty public land by enterprising landlords with city officials and the police bribed to look the other way. There is no sanitation or running water. The squalor is appalling. But even here there are acts of goodness. A neighbour, Rajaram, gives them one of his two buckets to carry water, in the circumstances an act of overwhelming generosity.

Eventually the bribes are not enough, and under the Emergency Powers of 1975 and as part of her Beautification Scheme, Indira's police bulldoze the *jhopadpatti*, and a few thousand more, including Ishvar and Omprakash, are added to Bombay's homeless.

Indira Gandhi is everywhere. Mistry has introduced her in the novel slowly, subtly. At first, Ishvar and Omprakash, and the reader, are only aware of posters and slogans. But her presence becomes more insistent. At a hole-in-the-wall restaurant in the city, the two men ask about a huge Indira Gandhi photograph in the window:

"You have a new customer or what?"

"That's no customer," said the cashier. "That's the goddess of protection. Her blessing is a business necessity. Compulsory puja."

"How do you mean?"

"Her presence keeps my windows from being smashed and my shop from being burned. You follow?" (p. 360)

In a brilliant set piece, both comic and horrible, Ishvar and Omprakash will actually see Indira in the flesh. Along with thousands of others they are kidnapped for a day to attend a pro-Indira political rally. They are each paid five rupees, about a quarter, with one rupee deducted for a snack they never get.

The rally is a fiasco. Sacks of rose petals, meant to fall gently on the crowd, are dumped by the airplane in the wrong field and still in sacks. The crowd is too hungry to listen to Indira speak, in spite of the hired *goondas* who beat up anyone not paying attention. When Indira's son flies high over the crowd in a helicopter, both Mistry's astute use of symbolism and the arrogance of this terrible woman are made brilliantly clear.

At about the same time, Maneck is witnessing a scene at his college that is like something out of Germany in the thirties.

> The entire teaching staff had already lined up at the table, like customers at a ration shop. They obediently signed statements saying they were behind the Prime Minister, her declaration of Emergency, and her goal of fighting the anti-democratic forces threatening the country from within.
>
> As much as fear, Maneck felt a loathing for the entire place. But for his teachers he had only pity. They slipped away from the flag-raising ceremony, looking guilty and ashamed. (p. 288)

The middle and upper classes of India do not rise up to protest the danger to democracy. With honourable exceptions, when they do react to Indira it is with approval. Dina's businessman brother, discussing Indira's forced sterilization of the poor (officially called the Family Planning Programme), articulates a view commonly held by the moneyed classes, and not just in India:

"Probably started by the CIA – saying people in remote villages are being dragged from their huts for compulsory sterilization. Such lies. But my point is, even if the rumour is true, what is wrong in that, with such a huge population problem?" (p. 433)

Mrs. Gupta, the textile exporter for whom Dina does piecework, has the same faith in Indira's good sense:

"Now all those troublemakers who accused her falsely have been put in jail. No more strikes . . . and silly disturbances. . . . As I told you before, I prefer to deal with private contractors. Union loafers want to work less and get more money. That's the curse of this country – laziness. And some idiot leaders encouraging them, telling police and army to disobey unlawful orders. Now you tell me, how can the law be unlawful? Ridiculous nonsense. Serves them right, being thrown in jail." (pp. 83-84)

For Dina Dalal, her contact with the poor through her two tailors is a learning experience. She comes to understand the full implications of homelessness and the real import of the Emergency Measures. Initially aloof from her Hindu tailors, she comes to recognize their goodness, their humanity. She says herself, " 'It's the first time I actually know the people. My God – such horrible, horrible suffering.' " (p. 396)

The four people in the apartment become a family. It's not a perfect family – the sexually curious Maneck and Omprakash, both seventeen years old, try to spy on Dina as she bathes – but it's a chosen family nonetheless. Her acceptance of the two tailors means that she will now let them sleep on the balcony. The risk to her is great; it is the excuse the landlord craves.

She is acting against all reason, her heart has ruled, and in Dina's decision Mistry has accorded this woman an enormous measure of growth. There is a lovely moment when the rent collector, Ibrahim, a decent man forced by poverty into a job he hates, confronts Dina with the charge that she is operating a factory. The evidence is clear, he says; these men are workers. Dina denies the charge and announces them as her husband and her sons.

It will be through her chosen family that Dina will enter the most terrible of Rohinton Mistry's worlds, more terrible even than that of the

Untouchables or of the homeless. I am speaking of a world of no small population, the world of the Bombay beggars.

This empire of the disadvantaged, or at least a large part of it, is ruled over by Beggarmaster, one of Mistry's most powerful creations, and it is the stuff of nightmare.

It is Beggarmaster who organizes and protects Bombay's beggars in return for a commission. His star attraction is Shankar, often called "the Worm" because he is so close to the ground. Ishvar and Omprakash had seen him when they first arrived in Bombay.

> They passed a beggar slumped upon a small wooden platform fitted with castors, which raised him four inches off the ground. His fingers and thumbs were missing, and his legs were amputated almost to the buttocks. . . . "That's one of the worst I've seen since coming to the city," said Ishvar, and the others agreed. Omprakash paused to drop a coin in the tin. (p. 7)

Shankar, Ishvar, and Omprakash will come into intimate contact when they are all kidnapped by the police to labour for an unscrupulous contractor who has paid the necessary bribes to the Congress Party. Shankar explains how Beggarmaster, like his father before him, has stage-managed his theatre of horror, casting the parts, designing the afflictions.

> "Beggarmaster has to be very imaginative. If all beggars have the same injury, public gets used to it and feels no pity. Public likes to see variety. Some wounds are so common, they don't work anymore. For example, putting out a baby's eyes will not automatically earn money. Blind beggars are everywhere. But blind, with eyeballs missing, face showing empty sockets, plus nose chopped off – now anyone will give money for that." (p. 382)

When Beggarmaster arrives at the construction site to rescue his "Worm," the two tailors implore him to ransom them too. They will repay him with the income from three days tailoring a week. Their return to Dina and their contract with Beggarmaster will not only save Dina's little business, it will also put them all under Beggarmaster's protection.

Because of the arrangement, Beggarmaster often visits the apartment. When two *goondas* are sent by Dina's landlord to vandalize her home, Beggarmaster has their hands smashed and forces the landlord to pay compensation.

Beggarmaster enjoys his visits and becomes quite the family friend, sharing with Dina and the others the fruits of many years of reflection. He sees his world for what it is, hopelessly corrupt, and he works within it as best he can. He sees himself without illusion. As he says, " '[There is] a fine line between Shankar and me. . . . I did not draw it. . . . Freaks, that's what we are, all of us.' " (pp. 534-35)

Beggarmaster even shares with Dina and the others his vision of the ultimate begging team. He is something of an artist and is proud of the sketch he has made.

> They crowded around to look at the sketch: two figures, one sitting aloft on the shoulders of the other. "For this, I need a lame beggar and a blind beggar. The blind man will carry the cripple on his shoulders. A living, breathing image of the ancient story about friendship and cooperation. And it will produce a fortune in coins, I am absolutely certain, because people will give not only from pity or piety but also from admiration." (pp. 516-17)

His listeners do not condemn him; he is so monstrous that he has entered a dimension beyond ordinary morality. Maneck makes a very thoughtful response, "He's just a thoroughly modern businessman, with his eye on the bottom line." (p. 518)

We learn with horror that Shankar's mother was a beggar, beautiful in all things except that her father, disappointed that she was not a son, had cut off her nose. We learn with even greater horror that Shankar was not born as he now is. In one of the novel's most frightful passages, the reader is told what happened after Shankar's birth: "[A] few months later, the infant who was called Shankar was separated from her and sent for professional modifications." (p. 529)

Professional modifications, what a hellish phrase! It has given me more than one nightmare and it has deepened a mystery that has long preoccupied me. Given that Bombay's beggars, India's beggars, so often have planned

mutilations, why would anyone visit such a place for spiritual enlighten-
ment? As the Western middle-class youth journeys from the airport to the
ashram, is he or she blind? Does he or she not notice the homeless, the
disfigured, the dying? I cannot begin to comprehend such a degree of self-
indulgence.

When Beggarmaster finds out it was his own father, the previous
Beggarmaster, who had sired Shankar on the noseless beggar woman, he
becomes solicitous, even loving, to his half-brother. There is good even in
Beggarmaster, the gentle Mr. Mistry assured me, reluctant as he is to see
any human being as absolutely evil.

When Shankar is panicked by a lynch mob looking for a killer and
crushed by a car, Beggarmaster is distraught and arranges a sumptuous
funeral. But at the ceremony the businessman in him emerges in a delicious line of dark comedy, " 'There's only one thing worrying me, I hope
the other beggars don't assume this is standard procedure.' " (p. 584)

Ironically, Beggarmaster will be murdered by Monkey-man, a street
entertainer whose nephews Beggarmaster kidnapped and mutilated.
Beggarmaster could have escaped except for the weight of the moneybag
chained forever to his wrist. A very effective piece of symbolism on
Mistry's part, I thought. It made me realize that if a moneybag is chained
to your wrist, you are also chained to the moneybag. And I further thought,
as I'm sure I was meant to, of Dickens's Jacob Marley.

Before Beggarmaster is killed, Ishvar and Omprakash have decided to
take a little holiday. Everything seems to be going so well: Dina's business
is under Beggarmaster's protection and Maneck has completed his air-
conditioning course and flown off to a good job in Dubai. Now is the
moment to go back to their village and find Omprakash a wife. Ishvar is
very anxious that the family line continue.

It is a superb piece of plotting by Mistry to lift us all to such great
heights of optimism before the horror to come.

In the village Omprakash commits a supreme error. Faced with
Dharamsi, the *thakur* who murdered his family, Omprakash cannot resist
spitting at him, and Dharamsi answers with five syllables of quiet menace:
" 'I know who you are.' " (p. 606)

I waited with dread for what would come next. Ishvar and Omprakash
are among those rounded up at random for forced sterilization, a part of
Gandhi's Family Planning Programme. Both receive vasectomies. But

there is hope – Ishvar believes there is always hope – when a fellow victim assures them that the operation is reversible. It is at that moment that Dharamsi, both local Congress Party boss and overseer of the sterilization program, arrives at the hospital tent to check the daily total. He sees Omprakash among the patients and orders a doctor to diagnose a testicular tumour and castrate him. The doctor is reluctant but turns pale when Dharamsi whispers a threat that is all the more terrible because we do not know what it is. But we can imagine.

The young, mischievous Omprakash becomes a eunuch. His uncle will also suffer. The needles were not sterilized before his vasectomy, his groin is infected, and his legs must be amputated.

After two months of difficult recuperation, both uncle and nephew return to Bombay. They are now the two-man team of beggars of which Beggarmaster had dreamed. But out of the horror comes the most beautiful line of the novel. As the fat eunuch pulls his crippled uncle through the streets of Bombay, he thinks: "How light is my uncle . . . light as a baby, pulling him is no strain at all." (p. 630) I found it impossible not to weep.

That moment could have been the end of the novel, but Mistry adds an epilogue.

In 1984 Maneck returns from Dubai to Bombay to find that Dina, her business failed because of the loss of her tailors, has become her brother's household drudge. He also sees the eunuch and the cripple begging for alms. Numb with horror, he cannot speak to them. All he can do is go to the train station and jump under a train.

I talked to Rohinton Mistry about the suicide. "Of the four characters," I said, "surely Maneck suffered the least. Why would he kill himself?"

After some reflection Mr. Mistry said, "I don't know. My interest in writing is in creating character. After a while, my characters have a life independent of me. I began to suspect two-thirds of the way through the novel that Maneck would do something terrible."

I pressed him on the point and he continued. "In hindsight I suppose that Maneck was far less prepared than Ishvar and Omprakash to face the horror of life. He wasn't prepared for the horror."

As I listened to Mr. Mistry, I thought back over Maneck's character as it had been revealed throughout the novel. I realized how delicate Maneck had been, how prone to depression and melancholy. I remembered how he had considered suicide much earlier in the novel, after he had been so cruelly bullied by his fellow students at the hostel and when he faced the loss of his friend Avinash, tortured to death by Indira's police. Mr. Mistry's final word on the reason for Maneck's suicide was that it was "unknowable," but I think he was being kind to me; I think he had prepared us for it by a brilliant delineation of character. I had just not read carefully enough.

We talked about Mr. Mistry's career. In 1975 he came from Bombay to Toronto at twenty-three with an M.A. in Mathematics to work at a bank, where constant promotion delayed the beginning of his writing career. He agreed when I said that both his first novel, *Such a Long Journey* (1991), and *A Fine Balance* had, I believed, the same theme, how an individual may preserve his integrity in the face of a society unbelievably corrupt.

I congratulated him on all the ingenious devices he had used to unify such a massive work, the sustained metaphor of life as a patchwork quilt, for example, each patch a memory, or his use of a Greek chorus in the person of Valmik the lawyer. It was Valmik's comment that inspired the title *A Fine Balance*: "'There is always hope – hope enough to balance our despair. Or we would be lost.'" (p. 652)

I told Mr. Mistry that I found so much goodness in the novel, and he replied, "Yes, yes, I am glad that you saw that, so many critics have seen only the cruelty."

I also told him I thought that in moving from the tiny Parsi community of his first novel to the whole spectrum of Indian society in the second, he had created a masterpiece even more textured, even more satisfying than the first.

It was then that we began to talk about the final scene of the epilogue, when Ishvar and Omprakash visit Dina in her brother's kitchen, as they do every day in her brother's absence.

Ishvar made a clacking-clucking sound with his tongue against the teeth, imitating a bullock-cart driver. His nephew pawed the ground and tossed his head.

"Stop it," she scolded. "If you behave that way on the pavement, no one will give you a single paisa."

"Come on, my faithful," said Ishvar. "Lift your hoofs or I'll feed you a dose of opium." Chuckling, Om trotted away plumply. They quit clowning when they emerged into the street.

Dina shut the door, shaking her head. Those two made her laugh every day. Like Maneck used to, once. (pp. 712-13)

I told Mr. Mistry how transcendental I found the scene, how full of fellowship and communion, how beautiful and how moving in its triumph of the human spirit. I asked him if he was as moved as I was by his creations. I quote his answer in full: "As I write about my characters, I must stay in the middle distance. I can't weep for them, I can't get involved – but I can weep for them afterwards."

And so can I. And so I do.

THE LONELY PASSION OF
JUDITH HEARNE

Brian Moore

(Toronto: McClelland & Stewart, 1964, reprinted 1992)

The great Irish-Canadian novelist Brian Moore died at his home in California of pulmonary fibrosis on January 10, 1999.

He came to Canada in 1948, stayed here for eleven years, became a Canadian citizen, but lived the last forty years of his life in the United States, first in New York and then in Malibu Beach. He always kept his Canadian citizenship, however, made frequent visits to his friends in Montreal, and spent the last five summers of his life on the coast of Nova Scotia.

I remember meeting Brian Moore twice over the years, but our conversations were never about matters of import. The one point of interest I do recollect is that he corrected my pronunciation of his first name. He insisted on "Bree-an" in the Irish Gaelic fashion. I learned much more about him from an excellent biography, *Brian Moore: The Chameleon Novelist* (Toronto: Doubleday, 1998) by a Montrealer, Denis Sampson.

Before I turn to *The Lonely Passion of Judith Hearne*, I would like to explain why Brian Moore left his native city of Belfast in 1942 at the age of twenty-one, never to live there again.

He hated Belfast; he called it "a claustrophobic, provincial back-water . . . 'trapped in the nightmare of history.'" (*Brian Moore,* Sampson, p. 10) Physically he would never return, but he came back to it again and again in his writing, particularly in *Judith Hearne* and the four novels that followed.

Why did he hate the city so much, and why did he describe it as "trapped in the nightmare of history"?

To answer these questions and to understand the place of Belfast in today's novel, where the city is so important as to be almost one of the characters, we have to remember a few facts about Irish history.

Ireland had been a possession of England since the conquest of 1171, and the Irish had always hated their English overlords. The hatred became even more acute in 1534, when Henry VIII declared himself head of the Church of England while Ireland remained steadfastly loyal to the Roman Catholic Church.

The problem was exacerbated as Henry and his successors gave English and Scottish settlers land grants in Ireland, especially in the north, until there was a solid Protestant presence in the Irish province of Ulster.

The hatred in Ireland between native Catholics and Protestant imports grew even worse in the late seventeenth century. In 1688 the English suspected, with good reason, that King James II was a secret Catholic, plotting to return England to the embrace of Rome. After they deposed him in favour of his Protestant Dutch cousin, William of Orange ("King Billie" to his later admirers), James fled to Ireland, declared himself Catholic, and raised an Irish army to reclaim his throne. Both James and his army were soundly thrashed at the Battle of the Boyne in 1689, a victory still celebrated annually with bloodshed as the Protestant Orangemen flaunt their triumph by parading through the Catholic sections of Northern Irish cities.

The hatred never lessened over the centuries of British rule and the violence grew, culminating in the Easter Rising in Dublin in 1916. By 1921, the British government saw no choice but to partition Ireland. There were more than one million Protestants in Northern Ireland whose families had lived there for up to three hundred years, and they wanted no part of an independent Catholic Ireland. Thus six counties of the province of Ulster were retained as part of the United Kingdom, while the rest of Ireland became the Irish Free State, later the Republic of Ireland.

The problem that remained was twofold. Many in the South believed Ireland to be indivisible and were prepared to fight for the principle, and in the Protestant North, still a part of the United Kingdom and with its own capital of Belfast, there was a vociferous and very unhappy Catholic minority.

That was "the nightmare of history" that Brian Moore was born into in 1921, the year of the Partition Treaty, in a Belfast with a population of about half a million, two-thirds Protestant and one-third Catholic.

This nine-hundred-year history explains the venom with which Belfast Protestants and Catholics regard each other. I am not speaking of the fanatics of the Catholic Irish Republican Army or the Protestant Ulster Defence Force, I am speaking of the ordinary people of Belfast. I am speaking of Moore's protagonist, Judith Hearne, a member of Belfast's Catholic community in the fifties, who says of a neighbour, Mrs. Strain, whom she suspects of gossiping about her, "'You might know, being a Protestant, she wouldn't have one ounce of Christian charity in her.'" (p. 33)

As Moore said to his biographer Sampson,

> "It occurs to me that there is something sick about Belfast. Perhaps it has always had this sickness. Perhaps it is incurable. . . . The same old riots we had in my childhood. Mobs of rampaging Protestant *lumpenproletariat* trying to terrorize their equally ignorant Catholic *lumpenproletariat* neighbours. . . . Ordinary people set against ordinary people because there is something old and rotten still alive here." (Sampson, p. 201)

Brian Moore was brought up as one of the Catholic minority of Belfast, but his father was a pillar of society. A prominent surgeon, he was the first Catholic to be nominated to the senate of Queen's University, Belfast. Moore's mother, Eileen McFadden, was a former nurse and a country girl who had been brought up by her uncle, a Gaelic-speaking priest. Moore was much closer to his mother than his father – a stern, Victorian, distant man who made no secret of his disappointment with his son.

Sent to a strict Catholic school, which he hated and where he was beaten every day, Brian Moore lost his faith in the Church very early. Worse, he failed his high school leaving exams, his matriculation, which meant he couldn't go on to university and become the doctor his father wanted him to be. Moore also hated the household Catholic politics that held both Franco and Mussolini to be great Christian gentlemen.

Thus when Brian Moore left Belfast for England, a year after his father's death in 1942, he was carrying a tremendous amount of psychological baggage with him, childhood memories of a faith, a father, and a city he had found narrow and repressive. He was also burdened with a low self-esteem because of his father's frequently expressed disappointment.

After he left Belfast, Brian Moore worked as a civilian for the British war effort, first in England and then in Europe. When the war was over, he stayed on in Europe, working mainly for refugee relief. He saw Auschwitz and he saw the Communist takeover in Poland. He left Europe in 1948 for Canada to follow a Canadian relief worker with whom he had fallen in love. Nothing lasting came of the relationship, and after a year in Ontario he moved to Montreal. He married and he began to write, for money. He wrote thrillers under pseudonyms and became an editor at the *Montreal Gazette*.

With the money he made from his popular thrillers, he now felt able to write *The Lonely Passion of Judith Hearne*, his first serious work, which was published in 1955. In part it was an attempt "to write Belfast out of my system." (Sampson, p. 91)

He was very aware of the words of the great François Mauriac, "For the novelist, the door closes at twenty," (Sampson, p. 10) and didn't want Mauriac's dictum to be the truth of the whole of his writing career; that it be in essence no more than a constant re-examination of his growing-up. But it would take him another four novels to exhaust his experience of Belfast and escape to North America. Only after *The Emperor of Icecream* (1965) would he be able to take on other cultures and other perspectives and set his next fifteen novels in Poland, Haiti, Vichy France, nineteenth-century Algeria, et al., becoming finally what Sampson calls "the chameleon novelist."

Judith Hearne owes much to James Joyce, Brian Moore's literary hero. In "Clay," from Joyce's collection *Dubliners*, there is a middle-aged spinster who finds both solace and humiliation in her visits to a family. But I think Moore's ambition was even greater. He wanted to do what James Joyce had done with Leopold Bloom in *Ulysses*, to take an ordinary person and show the epic, cosmic conflicts that are under the surface of the most seemingly ordinary of lives.

Moore also wanted to write about his own loss of faith and his own loneliness. But he wanted to avoid autobiography, and so, in his own words, " 'I decided to write not about an intellectual's loss of faith but of the loss of faith in someone devout, the sort of woman my mother would have known, a "sodality lady".' " (Sampson, p. 88)

Why did he choose a woman as his protagonist and not a man? Creating a believable character of the opposite sex is a difficulty few novelists can overcome. Dickens certainly never succeeded.

But Brian Moore was always very comfortable with women. He had been close to his mother, and of his eight siblings, six were sisters. Also he had a real-life model to work from. As he told his biographer,

> "I was trying to write short stories and I thought of this old lady who used to come to our house. She was a spinster who had some Civil Service job to do with sanitation and she lived most of her life with her 'dear aunt.' They'd not been 'grand' but they had pretensions, and she had very genteel manners. So I wrote a story about her; but when I'd finished I wasn't really happy with it. I can't tell you at what point that became my first novel. I know I then wrote a number of stories that weren't finished and, when I finally sat down a few years later and decided I wanted to write about someone losing their faith, it was then I remembered Miss Keogh – Mary Judith Keogh was her real name – and I remembered that little story about her. I could hear her voice, I could envisage where she lived." (Sampson, p. 89)

Now that I have pointed out Judith Hearne's antecedents in literature and in real life, it is time to meet Judith Hearne herself.

The time, according to the novel, is the early fifties. I know this from only two brief references in the novel, one to the Second World War as being recently over and the other to Queen Elizabeth II. But the exact year is unimportant, since this is really the Belfast of Brian Moore's childhood in the thirties. Moore makes it clear that he hated Protestant self-righteousness as much as he hated Catholic repressiveness:

> [T]he drab façades of the buildings grouped around the Square, pro-claiming the virtues of trade, hard dealing and Presbyterian righteous-ness. The order, the neatness, the floodlit cenotaph, a white respectable phallus planted in sinking Irish bog. The Protestant dearth of gaiety, the Protestant surfeit of order, the dour Ulster burghers walking proudly among these monuments to their mediocrity. (pp. 94-95)

Our protagonist Judith Hearne has just moved into a boarding house on Camden Street, a shabby, run-down part of the city where the once-

genteel family householders have now been reduced to renting out rooms
to boarders. In her own sad, run-down faded gentility, Judith Hearne with
her pretensions to middle-class respectability is much like the house and
the street and the city she lives in.

Judith is unmarried and forty-something years old. She has a tiny
annuity of forty pounds a year and a dwindling number of pupils to whom
she teaches piano and embroidery. We learn later that this is her sixth move
in a few years and we wonder why. Why move so often from one shabby
room with inadequate meals to another just as shabby? We sense a mystery
behind this lonely soul as we meet her unpacking her few household goods
and her two household gods, a cheap oleograph of Jesus and His Sacred
Heart and a photograph of her late aunt D'Arcy, who brought her up after
her parents' death. To Judith Hearne, these are not merely reminders of
faith and family life, they are actual living presences.

She will place her aunt's photograph "so that her dear aunt could
look at her" and the oleograph, the Catholic perception of Christ, so that
the eyes of Jesus, "kindly yet accusing," can follow her every action in the
little room.

Her possessions unpacked, Judith Hearne goes downstairs to meet her
landlady, Mrs. Rice (Mrs. *Henry* Rice, since she derives her whole identity from her late husband), and her fat, flabby, unemployed adult son
Bernard, a would-be poet.

In one succinct paragraph, Brian Moore paints a superb portrait of a
loving, destructive mother:

> "Bernie's a little delicate, Miss Hearne. He had to stop his studies a
> while back. Anyway, I think the boys work too hard up there at
> Queen's. I always say it's better to take your time. A young fellow like
> Bernie has lots of time, no need to rush through life. Take your time
> and you'll live longer." (p. 10)

Mrs. Rice is of course a Catholic. There is no way that Judith Hearne
could board with the Protestant heathen. To make her new lodger feel at
home, Mrs. Rice tells a story of the local priest, whom Miss Hearne has not
yet met. Mrs. Rice tells Judith Hearne how Father Quigley refused the offer
by a former brothel keeper of a new altar rail for the church. He flung the

offer back in the brothel keeper's face, thundering that the faithful could never kneel "with their elbows on the wages of sin and corruption." (p. 13)

Both the women praise the father's Christianity and neither understands when Bernard quotes Mrs. Brady's reply to the priest: "'[W]here do you think the money came from that Mary Magdalene used to anoint the feet of Our Blessed Lord? It didn't come from selling apples.'" (pp. 13-14)

Judith Hearne can't remember for the life of her where Mary Magdalene got the money, but she knows "it was an out-and-out sin to quote Scripture to affront the priest." (p. 14)

Judith Hearne does not know the story of Christ. She knows only the rigid piety of her upbringing, the obsequious subservience to the priests who told her all they thought she needed to know about the Gospels. Her version of faith has nothing to do with Christ or spirituality; it has to do with ritual and superstition and ignorance.

Bernard Rice is an interesting figure. He is lazy, physically repulsive, and a seducer of young girls, notably Mary, the boarding-house maid. But he also functions in the novel as the jester, the speaker of truth. It is he who will articulate in blunt fashion the religious doubt that will later creep into the mind of Judith Hearne. Brian Moore confessed to his biographer that he had modelled Bernard on his own young self and his own voracious, youthful sexual appetite. Bernard's outer repulsiveness is a physical representation of Moore's inner shame at his academic failure and the disappointment he had caused his father. (Sampson, pp. 92-93)

Judith Hearne of course sees none of this. All she sees is an eccentric character. Better still, she sees Bernard as a *topic*, someone she can talk about when she visits the O'Neill family for tea on Sunday afternoons.

It's the one bright spot of Judith Hearne's week. She had known Professor O'Neill in her childhood, and now he and his wife, Moira, and their children receive this lonely woman for a few hours every Sunday. For the father and children it is a painful act of charity, and they seek any excuse to leave the room and the presence of the visitor they call the Great Bore. Only the loving kindness of Moira O'Neill keeps the charade going, and I found it overwhelmingly sad that Judith Hearne actually prepares topics of conversation so that she might be found an interesting companion. The Father Quigley story is heaven-sent, but she decides to delete the reference to Mary Magdalene.

As the first chapter ended, I remember thinking, "It doesn't get better than this." With only a few strokes Moore has created a brilliant depiction of loneliness and ignorance.

Then I began the second chapter and the novel, unbelievably, got better. In one detail of Judith Hearne's getting up the next morning, Moore evoked the whole sexual repression of her convent upbringing. She put on her clothes *under* her nightgown! (p. 19) I was still admiring Moore's mastery when he presented me with what may be the saddest, most moving scene of the novel. It is when Judith Hearne goes to the mirror to brush her hair.

> Her angular face smiled softly at its glassy image. Her gaze . . . changed the contour of her sallow-skinned face, skilfully refashioning her long pointed nose on which a small chilly tear had gathered. Her dark eyes . . . became wide, soft, luminous. Her frame, plain as a cheap clothes rack, filled now with soft curves, developing a delicate line to the bosom.
>
> She watched the glass, a plain woman, changing all to the delightful illusion of beauty. (p. 20)

And now, supported by the two crutches of her religious faith and her imagination, she goes down to meet her fellow paying guests and the family of her landlady. At least for the moment, this plain woman is secure in the dream world she has created to defend herself against her fear that life has passed her by. There is in fact a third pillar of her existence, one apart from religion and imagination, that has not yet come into play. Brian Moore is a master of narrative building and he will not introduce Judith Hearne's secret vice until more than a third of the way into the novel. It is only then that we learn why Judith Hearne has moved so many times, why she is losing her piano and embroidery pupils, what exactly is the rumour that the Protestant neighbour has been spreading about her.

Judith Hearne is a drunk. She keeps whisky and bottles of cheap "tonic" wine in the tin trunk under her narrow little bed. When faith and imagination fail her, she turns to her third solace. But it has been six months since her last binge, and now, as she goes down to her first breakfast in the house, we have as yet no knowledge of her weakness.

At breakfast there is Mrs. Rice the landlady, her repulsive but insightful son, Bernard, and Mrs. Rice's brother, James Madden. James Madden is going to be a major player in Judith Hearne's little drama. Twenty-nine years earlier he had left Ireland for the United States, but he made no fortune. Brian Moore writes in the third-person omniscient, so when his focus is on James Madden, we are privy to James Madden's lack of self-esteem. In nearly thirty years in the United States, the best job he had ever had was as a doorman at a New York hotel. In his own eyes he is a failure in two countries and at ease in neither. I sensed here a touch of Brian Moore's own expatriate loneliness.

Madden had been married, even had a daughter, but his wife had died soon after childbirth and his daughter was embarrassed by the father her realtor husband called a dumb Irish mick. His only good luck had been the accident when a city bus ran over his leg, leaving him lame but with an out-of-court settlement of ten thousand dollars, enough to take him back to Ireland, away from his ungrateful daughter, but not enough to live on for the rest of his life. Mrs. Rice accepts her brother staying with her free only because she hopes he will invest his nest egg in an upgraded guest house they could both run.

James Madden is in many ways the male counterpart of Judith Hearne. He tries to present a genteel appearance, but his clothes are loud and his false teeth too big. Like her, he uses his imagination to mask his failure, hinting at a successful career in the hotel business.

Neither Madden nor Judith Hearne has a real friend. Judith had one once, Edie Marrinan, who introduced her to the comfort of alcohol, but Edie is now in a cold, cheerless nursing home. James Madden does have one acquaintance, the dreadful, racist Major Mahaffey-Hyde, but the major is a friend to anyone who will pay for the drinks.

At their first breakfast together, each is initially taken in by the other, she by his talk of the glamour of Broadway, he by her last few rings and her gold watch, which in fact no longer works. Madden is also attracted by Judith Hearne's willingness to listen to him. So few people seem interested.

I loved the contrapuntal relationship of two middle-aged failures; I thought it gave the novel perfect balance. But there is one major difference between the two major characters. It derives from their different sexes.

James Madden, as a man, has recourse to the comfort of violence. When he discovers Bernard and the maid naked together, he lashes out at the girl in what is clearly an orgy of self-hatred. The girl fears the loss of her job and cannot resist either the attack or the later rape, neither of which has anything to do with sex but everything to do with power as Madden gives vent to all his repressed feeling of inadequacy. Indeed there are incestuous undertones, for Madden also sees in the maid the daughter who rejected him.

Judith Hearne has no such outlet for her repressed desire. All she can do is focus her hopes on James Madden. Her imagination allows her to envisage marriage – at last! She can even see the paragraph in the newspaper:

> Mr. and Mrs. James Madden, of New York, sailed from Southampton yesterday in the *Queen Mary*. Mr. Madden is a prominent New York hotelier and his bride is the former Judith Hearne, only daughter of the late Mr. and Mrs. Charles B. Hearne, of Ballymena. The honeymoon? Niagara Falls, isn't that the place Americans go? Or perhaps Paris, before we sail. (p. 29)

Thus the friendship blossoms, each of them living an illusion: she believes he'll marry her, and he believes that she'll invest in his dream of an American-style restaurant for American tourists in Dublin.

They even go to Sunday Mass together. The Church is such a comfort to both of them in its different ways.

It's one of my favourite scenes. Madden is recovering from a hangover and his memory of attacking the maid the night before. He's looking forward to confession after the service, most of which he sleeps through. "Confession and resultant absolution were the pillars of his faith. He found it comforting to start out as often as possible with a clean slate, a new and promising future." (p. 61)

Judith Hearne is in raptures. She is at the church with a man who wants to marry her, "a man who had kept his faith and said his beads." (p. 62)

And then we have the sermon delivered by Father Quigley, of whom we have already heard. It is a remarkable sermon, remarkably free of any Christian charity.

> "Plenty of money!" Father Quigley roared. "Plenty of money! Plenty of time! Plenty of time! Yes, the people of this parish have both of those things. Time and money. But they don't have it for their church! They don't even have an hour of a Sunday to get down on their bended knees before Our Blessed Lord and ask for forgiveness for the rotten things they did during the week. They've got time for

sin, time for naked dancing girls in the cinema, time to get drunk, . . .
time to spend in beauty parlours . . . time to dance the tango and the
fox-trot and the jitterbugging, time to read trashy books and indecent
magazines, time to do any blessed thing you could care to mention.
Except one.

"They - don't - have - time - for - God."

He leaned over, grabbing the edge of the pulpit as though he were
going to jump over it.

"Well," he said quietly. "I just want to tell those people one thing.
One thing. If you don't have time for God, *God will have no time
for you.*

"And speaking of time, your time will come before the judgement
seat of Heaven. Don't worry about that . . . what will God say to them
on that terrible day? What will He say? Will it be, 'Come, ye blessed
of My Father, inherit the kingdom prepared for you?' Will it be that
now? Do you think it's likely? Or will it be, 'Depart from Me, ye
cursed, into everlasting fire that was prepared for the devil and his
angels?'" (pp. 66-68)

The intense pleasure it must give to threaten hundreds of people with
eternal damnation! It is the power trip to end all power trips. I'm surprised
that more people don't go into the ministry.

Now, a sermon like that is great to deliver, it's full of sexual rhythms
and fear and great emotion. But of course it has nothing to do with spirituality or Catholic theology. Do remember that nothing in this novel or what
I say about it is in any way an attack upon Christ or His Church. Father
Quigley, when he speaks of God turning his back on sinners, is not God's
priest. This has nothing to do with gentle Jesus who turned to the thief on
the cross and said, "Today thou shalt be with me in Paradise." Father
Quigley's version of religion is one of fear and bullying, not of love. But
this is the version that Brian Moore remembers from his Belfast childhood,
and it is the faith that created Judith Hearne and James Madden.

Judith Hearne only has one doubt about James Madden: he is obviously
"common." Her aunt D'Arcy had warned her about "common" men, and
when Judith had her one gentleman caller, her aunt saw him as "common"
and Judith was obliged to send him packing. Manus McKeown had been
her one chance until now, and Judith flares up at her aunt's living presence

in the photograph, "[I]t's all your fault that I am where I am today, being insulted by some fat old landlady and living in furnished rooms." (p. 101)

She is right of course. That selfish old woman had wanted to keep Judith for herself as an unpaid servant, and Judith is justified now in turning her aunt's face to the wall. But the damage has been done and the nagging doubt won't go away.

The intensity of the doubt drives her to her tin trunk and an all-day binge of drinking and singing, heard by everyone in the house. "Everyone" includes two other paying guests, Miss Friel the teacher and Mr. Lenehan the clerk. They have been acting as a Greek chorus, commenting on the budding romance. Brian Moore even gives them one deliciously spiteful chapter of their own.

> Mr. Lenehan: One ould fraud suckin' up to the other and the pair of them canoodling, it would turn your stomach . . . the best joke . . . neither one of them has a five-pound note to their name. (p. 84)

> Miss Friel: That American. . . . A big vulgar ill-spoken brute and the smell of whisky off him would have killed a cat. . . . Fifty? He's nearer sixty. . . . [The woman is] a decent enough soul, although, God knows, a temptation to no man . . . this poor woman is flattered by his attention. (p. 85)

The Machiavellian Bernard sees his chance. He wants to get back to the calm that existed before James Madden and Judith Hearne came to the house, he wants to return to being the centre of his mother's universe. To bring that about, he decides that he must first destroy Judith Hearne.

First he acts as the harsh teller of truth: "'You're waiting for a miracle. Look at yourself: a poor piano teacher, lonely, drinking yourself crazy in a furnished room. Do you want to thank God for that?'" (p. 170)

Then, like Othello's Iago, he lies to her, telling her that Madden loves her but fears she finds him inferior. Bernard knows he is provoking Judith Hearne to demand marriage and he knows that Madden will reject her.

Bernard is sowing his seeds on fruitful ground. Judith Hearne is already in spiritual crisis. Madden is not responding to her timid advances and she is beginning to question her religious faith. What kind of God would not reward her with a man as compensation for all her years of repressed desire? If she cannot rely on God to reward her piety, how can she trust anything? Terrible doubt assails her and she starts to question the very centre of her faith, the miracle of the Mass.

Suppose, she thinks,

> In the tabernacle there was no God. Only round wafers of unleavened bread. She had prayed to bread. The great ceremonial of the Mass, the singing, the incense, the benedictions, what if it was show, all useless show? What if it meant nothing, nothing? (p. 130)

Just as terrible, she thinks of all she has denied herself over the years. In her mind she rehearses the three experiences that make up her pitiful sexual history. She once saw a handsome boy on a beach with an erection in his swimsuit, a doctor's trousers had once brushed against her during a medical examination, and she had seen Victor Mature wearing only a loincloth in the movie *Samson and Delilah*. (pp. 131-32)

Unconsciously, she echoes the words of Father Zosima in *The Brothers Karamazov* as she cries out, "[S]upposing nobody has listened to me in all these years of prayers. Nobody at all up above, watching over me. Then nothing is sinful. There is no sin. And I have been cheated." (p. 131)

Then out of this tormented woman pours one of the most brilliantly constructed streams of consciousness I can remember reading, perfectly pieced together out of the snippets of poetry and film scenes that have remained deep within her, melded into her pathetically few sexual memories. The normally fastidious Moore lets grammar and syntax go hang, with

> . . . the sin, permissible then. Nobody above. Nobody to care. Whiteness hers, he seized, revelled in. Virile he, his dark flashing eyes, they lifted beakers of wine and quaffed them, losing themselves in the intoxication of love, homage to Bacchus, lusts of the flesh. . . .
>
> No sin in it. It would be passion, sublime freedom . . . tearing at my dress, ripping it away, his toga thrown aside, his huge hands feel me, press me close, his body, muscled, hard. And drunken, that wonderful cheerfulness, gay laughter, quaffing the wine, forgetfulness. Sweet oblivion. O Thou. A loaf of bread, a jug of wine and Thou beside me in the wilderness. Paradise enow. (pp. 131-33)

Momentarily she regains control but the edifice is crumbling, and when she does confront James Madden and he rejects her, her carefully constructed world falls apart.

She gets drunk again and all hell breaks loose. Accusations are hurled in every direction. James Madden informs on Bernard and his affair with the maid; the maid informs on Madden. Madden, the maid, and Judith Hearne are all ordered to leave. *Everyone* in the boarding house is a loser in this Belfast of losers.

The maid loses Bernard and her illusion that he will marry her. Mrs. Rice loses any chance of her brother's money. James Madden loses his free lodging. Bernard loses his mother's unconditional indulgence. The boarders lose Judith Hearne as an object of vicious, witty gossip. And Judith Hearne loses everything: her hope for a man, her last remnant of gentility, and most cruel of all, her religious faith, her belief that her reward would come on Earth.

She goes to see the only three people who have played any significant role in her life.

The first is Edie Marrinan, her old drinking companion. As she looks at Edie, abandoned by her family as all the women of the institution have been abandoned, Judith knows, like King Lear looking at the beggar, that she is seeing "the thing itself," humanity stripped of all pretension and humanity without the illusion of hope.

Her second visit is to Moira O'Neill, whom Judith Hearne secretly always thought so common and whose husband Judith secretly wished were her own. Bereft of all her support except drink, Judith pours out the truth for the first time in her life.

> "I have come to you," she cried. "You, of all people. And I never liked you, Moira, that's the truth, I never liked you."
>
> *In vino veritas*, Mrs. O'Neill said to herself . . . she too felt as though she must cry. For after all, she thought, drunk or not, it must cost her something to say that to me. Because now she can never pretend again. . . .
>
> "Moira, I've lost my faith. And I've left Camden Street and I'm living in the Plaza Hotel and everything's finished, Moira, everything." (p. 212)

Finally, Judith Hearne goes to see the priest in his presbytery, and to him she opens her soul: "'Father, if there isn't any other life, then what has happened to me? I've wasted my life. . . . What's the good of anything, unless it's more than bread. More than bread, do you understand, Father?'" (pp. 221-22)

But Father Quigley is not God's priest and all he can do is to threaten.

"Now, what nonsense is this, woman? It's the drink talking in you. Aren't you ashamed of yourself, drinking like that, making a public spectacle of yourself, a well-brought-up woman like you? . . .

". . . Oh, what a terrible thing to let drink take hold of you like that, you should be down on your bended knees, praying for forgiveness. A terrible, terrible thing!" (pp. 221-22)

With nothing left to cling to, Judith goes into the church and makes a drunken assault on the tabernacle in a final attempt to find God and not just unleavened bread. And then she collapses. What I found interesting is that Brian Moore records that Christ did appear to this suffering woman, but "she could not see His face." (p. 227) Moore is careful to distinguish between Christ and what He offers and the Belfast Church of Moore's childhood.

In total breakdown, Judith Hearne is admitted to the nursing home where Edie is an inmate. Her room will be paid for by the saintly Moira O'Neill. Moira visits and Judith thanks her, not for her friendship, but for what Judith now acknowledges as charity. With the pretences stripped away, Judith Hearne sees all things clearly.

She puts up her two little pictures: the Home permits some decoration. But now they are souvenirs of a past life, not living presences.

Brilliantly, Moore has her look in a mirror, as she did at the beginning of the novel. No longer does her imagination make her beautiful: "Old, she thought, if I met myself now, I would say: that is an old woman." (p. 236)

She now faces the truth, and we see her just as stripped and bare as Lear, and after as terrible a journey. It has not been a physical journey but rather a journey within herself. Interestingly, chronology is unimportant within the novel. It is as if time stands still while Judith Hearne undergoes her passion, her crucifixion.

And yet, at the end of the novel, the final action of Judith Hearne is to smile.

How can she smile? I know that many readers see her at the end as a woman crushed, totally defeated.

But I do not see it so. I believe that Judith Hearne smiles because she is free. Free of illusion and pretence and ill-founded faith. Now, I believe, she understands the great truth, that authentic life begins only when there are no more lies, no more easy systems of belief that relieve us of any responsibility. As I thought about Judith at the end of the novel, I thought of what Bertrand Russell said, that our only hope is to build our future on a firm foundation of unyielding despair.

Judith Hearne's losses seem terrible, but she has lost nothing of value. Whatever she will make of her life in the future, it will be truer and better than anything she has known before.

FOXFIRE: CONFESSIONS OF A GIRL GANG

Joyce Carol Oates
(Toronto: Penguin, 1993)

Foxfire: Confessions of a Girl Gang is Joyce Carol Oates's twenty-third novel. She has also published numerous collections of short stories.

There are many critics who find her too prolific. It is somehow not respectable to write too much; the critics suspect that standards are being lowered. Too many people believe that the writer should be either out drinking deep of life's experience or alone, starving in an attic. A novel should be produced out of agony every few years or even every decade.

It is an absurd view. How does it account for Emily Brontë and *Wuthering Heights*, the greatest of the world's love stories and wholly imagined by a young woman who rarely strayed out of her Yorkshire vicarage? How does it account for the output of Dickens or Zola or Trollope? How does it possibly account for the married businessman and property speculator who could imagine the existential loneliness of Lear while writing commercially successful plays at a rate of more than one a year?

It is fortunate for Joyce Carol Oates that she has managed to keep her total output a relative secret. She has published many more novels under other names, notably as Rosamond Smith, a variation on her husband's name, Raymond Smith.

Let me make my position clear. Joyce Carol Oates is a prolific writer, but she is also a superb writer. She has the gift of Dickens, the ability to create a multi-dimensional character who comes to life in the reader's mind. This, surely, is the first duty of the novelist.

She has won a Guggenheim Fellowship, a National Book Award, and is frequently the runner-up for the Pulitzer Prize. I am convinced that if Joyce Carol Oates had written only six to ten novels she would be hailed as the definitive chronicler of mid-twentieth-century America.

Let us consider the person of Joyce Carol Oates for a moment. She was born in Erie County, New York State, in 1938. She was a teacher in Detroit in the early sixties and published her first novel in 1963. She now leads what she describes as a very conventional life with her husband and children in Princeton, New Jersey, teaching university and writing every day.

Her particular study is the individual American life set against the background of mid-twentieth-century political and cultural mores. She often focuses on what she perceives as the contrast between the material prosperity and spiritual poverty of American life and on the great divide between appearance and reality in American middle-class existence.

She will often dissect a dysfunctional family, and sometimes pushes her characters to the very edge of breakdown. Because of her interest in extreme psychological states, she is occasionally referred to as a neo-Gothic writer.

Her preferred setting is a fictitious area in upstate New York she calls Eden County in an echo of her own place of birth. *Foxfire* is set in Hammond, Eden County, in one of the poorer sections, the largely blue-collar streets of Lowertown.

Our five main characters, all aged thirteen or fourteen, are in the ninth grade of Perry High School.

Led by the charismatic Margaret "Legs" Sadovsky, they meet to form a secret gang on January 1, 1953. The aim of the gang is to destroy the oppressor, although at the beginning the oppressor is very ill-defined. Some of the targets are obvious, like their math teacher, Mr. Buttinger, who harasses the pretty, prematurely developed Elizabeth O'Hagan. The girls paint a purported confession by Mr. Buttinger on the passenger side of his car so that he drives all over town before realizing what has been done to him. The humiliation is too much and he leaves the school.

Another obvious candidate for punishment is the great-uncle of another gang member, Maddy Wirtz. A would-be writer and the narrator of our novel, Maddy longs for a broken-down typewriter that her great-uncle is putting out in the garbage. He puts a price on it, however, five dollars, and keeps raising the figure, but always with the promise that it could be for nothing "if you're a good girl." (p. 69) He is lured by the girls to lower his pants in the back of his store, only to receive a good beating and a handful of dollar bills scattered on and around his battered body.

The girls widen their activities, without yet clearly defining their ultimate goals. They are still at the level of little girls, striking out at those who hurt them. They sense that the enemy is larger than just a bullying or predatory teacher or relative, but they don't really understand the anti-capitalist slogans they chalk up on neighbourhood businesses at Halloween, or even their own motives in giving money to the poor.

Neither they nor we have to search for a motive when the girls loosen the teeth of a group of boys who are harassing three new gang members. During the confrontation, the high school principal sees Legs intimidating the boys with a switchblade, expels her on the spot, and calls the police. Legs will spend fourteen months in a girls' institution, usually in isolation for defying the authorities, until she pretends to cooperate in order to secure her release.

After her release, Legs resumes the leadership of the gang. She also befriends Muriel, the pregnant former girlfriend of Legs's father, Ab Sadovsky, and the girls all live together as a commune in a house rented in Muriel's name. The girls' activities take on a more overtly political aspect – the novel is in large part a chronicle of their growing political awareness – and they begin to take battered women into their home, while continuing to punish the manifestly wicked, like the man who prostitutes his own retarded, deformed sister.

To finance what has become an abused women's shelter they are in urgent need of money. Muriel alone needs five thousand dollars for post-natal care and rehabilitation from alcoholism. Their solution is to kidnap a rich man for ransom.

Legs had been befriended by a prison visitor, a wealthy young woman doing her share of charity work. Legs, accompanied by Violet, a very attractive new gang member, arranges to meet the girl's father. His chauvinist reaction is the one they anticipated, and he invites them for a late-night car ride. Instead of receiving the sexual favours he had hoped for, Whitney Kellogg Junior is bundled into the trunk of the car and a ransom note is sent to the family. In a struggle with the girls, Kellogg kicks out and

Violet accidentally shoots him in the chest. Legs calls an ambulance and then flees, as do all the other gang members. Some are caught, but Legs is never seen again.

The girls go their separate ways. More than thirty years later, a fifty-year-old Maddy Wirtz comes across the diaries she kept from 1953 to 1957, the years of the FOXFIRE gang. ("FOXFIRE," by the way, is a contraction of "The Foxes of Fairfax Avenue," Hammond's main street. The powerful contraction is the brainwave of Legs, who claims to have seen it as a vision in a dream.)

Maddy decides to compile the diaries into a chronicle, which is, in fact, this novel. The only information she has post-1957 on Legs is a 1961 newspaper picture shown to her by Elizabeth O'Hagan. The photograph is one of Fidel Castro at a victory celebration in Havana. In the background is a person who bears a striking resemblance to the long-lost Legs Sadovsky.

There you have the bare bones of the novel, the gang's adventures over a four-year period. Taken at its simplest level, it is an exciting and fast-moving adventure narrative with a strong Robin Hood element of retribution visited upon the sinful.

But the very least reflection tells us that something much more profound has gone on. Let us retrace the four years of the gang, beginning with an event that took place even before the gang was formed.

The time is late 1952. An Uppertown Hammond congressman has been invited to give an inspirational address to the students of Perry High. The speech is poorly constructed, ungrammatical, and full of platitudes:

> . . . so proud such an honor American way of life free enterprise blah blah those of us who served our country in the War this God-ordained sovereign nation THE UNITED STATES OF AMERICA as our patriot Commodore Stephen Decatur said *Our country! – may she always be in the right, and always successful, right or wrong!* this land of opportunity of life liberty and the pursuit of happiness triumphing against all enemies because ordained by God where anyone *yes I mean anyone boys and girls in this very auditorium this morning* can aspire to the Presidency itself you can aspire to the head of General Motors – General Mills – AT&T – U.S. Steel – a Nobel Prize-winning scientist a famous inventor only have faith, work hard study hard never be discouraged have faith! (p. 6)

The girls' reaction to the speech marks the beginning of their journey to political consciousness. Maddy Wirtz, "the one perceived as having the power of words," (p. 5) sums it up:

> [W]e so resented that asshole up there talking talking talking taking up the entire assembly expecting us to believe there isn't a special creation of God, or of man, to which we didn't belong, here at the shabby south end of Hammond in the worst damn public school in the district, we didn't belong and never would. (pp. 6-7)

The girls have never attended a consciousness-raising session, or a political lecture, or any meeting of the not-yet-born women's movement, but they know instinctively that what this white male visitor from the power structure says is not true. Young women like them do not have a chance at the golden apple.

We must remember the period. We are at the beginning of the Eisenhower era, the "happy days" of American history. Rock and roll had not yet arrived; it would be another year before Elvis would turn the world upside down with his first appearance on the "Ed Sullivan Show." Segregation was still legal, even in the U.S. Army, and the black man still knew his place. Dr. Martin Luther King Junior was not yet a household name. Betty Friedan and Gloria Steinem had not yet found an audience. The Vietnam War and the attendant protest was yet to come. No one perceived a threat from any direction to "traditional family values."

At the end of 1952 we are still in the era before women, blacks, the poor, and the young had begun to formulate their protest against a patriarchal society dominated by old white males.

I hear even now nostalgia for that time, and it is true that life was more certain, more orderly, more comfortable, and safer in the streets. All that was true, provided that you were a man and the right sort of man, white and with money. You could be comfortable too if you were a woman, provided you were the wife of the right sort of man or the daughter of the right sort of man or if an institution had decided to make you its token woman.

We are still in the early fifties, so the vocabulary of oppression, the vocabulary of the feminist movement for example, has not yet been developed. The five girls who originally make up the FOXFIRE gang know that they are victims but lack the political sophistication to define their victimhood. When they do form their gang, they do so in terms of a culture they are only just beginning to question. It does not even occur to Legs, their leader, that "foxes" is a male-coined, reductive, sexist term to describe pretty women.

The five are so much products of their culture that they take their nicknames from Hollywood and never question the screen-magazine world that so exploited women. Legs herself is "Sheena, Queen of the Jungle," Loretta McGuire is "Lana," after Lana Turner, and red-haired Elizabeth O'Hagan is "Rita," after Rita Hayworth. Not one of them sees the irony of taking the names of male-constructed sex symbols.

The girls have also been corrupted by the racism of their society, so at the beginning of the novel they have a racist vocabulary. They call the teacher who laid his hands on Rita (Elizabeth O'Hagan) "Niggerlips" Buttinger, and Goldie, one of the five founding members, will later object to the initiation of two black girls into the gang.

Joyce Carol Oates was careful not to create a homogeneous gang of identical characters. This is a collection of very different individuals, united in their sense of victimhood, but different from and distrustful of each other. Oates also had the wisdom to have the girls continually discuss, disagree, fight, reconcile, and come to new understandings. If a goal of the individual is to develop a strong sense of self, then it would be no victory for one of these girls to go from the tyranny of patriarchy to the tyranny of sisterhood.

There is superb, illuminating discussion within the gang as they progress from one level of understanding to another. Consider the case of Rita, whom we know already as the victim of her math teacher. Mr. Buttinger was not her first aggressor; she had already been the prey of two of her brothers and the boys' gang they belonged to.

> Rita O'Hagan, twelve years old, was the object of certain acts performed upon her, or to her, or with her, for most of a long August afternoon; and when, dishevelled and weeping, and leaking menstrual blood, Rita was released to make her way home, alone, her mother screamed at her and slapped her and did not then, or subsequently, inquire of her what had happened that afternoon – whether anything had happened at all. (p. 25)

When Rita tells Maddy, "'I don't *want* these things to happen, they just *do*,'" Maddy's answer is, "'It's because you cry, they like to see you cry . . . if you just wouldn't *cry*.'" (p. 24)

Goldie blames the victim in similar fashion, "'*She's* the asshole, letting him get away with it,'" (p. 46) the "him" being Mr. Buttinger.

But Legs places the blame squarely on the aggressor, replying to Goldie, "'*You're* the asshole, letting him get away with it,'" (p. 47) and then Goldie understands: "'Legs is right. If Rita wasn't there he'd pick on someone else and if that person wasn't there he'd pick on someone else till it got down finally to one of *us*.'" (p. 47)

Legs has the final word in the discussion and the word defines sisterhood: "*We're all Rita.*" (p. 71) Legs not only exonerates the victim, she persuades the others of the rightness of standing united.

At the delinquents' home, Legs realizes how women have imitated their oppressors, how many of them have been co-opted by the other side. One of the inmates, Dutchgirl, had "cultivated the bullying-suspicious manner of the guards . . . so she could . . . lay hands on weaker girls, challenge and connive with the stronger." (p. 148)

After Legs is released from the home and the horror of the "Room" in Isolation, where she had slept on "that thin smelly mattress stained with stale menstrual blood, aged grief, vomit, others' tears," (p. 141) she confides to Maddy, "'[W]e do have enemies, yeah men are the enemy but not just men, the shock of it is that girls and women are our enemies too sometimes.'" (p. 180) And we think back to when Rita was assaulted, and her mother, Mrs. O'Hagan's, "primary concern was that her husband know nothing since Mr. O'Hagan, a machine-shop worker, was inclined to melancholic binges of drinking and sporadic acts of violence, most of them domestic, when things troubled him." (pp. 25-26) Mrs. O'Hagan had screamed at and slapped her violated twelve-year-old.

Even before her confinement in the girls' home, Margaret Ann "Legs" Sadovsky had had her fill of violence. Her mother is dead and her father, Ab, is heavy-drinking and abusive. Legs bears on her chin a sickle-shaped scar her father gave her when she was ten. Even before the novel begins, Ab Sadovsky welcomes the decision of the Welfare Department that his home is "unsuitable for a minor." Legs is shipped off to her grandmother in Plattsburgh. We meet her first in November of 1952 after she has run home to Fairfax Avenue, initially to her friend, our narrator, Maddy Wirtz.

It is to Maddy that Legs proposes a pact of mutual loyalty. Legs – far, far ahead of the other girls in political insight – has already identified the enemy as patriarchy, but she knows that she cannot fight alone, and her pact with Maddy is merely a precursor to the foundation of FOXFIRE on New Year's Day, 1953. In the four years to follow, the world of lying politicians, fumbling schoolteachers, abusive family members, and timorous, enslaved women will tremble before the flame and the name of "FOXFIRE"!

FOXFIRE will be a true sisterhood, not just the female auxiliary of a boys' gang. Those auxiliaries already existed as a bank of available and promiscuous girls on which the male gang members could draw. This will be true sisterhood, and that's why at the initiation ceremony there is such an emphasis on the baring of breasts. This is a *female* movement, not the mirror image of a fraternity.

It is interesting that when the police arrest Legs, they ask her which boys' gang she is running with. The police assume that women do not have the capacity to act alone, even at the criminal level.

Legs is brilliantly perceptive: she knows how to exploit male weakness. Under her direction, the gang will take full advantage of dependable male urges. To finance their support of their sisters they will lure men to robbery and blackmail, ironically baiting the trap with an air of innocent vulnerability, a bait few men can resist.

In her crusade against patriarchy, Legs will come across many of its victims, not all of whom live on Fairfax Avenue. When she is at the reformatory, she meets Triss, molested by her stepfather; Bobby, imprisoned for holding stolen goods for her boyfriend; and, saddest of all, feeble-witted Bernadette, who was abandoned by her boyfriend and who in turn abandoned her baby. Joyce Carol Oates makes the point that the oppressed will often take on the characteristics of the oppressor, but Legs understands that does not make the persecution any less real.

The commune the gang creates after Legs is released not only helps abused sisters, it also creates an alternative to the traditional family, so long the underpinning both of our society and of the traditional English novel. More and more frequently, contemporary novelists have turned to the commune or even the chosen family as an alternative to the patriarchal family structure, which has permitted so much abuse.

Joyce Carol Oates has not only created a remarkable variety of young women, from the beautiful newcomer Violet to our own narrator with her occasionally acid tongue, she has created a rich selection of male characters, from the loutish Ab Sadovsky to the kidnap victim himself, Whitney Kellogg Junior.

Kellogg introduces a new element into the novel with his equation of capitalism and Christianity. How does he put it? Speaking as a successful Christian businessman, he says,

> "I mean we're *blessed* from the start. . . . If we so choose. If we make our decision for Christ. . . . If we don't crawl whimpering and whining casting blame on others . . . *some rise to the top and some do not . . .* 'God helps he who helps himself.'" (p. 283)

Poverty, in Kellogg's view, is the punishment God metes out to those who do not believe sufficiently in capitalism. He then goes on to attack the Commie-backed unions and "'that Jew-lover "F.D.R.".'" (p. 284)

I would have thought Kellogg was a bit of a caricature if I hadn't met him one summer in California. The man I met was not of course Whitney Kellogg Junior, but he said all the same things. He was the friend of a friend, and he invited my wife, Pearl, and me to dinner. Beside him sat his submissive wife and his two adorable children. Before the meal began, we were asked to hold hands while he said Grace. Pearl and I were so surprised that neither of us had the presence of mind to refuse. I remember even now the first words of the prayer, "O Lord, let tomorrow be a productive day and a day of economic success in Thy service." I realized that I was in the presence of a patriarch who had declared himself sanctified. It is also not often that I sit facing *The Collected Works of Rush Limbaugh*.

I should not really have said it is Whitney Kellogg who introduces the religious dimension of capitalism and patriarchy into the novel. Oates already did that in the person of Father Theriault, Legs's friend and counsellor and an alcoholic ex-priest. Father Theriault, as a young priest of twenty-four, had attended a Socialist Party Congress in New York City in 1909 and had suddenly become aware that God was to be found in fellowship and not in what Father Theriault perceived to be a patriarchal and paternalistic Church. Since 1909 his life has been an alcoholic fog through which he bellows a continual diatribe against the Church as established capitalism.

As he puts it to Legs and the girls,

> Did we know, Father Theriault went on, growing excited now, of the Church's betrayal of the faithful? of the Church's betrayal of Christ? of the Church's wealth, the Church's militancy, the Church's fear of truth? Did we know of the pitiless inquisitions through history continuing to this very day? this hour? (p. 55)

It is from this old former priest that Legs learns the vocabulary of the revolutionary class struggle. After the shooting of Whitney Kellogg Junior, Legs presumably went on to continue to fight the good fight in the mountains of Cuba.

And thus ends Maddy Wirtz's diary. At the end of the novel, Maddy tells us that she did meet one of the FOXFIRE girls again, twelve years after the Kellogg kidnapping and the breakup of the FOXFIRE gang. Rita brought her up to date on some of the members. Rita herself is married to a "sweet guy" and is happy with her husband and children. She has had no news of Goldie and Lana since their arrest but hears that the beautiful Violet, the latecomer to the gang, married rich.

On the very last pages of the novel, Maddy brings us up to date on her own life. She tried marriage. It lasted three years. Now she is a university graduate doing interesting work for an astronomer in New Mexico. She realizes that she, Rita, and Violet have all made compromises with the patriarchal world around them. But at the same time we realize that the flame that illuminated their adolescence for a few brief years, the flame with which Legs tattooed them at their initiation ceremony, has not been completely extinguished. All of them were marked by their years of rebellion. Legs had warned them about being betrayed by their own sexual natures. As Maddy recorded, FOXFIRE had no objection to men as friends, "as long as they were *friends*, not *boy friends*." (p. 167) It was not celibacy that was advocated, it was a caution not to enter a traditional male-female relationship. I have the strong sense that Rita and even Violet married because they *chose* to. So did

Maddy, and when she chose to, she ended the marriage. The FOXFIRE gang and the sisterhood and the commune showed them that the traditional family is not the only framework in which one might live. All the FOXFIRE girls, including those of whom Maddy has had no news, must know, because of Legs's teaching, that other options are available. To that extent, Joyce Carol Oates has deconstructed the traditional values that have been so embedded in the novel as a middle-class literary form.

Ironically, in spite of its deconstructionist attack on patriarchy, the structure of *Foxfire* is the very classical one of tragedy. It satisfies all the criteria, assuming Legs Sadovsky to be the protagonist.

A person of strong character faces a world she cannot accept and she defies it. The struggle is magnificent, but the protagonist must inevitably be defeated. The world is too powerful, and we see the inevitability of the hero's loss while we rejoice in the struggle. The magnificence of the defiance is more important to us than the defeat. It is the mark of tragedy that the narrative will end with a judgment on the protagonist rendered by the survivor of highest rank. In terms of the FOXFIRE gang, that would be Maddy, and it is indeed she who will deliver the final lines.

But, as I reflected on Legs Sadovsky as a tragic hero, I realized that Joyce Carol Oates had gone one daring step further. She had created not only a perfect tragic hero, she had created an epic hero.

The epic hero is the protagonist who embodies the struggle of a whole class or a whole people. The epic hero is the protagonist with whom all ages can identify, the hero who is the incarnation of the hopes and dreams and aspirations of a whole people, while remaining an identifiably real and human person. Traditionally in literature, the epic hero, apart from embodying the struggle of the oppressed, has certain identifying characteristics.

The epic hero will always have a mysterious birth, see visions, perform superhuman deeds, have a mystical counsellor, and at some crucial point in his or her life go into a lonely place to enter into communion with his or her deepest self and receive the revelation of a profound and pure truth.

Consider how well Legs Sadovsky fits that description.

As her father, Ab, tells her on his second visit to the reformatory, Legs was born to her mother, then unmarried, *after* she went for an abortion. She had left the abortionist dripping blood, having, one would have thought, ended the pregnancy. There we have the mysterious birth.

You will remember too that Legs always claimed to have received the name of the gang as a vision within a dream. The epic hero is always assigned a mission within just this kind of mystical revelation.

For all his human weaknesses, we can reasonably accept Father Theriault as Legs's advisor and spiritual guide, the modern equivalent of Arthur's Merlin.

The whole gang saw Legs leap twelve feet down from a culvert, and there is the suggestion that at the beginning of the novel Legs had walked the three hundred miles from Plattsburgh to Hammond. Maddy certainly has the impression that Legs can fly across rooftops. These are the necessary superhuman deeds of the epic hero.

The absolute certainly that Oates has created an epic hero came to me as Legs experiences her epiphany in the isolation of the "Room" at the reformatory. We are prepared for the moment on p. 153, when she says, *"I'm getting stronger, I can feel it,"* and the moment arrives when she feels herself one with the hawks, high and free in the immensity of the sky. *"Masters of the air. I am one of you."* (p. 171)

The "Room" is the underworld of Ulysses, it is the mountaintop or the cave or the desert place of the founders of our religions. Maddy is the traditional chronicler of the larger-than-life epic hero, writing decades after her disappearance, telling of long-ago events when she led her people against the oppressor.

It may be hard to believe that Joyce Carol Oates intended this young woman to be perceived as a hero of epic proportions, but the chronicler's words at the beginning and end of the narrative leave little room for doubt.

[E]verything she did especially as time passed was magnified onto a giant movie screen, in Technicolor, not fading away like the things most people do, and dying. (p. 5)

Is she – *are* you, Legs – in any Time at all? (p. 327)

Legs Sadovsky has exited from the personal into the eternal. She has become part of the ages. She is not only Ulysses, she is Robin Hood, she is Zorro. Wherever there is oppression and injustice, there will be Legs Sadovsky.

In a North America where the American Congress and Senate, like the Canadian House of Commons, are dominated by white males (in the United States by white, male Republicans), where the religious right and the National Rifle Association are gaining more ground every day, where all the pro-woman, pro-equality legislation of the last thirty years is under threat, I say, "Come, Legs Sadovsky, come from wherever you are waiting, we need you now more than ever!"

IN THE MEMORY OF THE FOREST

Charles T. Powers
(Toronto: Penguin, 1998)

Since *In the Memory of the Forest* is the only novel Charles T. Powers wrote, I feel that I should begin with a brief note of biography.

Powers was born in the small town of Neosho, Missouri. After studying at Kansas State University, he went on to a brilliant career in journalism. For more than twenty years he wrote for the *Los Angeles Times*. For twelve of those years he headed their African bureau, headquartered in Nairobi, Kenya. During that period, while reporting on Idi Amin, he was imprisoned and tortured in Uganda.

In 1986 the *Los Angeles Times* made him head of their Eastern European bureau. For five years he lived in Poland, made an extensive study of Polish history, and amassed the historical background he would need later to write *In the Memory of the Forest*.

In 1991 he returned to the United States, quit journalism, and settled in the peace and quiet of Vermont in order to write his novel.

It took him five years. On October 2, 1996, at the age of fifty-three, just after *In the Memory of the Forest* was published, he died of a rare blood disease, possibly contracted years earlier in Africa. He is survived by a daughter.

Since the novel contains so many references to the relations between Jews and Gentiles in Poland before and after the Second World War, I feel I must give some time to a consideration of Polish history and of the Jewish presence in Poland. I will try to be as objective as possible.

Poland came into existence as an independent nation over a thousand years ago in 966 under Mieszko, its first king. By the fourteenth century, under King Kazimierz Wielki, known to the West as Casimir the Great or Casimir III, Poland had become the first European nation to have a unified code of laws. So advanced and forward-thinking was Casimir III that he realized his ever-growing nation needed outside help to stimulate trade, banking, and economic development.

Casimir knew that the Jews in the German-speaking states of Central Europe were suffering under Church-incited pogroms. The priests were encouraging the old anti-Semitic blood libel, that Jews were killing Christian children for their blood – according to traditional Church teaching a necessary ingredient in the making of matzohs for Passover. Casimir gave the Jews of Central Europe a safe haven in Poland. Tens, later hundreds, of thousands of Jews migrated into Poland in the fourteenth and following centuries. As farmers, merchants, and, later, bankers, they were part of Poland's expansion into one of the most powerful countries in Europe.

There was anti-Semitism in Poland, as there was everywhere else in Europe, largely fostered by the Church, which branded the Jews as Christ-killers. But Jews were under the protection of the Polish monarchy. In 1534, for example, King Zygmunt I resisted Church demands that Jews wear distinctive clothing. Yellow stars were suggested. Under royal protection, therefore, Jews were a part of Poland's Golden Age, from Casimir III almost until the destruction of Poland in 1795.

The situation of Polish Jews changed drastically in the eighteenth century when in 1762 Catherine the Great seized power in neighbouring Russia. Poland had been weakened by infighting among its nobility, each faction backing a different candidate for the Polish throne and calling in support from outside countries, and so was in no position to withstand the imperialist ambitions of its powerful Russian neighbour. In three successive partitions, Catherine the Great divided up Poland between herself and her allies, Austria and Prussia. In the third partition, in 1795, what was left of Poland was swallowed up completely into Catherine's Russian empire.

From 1795 until the end of the First World War in 1918, Poland ceased to exist as an independent country. Russia had nailed Poland to the cross. The more than one hundred years of Russian oppression were marked by many violent Polish uprisings, all of them gallant, all of them bloody, all of them unsuccessful.

Catherine the Great and her successors initially felt that for economic reasons they needed the Jews in their empire, but they didn't want the defiling presence of the Christ-killers too close to the delicately Christian heart of Holy Mother Russia. Accordingly, the Jews, with very few exceptions, were permitted to live only in the occupied territories on the western edge of the Russian empire. A Pale of Settlement was established from the Baltic provinces in the north down through Belorussia and Poland to the Ukraine.

The situation became very serious in the nineteenth century for the Jews of the Russian empire, the majority of whom lived in Poland. Czar Nicholas I alone passed more than six hundred different anti-Semitic decrees, and Czar Alexander III, echoing the advice of his chief minister, said of his Jewish subjects, "I will convert a third, starve a third to death, and force the remaining third to emigrate."

The situation became even worse in the twentieth century under the last czar, Nicholas II. When Russia lost its war against Japan in 1905, Jews were made the scapegoat. Pogroms instigated by the Moscow government and encouraged by the Church became more frequent. The organization of anti-Semitic societies known as the Black Hundreds received official government subsidy and the czar wore a Black Hundreds pin in his lapel.

The Jewish position in Poland was particularly dangerous. Absentee landlords, including both Polish and Russian aristocracy, used Jews as buffers between themselves and the peasantry they were exploiting. Jews were limited by law in the Russian empire to a very small number of occupations, one of which was estate management. Thus the Polish peasant, ground down by both the landowner and the Czarist government, never saw the face of his real oppressors; all he saw was the face of the Jewish estate manager. Encouraged as it was by both Church and Czarist government, anti-Semitism was rife among all the peoples of the Russian empire.

In Powers's novel, eighty-seven-year-old Mrs. Skubyszewska is one of the few villagers who remember how it was in the old days in the village of Jadowia before the Second World War, and even before the First World War. She describes it to Father Tadeusz, a relative newcomer to the village:

The Jews purchased grain and eggs and vegetables – produce – from the farmers. And from their own traders they bought goods from the city. They baked bread and repaired shoes. They sold needles and buttons, candy, tea. They gave credit. They lent money. Oh, no, they were not rich. Of course, some said they were, but if it was true you couldn't see it. . . . No, no, they were not rich. They were poor as everyone, just different poor. They sold, the Poles plowed. . . . The Jews could all read, or most could. They educated their children. Not so the peasants, not so much. That was a difference. (p. 173)

Mrs. Skubyszewska, I think, describes the situation accurately. The great differences between the Polish Gentiles and the Polish Jews, apart from religion, lay in occupation and in education. The Poles had a deep and fierce attachment to the land they worked. The Jews could never develop that – their history under the czar had shown them that they could be expelled from any village at any moment. In any case, in many areas they were not permitted to own land.

As for education, Jews *had* to learn to read. The study of Torah was and is the essential duty of every adult Jew. The same was not true for Polish Catholics; they had no need to read to perform their religious duties. Their priests would tell them what they needed to understand and to believe. I was reminded of the situation in Quebec before the Quiet Revolution of the sixties, when it was not in the interest of the Church or of political leaders like Maurice Duplessis to have a literate population.

Then comes the First World War and the Russian Revolution. The collapse of the Russian empire meant that Poland could declare itself a free nation under the leadership of the great Jozef Pilsudski. From 1918 to 1922, and again from 1926 to his death in 1935, Pilsudski wielded almost dictatorial power.

During the Pilsudski regime, the lot of Poland's Jews improved. Pilsudski's vision of Poland was inclusive: everyone who lived in Poland was Polish, including the minorities, including the Jews. But after Pilsudski died the situation for the Jews changed. Pilsudski's successor, Edward Smigly-Rydz, was a weak man who gave in to those anti-Semitic impulses that derived from Czarist occupation and, regrettably, the traditional teaching of the Catholic Church.

In 1936 the new prime minister declared to the Polish parliament, the *Sejm*, that the economic conflict between Poles and Jews was a struggle for Poland's survival. Two months later, Smigly-Rydz demanded that the League of Nations allocate colonies to Poland so that Poland's Jews could be shipped to them. Jews at the time made up about 10 percent of Poland's population of thirty million.

In the same year the Catholic primate of Poland, Cardinal Hlond, published a pastoral letter that was read in every pulpit. It said:

> It is a fact that Jews oppose the Catholic Church, are steeped in free-thinking, and represent the avant-garde of the atheist movement, the Bolshevik movement and subversive action. The Jews have a disastrous effect on morality, and their publishing houses dispense pornography. It is true that Jews commit fraud, usury, and are involved in trade in human beings.

With the Church fanning the flames of an anti-Semitism nourished by more than a century of Russian Czarist occupation, it is hardly surprising that the situation worsened.

At the universities Jews were forced to sit on yellow benches at the back of lecture halls, and the Polish doctors' and lawyers' associations jointly passed a membership code based on the German model which restricted new membership in their profession to "Poles of Polish descent."

We come then to September 1939 and the German invasion of Poland. Under a secret clause of the Molotov-Ribbentrop Pact, Germany and Russia agreed to divide Poland between them. For the second time in history, Poland would be crucified. In western Poland, Germany imposed a barbarous administration called simply the General-Government. Poland was even to be denied the dignity of a name. The intention of the Germans was to murder all Polish intellectuals, the officer class, and all potential Polish leadership. The Germans intended to reduce the Polish people to slave labour for the German Reich. Fortunately, some Poles and some remnants of the Polish army were able to escape to England to form a government-in-exile. Others remained in Poland to form an underground Home Army.

In eastern, Russian-occupied Poland, the Russians imposed Communist government and, just like the Russian czars before them, used Polish Jews as often as possible as their front men, their administrators and political commissars. Many Polish Jews had in fact welcomed the Russian armies as liberators, still seeing communism as the ideal by which all of us might move forward to a better world. It was at that time an understandable attitude, but it exacerbated the tensions that already existed between Polish Catholics and Polish Jews.

I do not have to dwell on the horrors that took place in occupied Poland. We all know that three million Polish Catholics were murdered by the Germans and Russians, 10 percent of Poland's Christian population.

We all know that three million Polish Jews died in the German death camps, 90 percent of the pre-war Polish Jewish population.

In many cases, Polish Catholics saw Polish Jews as agents of the new Russian Communist oppressors, just as they had earlier perceived them as agents of the Czarist aristocracy. Human nature being what it is, it is not surprising that many Poles did not resent, and even applauded, the German *aktions* against the Jews. But paradoxically, it was the Polish government-in-exile in London in 1942 that first informed the Allied Powers of what was happening to the Jews of Eastern Europe, and it was the Polish government-in-exile that first used the word "martyrdom" in its communiqué.

The Allies did nothing. They would not even bomb the railway lines to Auschwitz.

I must point out that almost no nation came out well from the Holocaust. Poland may have wanted to get rid of its Jews before the war, but it is equally certain that almost no nation wanted to take them. The Evian Conference of 1938 made that very clear, with Canada, Great Britain, France, and the United States, among others, proving beyond doubt that Jews were not welcome. I also remember that Sir Oswald Mosely, the leader of the British fascist and anti-Semitic movement, had hundreds of thousands of blackshirts under his command. There would have been no shortage of anti-Semitic collaborators if Hitler's invasion of England had been successful. I must also point out that Poland was the only occupied nation that did not raise at least one division of volunteers for the German SS.

We come in our historical review to the end of the war in 1945. Once again, Russia would nail Poland to the cross. The Russians, by radio, encouraged the Polish Home Army of Resistance to rise up against the German occupiers in Warsaw, promising to rush the advancing Russian armies to its aid. Once the Polish revolt began, the Russians halted on the other side of the Vistula and just sat back, letting the Nazis do their work for them in slaughtering Polish resisters and, of course, Polish leadership. The way was then clear for Russia to impose its own Polish puppets on the Polish people in a Moscow-controlled Communist government.

Once again the Russians would use Polish Jews wherever they could as their front men, as the administrators and the commissars, as the buffer between the Russian masters and the Polish population.

Conditions in post-war Poland were horrifying. The country had just lived through six years of German barbarism, and the sad truth is that suffering does not bring out the best in people. Some Polish Christians acted nobly, however. There is a Jewish woman in Israel, Edith Tzirer, who remembers how it was when she was fourteen and tottered out of a liberated concentration camp near Cracow. She was weak from starvation and ravaged by tuberculosis. A young priest gave her bread and carried her on his back for three kilometres to a train and medical attention. That same young priest, Karol Wojtyla, would perform other acts of brotherly love in memory of the Jewish friends of his childhood.

But Karol Wojtyla, later Pope John Paul II, was not typical. All too often those who had suffered were cruel to others who had suffered. When in 1946 a few Polish Jews, the pitiful remnants of the camps, tried to return to their ancestral home of Kielce, fifty-five were murdered, many were crippled, and the rest had to flee.

At the end of the war, our best estimate is that out of a pre-war three million, fifteen thousand Jews remained in Poland. In 1968, the Polish government, under orders from Moscow, compelled most of the fifteen thousand to seek exile. The Soviet Union was entering one of its virulently anti-Semitic phases and had committed itself to the Arab cause in the power struggle in the Middle East. By the time of our novel, 1990 or 1991, there were perhaps three thousand Jews left in Poland, many elderly or infirm.

Let us now approach the novel. We can fix the date of the action fairly accurately from references in the text to Gorbachev, in power in Russia since 1985, to George Bush as the American president, and to Poland's newly elected president, Lech Walesa. With a new anti-Communist president in Warsaw, reform is in the air, but it is coming only slowly to the village of our story.

The fictitious village of Jadowia is situated at the junction of two main roads, "a village, as the expression goes, of a hundred 'chimneys,' but that count was generous." (p. 26)

Most of its inhabitants in 1990 were not born in Jadowia. Our narrator, the farmer Leszek Maleszewski, is exceptional in that he and his father and grandfather, like their ancestors before them, are native to the village. Most of the people, like the local priest and his assistant and the Party boss, had come from elsewhere after the Second World War.

It is generally known that

> There were houses here that were Jewish shops before, whose front shutters had opened once onto counters where fresh loaves were stacked, meat was trimmed, clocks repaired, cloth cut, heels nailed on boots. Few who lived now under these same roofs . . . had lived here before, and the people who once occupied those houses and shops (their doorways now guarded, inside, by a crucifix) left behind no archive nor, so far as we knew, any descendant. (pp. 26-27)

But no one ever talks about the disappearance of 80 percent of the village's pre-war population. We are told that *jadowia* means "venom" or "poison" in Polish. (p. 13) The suggestion is that the name refers perhaps to the snakes prevalent in the area during the Middle Ages, or perhaps to the odour of decay rising from the marshes, but as I worked through the novel I began to think that the venom, the poison, refers to the poison of prejudice that seems to be lodged everywhere in the hearts of humankind, even in the hearts of the best of us.

Close to the village is the beginning of the great forest. It is evoked in the prologue as a place of "brooding, meditating gloom," with oak trees six or seven hundred years old, where the now-powdered bones of remote ancestors are encircled by the roots of ancient trees. Our narrator's grandfather is one of those who feels a unity with the land of his ancestors. "What mattered was the belonging – to a history that attached to a stretch of land . . . to struggles won and lost there; to its silences and its secrets." (p. 82)

At the beginning of the novel, our narrator introduces himself:

> My name is Leszek. Along with my grandfather, who is seventy-four . . . and the ghost of my father, who died of cancer, I am a farmer.

Together, we have twenty-six acres, scattered, in the Polish manner, in six locations, the farthest of them – planted in rye last year – set six miles from the house. We own twelve cows, fourteen pigs, a horse, a tractor, and a newly bought used combine. By local standards, we are reasonably prosperous and on good terms with our neighbors. . . . I am twenty-six years old and in need of a wife. (p. 14)

Leszek's mother is busy looking for a wife for him. On market days in Jadowia and the neighbouring villages she boasts of his virtues, that he can both read and write and doesn't drink. I thought that spoke volumes about the young men of rural Eastern Europe, where functional illiteracy is high and vodka the universal curse.

Many of the characters in the novel are habitual drunkards. One of Leszek's neighbours, Pani Urban, is regularly beaten by her drunken son. She has no husband to protect her since the one she had froze to death, drunk in a ditch. Even the veterinarian, Karol Skalski, is a drunk. He is married to Jola, the local beauty, who is finding comfort in the arms of our narrator, Leszek Maleszewski.

Theirs is a beautiful, idyllic love. They lie together and watch the glories of the sunsets and the beauty of the forest, both exquisitely described by the author. In the conversations between Leszek and Jola I found Charles Powers's delineation of character absolutely superb. We are given all the brutal practicalities of a farmer's daily life, but it is Leszek who has the fantasy of making another life with Jola in a different place. It is Jola, the mother of three children, who understands the demands of reality.

I found Jola so interesting, so perceptive. During one pause in their lovemaking, she tries to explain to Leszek that as a woman she has no choice but to be more practical than a man. She uses as an example a ninety-year-old woman, Pani Slowik, abandoned by her children and living on bread dipped in bacon fat in a broken-down shack at the edge of the village.

Men can live in huts, and they know how to make it okay. If they live like that, it's just that they're eccentric, maybe even crazy, and it's okay. Somehow they take care of themselves. Even if you feel sorry for them, it's different. For a woman, it's pitiful. I look at Pani Slowik, and it's terrifying. (pp. 74-75)

Every woman, Jola says, fears coming to such an end: it's "not a fore-
gone conclusion, just a possibility. A distinct possibility."

As a background to their passionate relationship there is political
turmoil in the village. Jablonski, the Party boss of the village since he
came from Cracow ten years earlier, is fighting for his survival. For ten
years he has ruled his little kingdom with a very simple administrative
structure. He has appointed himself head of the Farmers' Cooperative
and installed his puppet Zbigniew Farby as *naczelnik*, or mayor. The
village constable is the obedient and simple-minded Krupik. Jablonski
also has a network of errand boys and informers, notably the local
plumber, Andrzej.

Once, long before, Jablonski had believed in socialism, but that day is
long gone.

> The system, what was it anymore? He had a clean, clear conception
> of it once, but that seemed to have gotten lost in the day-to-day busi-
> ness of nursing it along, adjusting to the endless crises its managers
> inflicted upon it. For years it had been like a broken-down car, its last
> miles wrung out, worked over by incompetent mechanics. (p. 48)

What a marvellous simile for the last years of communism.

We learn how this great, lumbering political system had functioned,
particularly at the local level. The party bosses, people like Jablonski,
would meet in smoky back rooms, surrounded by whores and sweating
from vodka, and barter at the most primitive level – tractors for cement,
cement for bricks, and so on. The system only worked at all because the
local bosses had taken unto themselves the right of petty theft. And then
there were the obligatory speeches, full of Marxist gobbledygook.

> ". . . Luxemburgism," "adventurism," "utopian thinking," "material-
> ist provocations," each term a sort of shorthand strung together in a
> cryptology of nonsense, half-understood terminology straight from
> the Party's theoretical journal, which probably didn't understand it
> either. (p. 49)

Our narrator tells us the reality of the Communist experiment:

The meat shop sold only hog fat. People lived on cabbage and pota-
toes. We had no money, nor did our neighbors, which meant that
animals had to be sold for cash and not killed for food. Not that the
cash came to much, and, of course, there was nothing to buy with
it. You couldn't locate a bag of cement or a hundred bricks or a
pound of nails. You couldn't find a new milk bucket. When sickness
descended, as sickness always did, there was no medicine to buy
even if you had money for it. Most people couldn't afford a pair of
rubber boots; they traded old sweaters with holes in them for
twenty eggs. (p. 16)

Who in the West could have dreamed that the power of Stalinist Europe,
the Warsaw Pact countries, was built on foundations such as these?
Whether you saw communism as a threat or as the hope of a better world
to come, who could have imagined that the system was so inefficient and
so corrupt? Certainly not I. It is one of the great frustrations of my life that
Ronald Reagan foresaw the collapse of the Evil Empire and I did not. I still
can't believe that he was right and I was wrong.

With Walesa in power in Warsaw, Jablonski is now fighting for his survival, hoping only to avoid prosecution for corruption. He does have a
plan and he is not a stupid man, but he still gives way to moments of self-
pity as his world falls to pieces around him. I found one of these moments
very illuminating.

Yes, he thought, I looked after this benighted shit hole in the middle
of nowhere while a government of spineless compromisers minced
around in Warsaw begging for a chance to kiss George Bush's ass on
satellite TV and inviting the Great Electrician to beat them in an election. And here in Jadowia, while the standers on the street corner
bellyached about the price of bread, and Jew money-lenders in
Washington made sure it kept going up, it was me, Jablonski, who
kept the place running. (p. 101)

Jablonski has transferred the "usual" hatred of Jews in Poland to a
hatred of Jews in the West. The reason is obvious: by 1990 there were virtually no Jews in Poland.

Jablonski feels his power slipping away. He sees new enemies, Twerpicz of the self-appointed Citizens Committee for Reform, and Father Jerzy, the zealous assistant priest of the parish.

Father Jerzy represents that part of the Church that does not want democracy as much as it wants the return of power to the Roman Catholic Church. He wants an end to official atheism and state-subsidized abortion, he wants responsibility for education to be given back to the Church, and he wants a re-establishment of "family values," based on Catholic and anti-Semitic tradition. His is a voice from the past.

> "It is a poor *country*. It is poor because the Communists robbed the people for forty years. Suppressed the church. Encouraged the collapse of the family. Sent Bolshevik Jews and Stalinist tyrants to rule over our lives, to remove religion from the schools." (p. 86)

But apart from the political struggle there is new excitement in the village. Tomek Powierza has been found dead at the edge of the forest. The son of Stanislaw Powierza, Leszek's neighbour and surrogate parent since the death of his father, Tomek had always been a disappointment to his father, a hard-working farmer and an intelligent, practical, decent man. Strong but lazy, Tomek used to flit between Jadowia and Warsaw, only a hundred miles away, always involved in black-market activities – nothing violent but all illegal.

For the reader, there is a second mystery attached to the murder. This mystery concerns the man who found the body, Krzystof Czarnek, who manages the state-owned distillery just outside the village. We already suspect that some of the alcohol is being siphoned off illegally, almost certainly under Jablonski's direction. When Czarnek discovers the body, he doesn't report it. He simply arranges that one of the distillery drivers finds the body and informs the police.

But why doesn't Czarnek report the crime? It can't be that he wants to divert attention from the distillery, since it will be a distillery driver who finds the body. It must be that Czarnek, who lives alone outside the village, wants to divert attention from *himself*. But why? I held the question in my mind as I read on.

Not content with two mysteries, Charles Powers creates a third and a fourth. Some of the houses and barns in the village are vandalized, and the damage is always the same: a foundation stone is taken and, in the case of the houses, the frame of the doorway is ripped away, especially that part of the doorway to which a crucifix has been attached. At the same time, Leszek's grandfather is secretly taking his cart into the forest and hiding long, flat stones under the leaves. The forest is a good place to hide secrets and memories.

The villagers are united in their mystification and they remember what they rarely discuss, that the Jews of the village were rounded up when the Germans came, penned for days like animals in the village square, and then shipped off, starving, to nearby Treblinka. Are the Jews coming back to claim their property? But why would they vandalize first? Perhaps someone is still looking for Jewish gold.

Certainly, in spite of the fact that there are no Jews in the village – and few in Poland – the old stereotypes have persisted. High school students out for a lark will still deface walls with "Jews to the gas." Even Stanislaw Powierza, an essentially good man, can on occasion come out with an obscene remark. When he and Leszek buy a flashlight in a nearby town, he tells Leszek he knows the vendor is a Jew because "I saw his tattoo. And he overcharged us." (p. 310)

Leszek's grandfather had already tried to explain Polish anti-Semitism to a wondering Leszek:

"They made demons out of the Jews, for their own reasons. Poles like to believe in demons and fairy tales. Demons are best. It makes them feel better. Gives them an excuse."

"For what?"

"For complaining. For surviving and not earning enough of the world's sympathy. For not being appreciated as victims. They feel like they got cheated out of it. The Poles are still here. The Jews aren't . . . there are things people don't want to remember. . . . Moving into their houses. Burning down their temples. Stealing the stones off their graves and using them to build houses, barns." (p. 183)

This last from a man who we know has been hiding long, flat stones in the forest. The mystery deepens!

Leszek's grandfather is a reflective man, but even he shares in the universal Polish hatred of the Russians, a hatred reflected in his favourite joke:

"If you were in a foxhole and you were being attacked on one side by Germans and on the other by Russians, which would you shoot first? 'The Germans,' he would say. 'Business before pleasure.'" (p. 107)

No one appears interested in finding out who killed Stanislaw's son, Tomek. The village constable is an idiot, serving only Jablonski, and the authorities see the murder as just one more example of the lawlessness sweeping across the whole of Eastern Europe.

I found that so interesting. After the fall of any dictatorship, whether it be of the left or right, there seems inevitably to be a dramatic increase in crime. I am thinking not only of Poland and Russia but of post-Franco Spain and post-apartheid South Africa. It is so much easier to suppress crime in a dictatorship with a ruthless police force and compliant courts than in a democracy where the police are bound by the rule of law and the rights of the accused. It seems odd that the price of democracy is a high crime rate.

Tomek's father, Stanislaw "Stashek" Powierza, the village priest, Father Tadeusz, and Leszek, our narrator, all realize there will be no serious murder investigation, so they undertake it themselves. Their inquiries will take them everywhere, and into the lives of everyone in the village, uncovering secrets not connected to the crime, secrets that the people concerned had thought were long buried in the silence of the forest.

As part of the investigation, while trying to retrace his friend Tomek's last movements, Leszek goes to Warsaw. He had spent eighteen months there previously but had been revolted by the city and had come back to Jadowia. Through Leszek's eyes we see the drabness of the workers' districts, endless, grey concrete blocks put up after the war to ring the city and offer workers' families cheap accommodation. Faceless places without character or humanity. We also see the great open-air markets, black markets. Socialist central control has broken down and Poles are fighting with Russians for vending space in the free-for-all. In 1990, Russian criminals are already moving in. Leszek meets two Russian smugglers, Yuri and Valentin, associates of Jablonski, but makes little progress and returns to the village where the move to unseat Jablonski has gained momentum.

Jablonski's puppet, Farby, begins to fear that Jablonski will offer him up as a scapegoat. He is a married man, but in his panic declares his long-hidden passion to his secretary, Zofia, and disappears with her to a hut in the forest, where they will make love and dream their dream. Their fantasy is of a little bourgeois heaven, a little chocolate shop. Marx and Lenin must be spinning in their graves.

It's strange how many people in the novel escape into fantasy. Dreaming must be one of the few refuges for those who have lived for years in a planned economy. Father Jerzy dreams of an officially Catholic Poland and an end to "Jewish Bolshevism." Leszek dreams of a new life with Jola. Even Yuri and Valentin dream of a little restaurant in Brooklyn, safe in the bosom of the Russian Mafia.

Jablonski dreams only of getting safely out of his current mess. He has one secret weapon, his box of secrets. They are the files he and his predecessor put together through their spies and informers.

And so Jablonski begins his self-protective blackmail. He tells Leszek that Leszek's late father, Mariusz, was an informer for the authorities, that he had spied on his friends and had even reported his neighbour Stashek Powierza for illegally cutting firewood. Jablonski's price for his silence is that Leszek give up looking into Tomek's death. Jablonski's threat becomes pointless as Leszek discovers that all the neighbours, including Stashek, *knew* his father was an informer; before his death, he had confessed. The odd thing is that no neighbour sought revenge. They neither forgot nor forgave the wrong done them. They simply accepted the imperfection, the human frailty, of their neighbour. The only way for the village to continue was to accept the past and move into a possibly better future. It was at this point that I began to glimpse what might be the real theme of the novel.

Jablonski is equally unsuccessful with Father Jerzy. He has files to show that the former priest of the village had cooperated with the Communist authorities. But Father Jerzy's attitude is that Jablonski publish and be damned. Let corruption be rooted out wherever it may be. The senior priest, more pragmatic than his zealous assistant, sees no point in raking up hurtful scandal, intercedes with the Bishop, and has Father Jerzy transferred to a far-off orphanage where his zeal can do less harm. Jablonski is thwarted; his files will not save him.

Our attention turns to another character. Indeed, he will take over the narration of much of the rest of the novel. Krzystof Czarnek, the distillery manager, is a solitary man who does not want attention drawn to himself. As he tells his story, we learn that the village of Jadowia has a secret Jew. In 1939, Czarnek was a little Jewish boy called Chaim. He and his parents and his three siblings were among those Jews rounded up and penned in the village square. Some of the Polish peasants helped the trapped Jews with food while others exploited them, selling food to them at extortionate prices. Some of the peasants approved of what the Germans were doing, others watched in silence.

Chaim slipped under the fence, and with Grandfather Maleszewski's assistance he was taken in by a local woman who had just lost a child. Chaim became Krzystof Czarnek, the son of Danuta, who warned him never to reveal his Jewish identity.

This was a good woman who was risking her life to save a Jewish child, and yet – and yet – in a paradox that is central to the novel's theme, she fed him the same intellectual poison that she had been fed by both religious and secular authority over the years. She asserted the authenticity of that Czarist forgery, the *Protocols of the Elders of Zion*, absolute proof in her eyes of the Jewish conspiracy to take over the world. She reminded me of Stashek Powierza, a good man capable of an anti-Semitic slur.

Czarnek has lived in torment for fifty years, knowing that he alone survived and believing that the rest of his family were gassed by the Germans.

Now the narrative voices change again and we find that Czarnek is not the only inhabitant of Jadowia to have endured fifty years of mental anguish. Leszek's grandfather will tell of his nightmare.

After the fall of Poland in 1939, he had become Captain Maleszewski of the Polish Home Army, known as the "Raven." He was there when the Jews were rounded up, and it was he who had organized the escape of the rest of Chaim's family. It was he who took them to the great field they had to cross at night to gain the safety of the forest. It was he who realized that there were German soldiers all around the field. It was he who understood that the only way to save the Resistance unit at his side was to divert the Germans' attention. It was he who shouted "*Achtung! Achtung!*" and directed his flashlight on the family halfway across the field. He effected the escape of his own men, but it was at the price of five Jewish lives.

He has lived with that horror for half a century and now he wants to make a memorial, a shrine, to the five Jews he caused to be martyred. To this end he has taken five tombstones from the old Jewish cemetery. These were the long, flat stones he had hidden in the forest. He cannot read Hebrew but he knows they are Jewish tombstones and they are the best he can do.

But this does not explain the vandalism of the houses and barns. To understand that, we must listen now, once again, to the voice of Czarnek. It turns out it is he who has been taking the foundation stones from the village buildings. The stones are in fact Jewish tombstones stolen and used as building material. Czarnek has been restoring them to the old Jewish cemetery and destroying the doorways of houses to reveal where the *mezuzahs* once were. We have already met one other Jew in the narrative, the vendor of the flashlight, the survivor of the camps. When Leszek hurried back to speak to him, the first Jew Leszek had ever met, anxious to understand what it meant to be a Jew in Poland, the old man told him, "'I am not a congregation of one. . . . We all breathe the air that's in front of our faces.'" (p. 309) If he were the protagonist of the novel, he would be the perfect satiric hero, coming to terms with the hostile world around him, making the compromises necessary for survival, refusing to stand alone against a hostile Polish world. He was a mirror image of Czarnek. Until now.

Now Czarnek will abandon the satiric and adopt the tragic stance, refusing to accept the world on the terms on which it is available to him, terms he has accepted for fifty years. Out of the copper coils of the distillery he fashions a great menorah that he erects in the old Jewish cemetery. Then he retires to his quarters in the distillery after uncovering the vats to release their toxic fumes. He pronounces the *Shema*, the great Jewish prayer that affirms the oneness of God, and settles down to wait for death. He has declared himself a believing Jew, and now, by gassing himself, he declares himself one with the family he believes was gassed at Treblinka.

The villagers wake the next morning to two startling new phenomena – Czarnek's illuminated menorah in the old Jewish cemetery and Grandfather Maleszewski's new shrine, built around five Jewish tombstones.

Charles Powers will now tie up the loose ends of all his mysteries. Jola decides to leave Jadowia with her husband and children to make a new start elsewhere. Stashek and Leszek catch Jablonski red-handed in arms-smuggling, and Jablonski's Russian associates reveal that Tomek was killed by Georgian smugglers, long since disappeared, just for the money on his person. What I found remarkable was that I didn't care. And I am certain that Charles Powers meant me not to care. The mysteries of Czarnek and the tombstones had long since monopolized my attention, and the author had responded perfectly to this by switching the narrative voice to Czarnek and Leszek's grandfather.

Jablonski will flee to Cracow to begin a new life of crime, his files will be burned, and his spies, like Andrzej the plumber, will be busy currying favour with the reform administration.

After a dramatic dash to Warsaw, Leszek reaches Jola in time to speak to her at the train station before she leaves. They make their goodbyes in a scene strongly reminiscent of the immortal airport scene in *Casablanca*, except that there is a reversal. It is Jola, the woman, who decides that duty must come before love. All that is missing is a declaration by Jola that "We will always have the forest."

Leszek will meet a nice schoolteacher from a neighbouring village and persuade himself that his father only turned spy for Jablonski in return for Jablonski's appointment of the secret Jew to the management of the distillery. So do we all manage our history to make it easier to live with.

Farby, Jablonski's puppet for ten years, will marry Zofia, his wife having left him in disgust, and they will realize their little middle-class dream. It is, I think, Charles Powers's gentle way of reminding us that there is little justice in the outcome of human affairs.

But the real conclusion to the novel is the sermon preached to his parishioners by Father Tadeusz after he has buried Czarnek in the old Jewish cemetery. Father Tadeusz has grown enormously in wisdom and understanding since he came to Jadowia two years before our novel began, filled with resentment at being transferred to a village at the back of nowhere.

"But there is another history," he said. "And there is another ten percent." The pitch and volume of his voice rose.

"A tenth of our population, people who used to live and work and walk among us. You know who I mean.

"They are gone now, and this is history, too.

"But it is also a sorrow. And it is this history and this sorrow which we have a harder time acknowledging. . . .

"For too many of us, what happened to those people was not a sorrow. It was a horror, but not a sorrow. Do you see that there is a difference?" . . .

"Our own, and *them*. Ours are Poles. *They* are Jews. We mourn for our own, as we should and must. Widows grieve for husbands, mothers for their sons. We have our own grief to suffer, to occupy us, and so it equates with theirs. They are canceled out." . . .

"We left their graves untended, forgotten, while looking after those of 'our own.'" (pp. 371-72)

Father Tadeusz does not ask that his parishioners seek forgiveness for any sins or crimes, whether of commission or omission. All he asks is that his people remember that there was once "another people" in their midst and that "their memory should be honoured." (p. 376)

His sermon appears to have had very little effect, except for an abusive missive addressed to "The Rabbi of Jadowia." (p. 377) His sermon "had released no outpouring of sorrow for the Jews. Father Tadeusz had not really expected that." (p. 376) Even Stashek Powierza, who had promised Father Tadeusz that he would look after the old Jewish cemetery, asks the priest not to bruit the news around, as "he didn't want to become known in the village as 'a lover of Jews.'" (p. 376)

The last lines of the novel, dealing with Leszek and his fiancée, seem anticlimactic. "I have grown to love her" (p. 384) is far from the passion Leszek knew with Jola.

A disappointing ending? Perhaps. Yet someone must have listened to Father Tadeusz or someone very like him. While there is still residual anti-Semitism in Poland (Lech Walesa always found it necessary to assert that he was of "pure Polish descent" and the same claim by others is still common), let us look at the positives.

Since January 1999, Holocaust denial has been a crime in Poland. In January 2000, the Roman Catholic Church in Poland marked its third Annual Day of Judaism with inter-faith dialogues in all the major cities.

The present foreign minister of Poland, Mr. Geremek, is a Jew. He and his mother were rescued by Polish Catholics who sheltered them throughout the war and are among the thousands of Poles honoured as Righteous Gentiles at Yad Vashem.

Of course there are still anti-Semitic Polish voices – Archbishop Jozef Glemp is a repeat offender – but there are other, powerful Polish voices. When the leader of the Polish American Congress made an allegedly anti-Semitic remark in 1999, thirty-nine prominent Polish-American church leaders and intellectuals took out full-page newspaper advertisements denouncing the remark and set up a rival, *inclusive* organization.

Finally, we have the statement made by Pope John Paul II at Yad Vashem on March 12, 2000:

I assure the Jewish people that the Catholic Church . . . is deeply saddened by the hatred, acts of persecution and displays of anti-semitism directed against the Jews by Christians at any time and in any place.

It is good that the pope said Christians and not just Catholics. We should not forget the special contribution to inter-faith made by the founder of the Protestant movement, Martin Luther, in his 1543 treatise "On the Jews and their Lies."

I was going to finish by indicating my admiration for Charles Powers in weaving together so many narrative strands, in conjuring up the beauty of the Polish forest and the drabness of the Polish capital, and especially in evoking the whole paradoxical complexity of Polish history.

But I thought it would be more fitting to end with a summary of one of the last sermons of Duncan Runcie, the late Archbishop of Canterbury. He spoke of how easy it was to continue ancient hatreds, how easy it was to seek revenge for real wrongs committed against us. But if there is to be any hope for the future and for our children, we must, without forgetting the past, stop seeing people as stereotypes. There must be no more generalizing, no more attribution of guilt or negative qualities to whole peoples. The Archbishop said that this requires a basic change in the attitudes of all of us. I cannot do better than to end with the Archbishop's final words: "And let that change begin with me."

BARNEY'S VERSION

Mordecai Richler

(Toronto: Vintage, 1998)

Mordecai Richler has often said that he sees his function as a writer as being an honest witness to time and place. In most of his ten novels, Richler has tried to bear honest witness to the Montreal he knew as a child, to that remarkable, close-knit, Jewish immigrant community that lay in a clearly defined area of about two square kilometres at the eastern foot of Mount Royal, hemmed in by the homogeneous French Catholic culture to the east and a white Anglo-Saxon Protestant culture to the west.

It was a community of fairly recent arrivals. At the beginning of the twentieth century, there were only seven thousand Jews in Montreal. By 1926, there were fifty thousand. By the time I arrived from London in 1964, the figure had grown to more than one hundred thousand, many of whom had prospered and moved to more desirable areas.

When Richler was born in 1931, the new Jewish immigrants were full of dreams of a better world for themselves, their community, and their children. Critics have sometimes accused Richler of creating characters larger than life. Not so – the people *were* larger than life. There will never be a generation like that again. Pent up by years of oppression in Eastern Europe, all their energies and aspirations burst forth in Montreal. No community will ever again produce so many writers, artists, sculptors, lawyers, judges, philosophers, political leaders, doctors, and business giants as did that *shtetl* at the bottom of Fletcher's Field.

Obviously, not all the creative energy would be channelled positively, and there were the confidence tricksters like Boogie Moscovitch of the latest novel, or the criminals like Jerry Dingleman of *The Apprenticeship of Duddy Kravitz*, or the immortal Duddy himself, who makes several delightful appearances in *Barney's Version*.

Montreal between the two world wars makes for a fascinating study. In 1988 I wrote the biography of a Russian Expressionist painter, Alexander Bercovitch, who came to Montreal's Jewish community in 1926 and died there in 1951. I spent two years researching both Bercovitch and the community. But more than that, I met and married Pearl Brownstein nearly thirty years ago. My wife is an exact contemporary of Richler. They graduated in the same year from Baron Byng High, the same school that Mordecai Richler immortalized as Fletcher's Field High. They grew up on the same crowded streets, and Pearl has given me innumerable and highly detailed tours of the area.

"My Auntie Annie lived on the ground floor of that triplex; my Auntie Minnie lived on the middle floor of that one over there; and just here there was a *khaleria* [terrible woman] who didn't like children." It was a close and loving family. Pearl's mother, Rose Brownstein, looked after her aging parents in her home and never lived more than a few minutes' walk from her sisters.

Many Jewish families, in order to give the children fresh air, would rent farmers' cottages in Shawbridge and Prévost in the nearby Laurentian mountains. Several families, often related by marriage, would sometimes club together and share the same cottage. On at least one occasion, my wife's family and the Richlers rented back-to-back cottages and shared the same outhouse.

When I married Pearl I was received into a large extended family, and when the cousins meet they love to talk about how it used to be. I have heard the reminiscences so often that I have come to believe I was there. Who can forget Bishinsky's and Hammerman's and Plage Laval?

That was the community, vibrant and exciting, to which Richler bears witness and into which he and his great protagonists, Noah Adler, Joshua Shapiro, and now Barney Panofsky were born. I tried to do it justice in my biography of Bercovitch:

     . . . families spilled out of the overcrowded homes on to the sidewalks. Women called out to each other from their balconies, and shoppers and gossipers filled the stores and the markets. Peddlers and fruit-sellers and icemen cried their wares and bargained with the mothers, careful with their pennies. The grassless streets bulged with horses and wagons and trucks and streetcars and racing, shrieking children and the whole noise of humanity at work and play. Only on Saturdays did mothers put families into their finery to take the fresh air on the promenade at the foot of Fletcher's Field. (p. 37)

This was Richler's world, but his family wasn't as happy as the others and their house was full of tension. His mother despised her husband, and his maternal grandfather, a Hasidic rabbi, beat Mordecai regularly with a leather belt for minor infractions of religious law. His parents finally divorced when Mordecai was thirteen. He didn't get much comfort from his paternal grandfather either; the man considered Mordecai such a failure as a Jew that he left instructions that Mordecai wasn't to touch his coffin when he died.

It really must have been a dreadful life for Richler in his teens. He loved his father but for years was estranged even from him after Mordecai declared himself an atheist. There was a later reconciliation with his father, but with his mother there was no tenderness and they didn't speak for decades.

After squeaking through high school and dropping out of Sir George Williams College, now Concordia University, Richler decided to go to Paris. Home life offered him nothing and Richler believed that Canada at the time was no place for an aspiring writer.

In 1950, at the age of nineteen, Richler left for Europe. He spent four years in Paris and then eighteen more in London. After a failed first marriage, he met and married Florence Wood, like himself a Montreal expatriate. Florence is now his friend, the mother of their five children, his editor, his critic, and the only person to read his work before its submission for publication.

Richler did not come easily to the subject he would finally make his own, Jewish Montreal. His first two novels were far too influenced by Céline, Malraux, and Hemingway. Even in his first Montreal novel, *Son of a Smaller Hero* (1955), he had not yet found his authentic voice. That came in 1959 with *The Apprenticeship of Duddy Kravitz*. Since then, Richler has won two Governor General's Awards, the Giller Prize for *Barney's Version*, and has twice been nominated for the Booker Prize.

Beginning with *Duddy Kravitz*, all his novels are informed by the same perfect ear for comic dialogue and have wonderfully funny set pieces and a host of marvellous secondary characters. And, most important, all his novels are driven by character rather than plot. That is particularly true of *Barney's Version*, in which the mystery runs a very poor second to the revelation of character.

I know that Richler arouses controversy, especially in Montreal, but you have to love a man who, after Jacques Parizeau's infamous claim that "money and the ethnic vote" cost the separatists the 1995 referendum on Quebec's future, would establish an annual award for the best fiction by a Quebec ethnic writer and call it the Prix Parizeau.

Let us now meet Richler's newest hero, the sixty-seven-year-old Barney Panofsky. His medical problems are becoming acute. He has an enlarged prostate and has already had a hip replacement. Worst of all, he is becoming forgetful and is terrified that he is entering an Alzheimer's twilight. While his failing memory still holds, he is anxious to set down, as he calls it, "the true story of my wasted life." (p. 1) He has three compelling reasons to write his version of events.

First, there is a book coming out by his old nemesis, Terry McIver, which he knows will label him a cuckold, an adulterer, a sycophant, and possibly a murderer. Not only must he match McIver's version with his own, he is desperate to redeem himself in the eyes of his beloved third wife, Miriam, and their children.

Second, Barney is still not sure what happened when his friend Boogie Moscovitch disappeared thirty-five years earlier in 1960. No body was ever found, but Barney was tried – and acquitted – for the murder.

Third, Barney has come to a depressing conclusion: "Life was absurd and nobody ever truly understood anybody else." (p. 417) Working on a memoir is a last great struggle against that conclusion, a last attempt to make sense of his life.

I also have the feeling as I read Barney's story that it is an elegy for loss. He is witness now to his own final decay, made all the more poignant when he remembers the dreams of his youth. How did he go from adolescent dreamer who read poetry aloud in bed to cynical producer of mindless TV? How did we all come to be what we are today? All Barney can do is say goodbye to his life and his lost loves as he rages against the dying of the light.

As Barney reviews his life, he will jump around a little in his chronology. It is sometimes confusing, but I found that it added authenticity. This is a sick, aging man who is trying desperately to put it all together. The liberties with time apart, the novel has a very traditional structure. It should surprise no one to hear that Jane Austen is Richler's most admired writer. *Barney's Version* is a perfect satire in the purest sense of satire; it is the study of an imperfect protagonist moving through an imperfect world. We are witness to all the compromises the protagonist makes with that imperfect world. There are no great tragic challenges to the order of things, and at the end of the novel nothing has really changed. The dominant feeling in all satire is one of sadness, even of rage, that the protagonist is no better than he is and that the world is no better than it is.

Satire is about the weaknesses and the foibles of the human race. The interest of satire is therefore always in character rather than plot. The great question posed by the narrative, whether or not Barney killed his friend, is answered very neatly and very surprisingly at the end of the novel, but the reader has long since become much more interested in the essence of Barney Panofsky.

The first aim of any novel is to create a whole, complex person who never existed before. Richler's gift is that he can create not only one main memorable character but also, like Dickens, a whole world of fully fleshed-out secondary characters.

One word of caution before we dissect Barney Panofsky. Our only material is that made available to us by Barney himself, and we must remember that Barney is a born storyteller. He is fond of "fine-tuning reality. . . . Dining out on a story, I tend to put a spin on it. To come clean, I'm a natural-born burnisher." (pp. 233-34)

I have the same problem. My wife calls what I do either exaggeration or wilful distortion, depending on the generosity of her mood. I prefer to describe it as my gift for effective narrative.

Given that Barney is prone to embellishing the past, given that his memory is often confused, and that all of us have a basically unreliable sense of ourselves, we would do well to be very, very careful as we read Barney's version of his past.

Barney was born in 1928 in the heart of Jewish Montreal. If his grandfather had had twenty-five more dollars, Barney would have been born in

New York. The story is one of Richler's many delightful and very funny digressions.

> I was born Canadian, I explained, because my grandfather, a ritual slaughterer, was short two sawbucks and a fin. It was 1902 when Moishe and Malka Panofsky, newly wed, went to be interviewed by Simcha Debrofsky of the Jewish Immigrant Aid Society in Budapest. "We want the papers for New York," said my grandfather.
> ". . . If it's the *goldene medina* you want, Panofsky, it costs fifty dollars American cash on the table."
> "Fifty dollars we haven't got, Mr. Debrofsky."
> "No kidding? Well, I'll tell you what. I'm running a special here today. For twenty-five dollars I can get you both into Canada." (p. 47)

Malka and Moishe Panofsky came to Montreal, where in the fullness of time they begat Izzy, Barney's father, who, as he grows up, dreams of becoming an RCMP officer. But he's too short. He's even refused by the Montreal police force until Jerry Dingleman, the leader of Montreal's Jewish mafia, whom we met in *Duddy Kravitz*, advises clipping a hundred dollar bill to his application. Izzy is accepted and eventually rises to the rank of Detective-Inspector. According to *Barney's Version*, Izzy is not only Montreal's first Jewish policeman, he is Montreal's only *honest* policeman. It isn't that Izzy doesn't want to be as corrupt as the next man, it's that he feels he carries upon his shoulders the reputation of the whole Jewish people. As he explains to his son,

> "[A]t the police school, where I was taught jujitsu and wrassling, the goys were always testing me. Irish *shikers* and French-Canadian *chazerim*. Dummies. Ignorantuses. I mean like I had at least finished seventh grade and was never held back, not once. . . . I had to be straight, Barney, I mean my name was Panofsky." (pp. 49-50)

Izzy Panofsky is a wonderful creation, Richler's best secondary character since Reuben Shapiro. Richler is superb at creating full-blooded characters with an appetite for life.

Izzy is at the centre of one of my favourite set pieces in the novel, the wedding of Barney and The Second Mrs. Barney Panofsky, the daughter of a wealthy Jew aching to be accepted by Montreal's gentile upper crust. Izzy is at the head table, regaling the rabbi and his future in-laws with stories of the brothels of Montreal's glory days: " 'Rabbi, you could eat off the floor. And, oh, they had beautiful beds and everything was systematically . . . you know what I mean? . . . You get a big pitcher in the room and as soon as you'd come in they wash it for you.' " (p. 210)

Ignoring the rapid departure from the table of the rabbi's wife, "grudgingly" followed by two other women, Izzy warms to his theme and hails a fellow guest: " 'Hey, Doc, didn't you say your name was Mendelsohn? . . . Shmul Mendelsohn. We used to call him "Grabby," because, well, do I have to draw you a map? . . . The peddler. Was he your old man?' " (p. 210)

Finally, Barney is able to get his father away from the head table and over to the bar. Izzy is in great spirits.

> "I thought they'd be all snobby here, but they're very friendly, it turns
> out. Boy, am I ever having a good time. What are you laughing at?"
> "Come here," I said, and I gave Izzy a hug. (p. 211)

First, I defy anyone to read that scene without laughing. Second, I confess to loving Barney at that moment. Compared to the *nouveau goniffs* at the head table, Izzy is such a joy, and I am thrilled that Barney is not ashamed of his father.

I was very sorry when Izzy died. He died as he had lived, on a massage parlour table, shortly after ejaculation. I rejoiced again in Barney when he described how he visited his father's grave in "the Chevra Kadisha cemetery and, as I do every year, emptied a bottle of Crown Royal rye whisky over his grave and, in lieu of a pebble, left a medium-fat smoked meat on rye and a sour pickle on his gravestone." (p. 46) We should all be so lovingly remembered!

In spite of having and loving such an exceptional father, Barney always felt something was missing in his childhood. Izzy was rarely home and Barney's mother was drifting into madness. She'd always been eccentric – Barney discovered later that she'd named him after a cartoon character. Barney only just managed to complete high school, but he was a voracious reader and dreamed of living a richer cultural life. Playing pool with Duddy Kravitz just wasn't enough.

Where else but Paris? But his two years in the French capital and its expatriate community are a great disappointment. As Barney says later,

> I've never known a writer or a painter anywhere who wasn't a self-promoter, a braggart, and a paid liar of a coward, driven by avarice and desperate for fame . . . I had lit out for the cultural territories, going to Paris, hoping to be enriched by associating with the pure of heart . . . and came home determined not to have anything to do with writers or painters again. (pp. 184-85)

Both Richler and his creation Barney went to Paris in 1950, and in the passion of Barney's denunciation I hear not only Barney's voice but Richler's. Over and over again, Barney rages against those whom the world calls great: Lillian Hellman was a liar; Picasso was a collaborator; Lewis Carroll was a pedophile; Frank Harris died a virgin; and Robert Frost was one mean son of a bitch. (p. 185) As Barney puts it, "every biography of one of the truly great proves that he or she was an absolute shit." This is the anger of both Barney *and* Richler, both of whom want to believe in the goodness of humanity only to have repeated proof of its imperfections.

What really drove Barney (and Richler) to distraction was the pretentious writer, self-consciously aware of his duty to posterity. And no one was more pretentious and pompous in that Paris crowd of the early fifties than Terry McIver. Like Barney, an expatriate Montrealer going through his Paris period, McIver, a would-be writer, already has his eye on history. His daily journals are already numbered to make things easier for his biographer. Terry McIver is being subsidized by parents who are too good for him, notably his father, who owns a left-wing bookshop on Ste. Catherine Street and who is constantly robbed by the very students whom he longs to convert. Barney sees McIver Senior as the most admirable of men, but all Terry McIver can do is mock his father for his idealism and for the grammatical errors in his letters. This thoroughly self-centred and self-serving person will go from spoiled son to successful, *subsidized* Canadian writer, assisted, as Barney says, by "mediocrity's holy trinity: the Canada Council, the Ontario Arts Council, and the City of Toronto Arts Council." (p. 97)

Some of the Paris expatriates were a lot more fun than Terry McIver. Leo Bishinsky, for example. Leo throws paint onto a canvas with a mop and invites a fascinated Barney to join in. " 'Really?' " says Barney. " 'Why not?'" says Leo. At sixty-seven, Barney wonders how many of Leo's masterpieces in the Tate and the Guggenheim are in fact original Panofskys. One of his works, he knows, is the proudest possession of a Canadian senator living in Montreal.

But best of all, in Barney's eyes, there was Boogie Moscovitch. In Paris on the GI Bill, he was a heroin addict, a lecher, a brilliant talker, and the author of just eight short stories. Barney adored him. He and Barney were inseparable. But what was their relationship? Was it one of friendship, one of equals? It's what Barney has always wanted to think, but McIver, Barney's sworn enemy, has always suggested that Barney was Boogie's sycophant, that Boogie saw Barney as no more than a kind of Man Friday. Barney, on the other hand, records McIver as being merely on the periphery of the expatriate circle. We don't like Terry McIver, although we only have Barney's heavily biased description to go on, but it doesn't mean that he never told the truth. The fact is that we can't be sure of what the relationship was between Barney and Boogie, and that uncertainty is one of the many delights of the novel. We can no more know the truth in the novel than we can in life itself.

And then there was Hymie Mintzbaum. At forty, he was older than Barney, Boogie, Leo, and the others. He was a loud, vulgar, name-dropping, old-style Hollywood movie producer, in Paris because of the Hollywood blacklist, but Barney is careful to note that he had a distinguished war record and supports without complaint an incredibly undeserving family, including worthless sons and a *schlemiel* of a brother-in-law. He and Barney have a lifelong love-hate relationship that barely survives their making a film together. What is interesting is what their relationship reveals of Barney's personality. With Barney well into his sixties and Hymie, a stroke victim, much older, they have a reconciliation dinner. It's another of Richler's great set pieces.

The waiter, following the orders of Hymie's granddaughter, is serving Hymie designer water and steamed vegetables and condescends to the dribbling old man – "'You're being naughty, Mr. Mintzbaum.'" (p. 231) Infuriated, Barney changes the order to roast brisket, latkes, horseradish, and Scotch on the side. Hymie, inarticulate because of his stroke, rocks with delight.

I loved Barney for the dignity he accorded the old man, and it reminded me of how he had treated his own father at the wedding to The Second

Mrs. Panofsky. Later, when Barney begins his descent into Alzheimer's, he will receive an unsigned, laboriously pencilled note from California, "Hang in old friend." (p. 414) Barney "read it and wept copiously." Such is the power of friendship.

When Barney was a young man in Paris he maintained himself by working for a shady import-export business, but never handling, in one of Richler's deliciously chosen catalogues, "arms, drugs or health food." It was then that he met his first wife, Clara. She announced herself as Clara Chambers, daughter of the senior partner at John Foster Dulles's old law firm. She is the quintessential old-money gentile, and Barney, the grand-child of immigrants, finds her irresistible. She has a filthy mouth and it is she who supplies Boogie Moscovitch with all the best ideas for the porno-graphic novels he is churning out for Maurice Girodias's Olympia Press. (I remember the Olympia Press publications, small green-covered paper-backs, brought into South Wales by sailors who disembarked at Cardiff and much sought-after by the fifth form at Bridgend County Grammar School for Boys.)

Yet Clara is strangely cold to Barney, always demanding that he wash before sex yet never offering the personal service with a pitcher that Izzy Panofsky had so valued. Barney doesn't discover until later that she is giving sexual pleasure to everyone in Paris except him. When she gives birth to a black child, the marriage seems over. Clara, clearly unbalanced, arranges a reconciliation dinner and a simultaneous suicide attempt. But Barney doesn't get the dinner invitation and consequently doesn't arrive to save her. And so the first Mrs. Panofsky leaves the stage. A mediocre painter and writer, she will become an icon of the feminist movement, which will at the same time demonize Barney. (I take it that we are all now thinking of Ted Hughes and Sylvia Plath.)

Now we meet Clara's father, no old-money lawyer but Cantor Charnofsky from Brighton Beach. What are we to make of the late Clara, who told Barney so often that her mother would suffer a stroke if she knew her daughter was sleeping with a Jew?

Describing his daughter's tempestuous youth, the cantor tells how he sent his twelve-year-old daughter to a doctor because of her premenstrual pain. When the child returned, she tells her father, "'He felt up my tits.'" (p. 150)

The cantor's reaction is to have his wife hold their daughter down while he washes out her mouth with soap and water. Then he arranges force-feeding and electroshock therapy. How could a child so slander "an honoured member of our congregation, a big contributor"? (p. 150)

It is a brilliant explanation by Richler of the adult Clara's denial of her father, her name, and her religion. How could we not understand that her hatred of her father, as a cantor the embodiment of her faith, would fester into self-loathing and promiscuity? The cantor, who destroyed his own child, can see no fault in himself; he can only blame Barney for not receiving the dinner invitation. Full of spite and an absence of logic, the cantor curses Barney: " 'Murderer. *Oysvorf. Momzer.* I wish *makkes* on you and your unborn children. Plagues. Deformities.' " (p. 153)

I can recall no other character in all of Richler's fiction who arouses such disgust. There is something terribly personal in Richler's hatred of the religious hypocrite, particularly the religious hypocrite who would hurt a child.

Shaken, not by the cantor's pathetic curse, but by the horror of Clara's history, Barney returns to Montreal, resolving to reform and walk in the way of the righteous. He becomes a TV producer with a money-making serial entitled "McIver of the RCMP." (Barney's revenges are often subtle.) When criticized for the lack of artistic merit in his work, Barney gives the time-honoured nationalist justification, a justification that his detractors are powerless to refute: "We are defining Canada to Canadians." It is Richler's point, not mine, that this meaningless expression has been used for decades to justify the waste of public money on dreadful but Canadian content. It's one of Richler's favourite hobby horses. What saves Barney, in our eyes, is that it is clear he doesn't mean it. (It is, in fact, a very difficult expression to say with a straight face.)

Now a solid Canadian citizen, Barney does all that his community might expect of him. He buys a house in Hampstead, an exclusive suburb only recently willing to accept Jews, and a cottage in the Laurentians. He even becomes a fundraiser for the Combined Jewish Appeal, where he meets the extraordinary Irv Nussbaum, who has perfected the art of collecting money from unwilling donors. In short, Barney is now ready to meet The Second Mrs. Panofsky.

The Second Mrs. Panofsky! It's very easy to laugh at her. The laughter begins at the wedding, with Izzy scandalizing the guests, Boogie Moscovitch snorting cocaine in the washroom, Terry McIver conspicuously making notes on Jewish social customs, and Barney leaving his bride every few minutes to check with the barman on Game Five of the Stanley Cup playoffs. But worst of all in this wedding from hell, Barney falls head-over-heels in love with one of the wedding guests. He leaves the wedding with the enchanting Miriam Greenberg, gets on the train to Toronto with her, and begs her to fly with him to Paris. Refused, he gets off the train at Montreal West and rejoins the wedding party.

Endlessly forgiving, The Second Mrs. P. overlooks his lengthy absence and it is off to Paris for their honeymoon. The indulged child of wealthy parents, she phones her mother every day. ("And why not?" I hear some mothers murmur.) Some of her conversations take up three pages of the novel and are miracles of trivia and banality. Even these both Barney and I could forgive, but every breakfast is a torment for Barney as his bride recounts every detail of the previous night's dreams. Is there anything more boring, more soul-destroying, than being given every detail of someone else's dream?

Yet the villain of the piece is not The Second Mrs. P., it is Barney. As he admits, "I dislike most people I have ever met, but not nearly so much as I am disgusted by the Rt. Dishonourable Barney Panofsky." (p. 166)

It is true that The Second Mrs. P. is a compulsive talker, compulsive shopper, and, later, a compulsive eater, but as Barney admits, she "had sufficient vitality for the two of us, and a comedic flair, or sparkle, all her own. Like that old whore Hymie Mintzbaum of blessed memory, she possessed that quality I most admire in other people – an appetite for life." (p. 191)

Later, after they separate, she will go back to study and to work with disturbed children, who adore her. Barney knows whose fault everything was: "The Second Mrs. Panofsky was not a bad person. Had she not fallen into my hands but instead married a real, rather than a pretend, straight arrow, she would be a model wife and mother today." (p. 192)

What Richler is doing with his portrait of The Second Mrs. Panofsky is attacking stereotyping. At first we are shown a portrait of a spoiled princess. But it's too easy a target, and Richler goes beneath the surface to reveal a kind, witty, socially useful person. Just as Richler shows just *why* Clara was the way she was, so he shows us what lies behind the facade of The Second Mrs. Panofsky. I find in this, Richler's tenth novel, a greater depth in his portrayal of women than in any of his earlier work.

Why is she always called The Second Mrs. Panofsky? I am sure that it is not because she is just a type, but rather because she is an individual and Barney has hurt her unfairly. Neither Barney nor Richler wish to hurt her further by actually naming her.

The marriage finally comes to an end in 1960, when Boogie Moscovitch turns up after years of travelling. With his great novel still unfinished, he has come to dry out from his heroin habit at Barney's Laurentian cottage. It is clear to us that Barney's vision of Boogie is inaccurate. We see Boogie for what he is, a sponging, spiteful, arrogant, profoundly unlovable person. Bur he still wears the aura of Paris in the fifties and Barney takes him in, only to discover him later in bed with the wickedly neglected Mrs. P.

Distraught, Mrs. P. rushes off to her mother and Boogie and Barney talk things over. There is an amazing lack of animosity – apparently Barney can forgive Boogie anything – and Boogie goes off for a swim to clear his head. According to Barney's version – and remember it is always Barney's version – he falls asleep on the couch, only to be woken up by a low-flying plane. Boogie has disappeared and will never be seen again alive. In the absence of a body, and with a bribed bishop as a character witness, Barney is acquitted, free to woo and win Miriam Greenberg. She accepts him in spite of the cloud that hangs over him, confessing that she had wished he had stayed on the train and flown her away to Paris.

And so begins more than thirty years of married happiness for Barney and Miriam. Clearly inspired by Richler's wife, Florence, Miriam is charming and kind, always finding waifs and strays and persuading Barney to give them jobs in his dreadful TV company. She can also be very, very funny. At one dinner with Barney and his pals, as they mourn the death of a sportswriter friend, she says, "'It must be the first time in twenty years she knew exactly where her husband could be found after ten at night.'" (p. 136)

Certainly she brings out the best in Barney. A part of it is their physical passion for each other. Richler combines that outrageously with humour in one lovely passage.

One memorable afternoon, we did it on my office carpet. Miriam had arrived unexpectedly, coming straight from her obstetrician, pronounced fit, six weeks after she had given birth to Saul. She locked the door, shed her blouse, and stepped out of her skirt. "I was told that this is where you audition actresses." (p. 59)

But of course Barney is his own worst enemy. He cannot share Miriam even with her friends, whom he alienates. Further, he cannot understand why she needs to go back to university, why she wants to go back to radio broadcasting. His love is stifling, overpowering, and she begins to respond to the flattery of one of her protégés, Blair Hopper, a pompous academic and American draft evader who turned up in their lives in 1969. For years, decades, he is there on the sidelines, praising her, admiring her, suggesting she publish.

The marriage would have survived even that if Miriam had not surprised Barney chatting up two young girls in a bar. Desperately hurt, she remembers her own father's womanizing and leaves for a surprise visit to one of their children in London to collect her thoughts. Barney, now in his sixties, defiantly tries to prove that he's still young and sleeps with a thirty-year-old. Afterwards, overcome with self-disgust, he confesses to Miriam, and that is the end of paradise, the end of the marriage. Their children are furious; only their daughter Kate demonstrates compassion for poor, foolish Barney.

Barney is still occasionally his old, boisterous self with a sense of humour, for which we can forgive him much. Or at least I can.

He continues those incredible letters, the letters he has written all his life to puncture the balloons of the pompous and the self-righteous. Among my favourites is the letter seeking support for a Black Hebrew movement in Israel which is trying to develop a gangsta-rap Haggadah. In another, addressed to a feminist foundation, he asks for help in promoting a female heavyweight contender to fight Mike Tyson.

There are dozens of fake letters in the novel, all of them extremely amusing and all of them very like the letters Richler has been sending for decades in real life. Perhaps the best, certainly the most suggestive, is the one he sends to Miriam's lover, Blair Hopper. Addressed to him care of his university faculty board, which means that everyone will see it, it says: "We acknowledge your return of our 1995 TOY BOYS calendar, but cannot send you a refund due to the many stains, and the fact that the August and September pages are stuck together." (p. 14)

But even Barney's humour cannot sustain him. He has lost Miriam and he feels her absence at every moment. There is one deeply moving passage:

I shut my eyes and summoned up Miriam as she appeared at my wedding to The Second Mrs. Panofsky. The most enchanting woman

I had ever seen. Long hair black as a raven's wing. Striking blue eyes to die for. Wearing a blue chiffon cocktail dress, and moving about with the most astonishing grace. Oh that dimple in her cheek. Those bare shoulders. . . . Miriam has been gone for three years now, but I still sleep on my side of the bed and grope for her when I waken. Miriam, Miriam, my heart's desire. (p. 364)

As we move to the end of the novel, it gains in power, in poignancy. As Barney becomes aware of his increasing frailty and mortality, a goodness seems to surge out of him. It had never been far beneath the surface. When he hears that his loyal daughter Kate has been rude to Miriam's lover, he tells her, " 'I won't have any of you taking sides. Blair may be a bit young for your mother, but he makes her happy and that ought to be good enough for the rest of us.' " (p. 131)

When Barney's arch-enemy, Terry McIver, dies of a heart attack on his way to the launching of the very book of which Barney is so afraid, "to my astonishment, I wept hot tears at McIver's funeral. We had once been young and footloose together in Paris, roistering provincials, and looking back, I regret that we never became friends." (p. 378)

When Miriam learns of Barney's decline, she comes to have lunch with him in Montreal. It's a lunch of happy memories; he praises her beauty, he wants her back – and then becomes confused and forgets that she had left him. Next comes the final indignity for this giant of a man, he wets himself. A little later we have the last sentence of the novel proper: "I couldn't remember Miriam's number." Richler's touch is delicate.

In the classic manner of satire, nothing has been resolved. Barney has found no great meaning in his life through his struggle to set it all down, nothing to contradict his belief that life is absurd and no one understands anyone.

Yet there is comfort – for us. Barney is not alone as he slips away into mindlessness. He is attended by his family and by those he befriended.

We realize that this outrageous rogue, so often the architect of his own pain, has been at least in part redeemed by the love and friendship he gave and in turn received.

After Barney enters his twilight, we have an afterword by his son Michael, the son who has footnoted his father's memoir. Some readers have seen great significance in Michael's footnotes, but I see them as a great joke by Richler.

They are, for the most part, conscientious, tedious, and unnecessary. What Richler is doing, surely, is attacking the kind of mediocre, pointless scholarship that Barney saw in the writings of both Terry McIver and Blair Hopper. Neither Barney nor his creator Mordecai Richler have any time for those whom Richler has often called academic drudges.

It is true that Michael picks up on some of his father's lapses – but who cares? The joy is in the smoothness of the narrative, the polishing of the story. What does it matter if Barney remembers the little hotel in the very centre of Paris as the Hôtel de la Cité and not by its correct name, the Hôtel Henri Quatre? (p. 62) (That by the way was an error I caught but Michael missed.)

The real point of Michael's afterword, other than to show how stuffy Barney's son could be, is to solve the mystery of the disappearance of Boogie Moscovitch. We are given two separate facts. In 1996, a survey team discovered Boogie's charred remains surprisingly far from Barney's Laurentian cottage. A little later, Michael, checking through his father's effects at the cottage, sees a plane, a water-bomber, swoop down low on the nearby lake, scoop up water, and fly away.

Suddenly Michael connects the two events. Boogie had been scooped up by the same water-bomber that had woken Barney, only to be dropped, broken, on some forest fire a significant distance away. The irony is that Barney, now an empty shell, can never know the truth. (One of Canada's best-known aeronautical engineers has assured me that a water-bomber cannot scoop up a body, but I am prepared to allow Richler to fine-tune the narrative.)

The mystery is solved, but it is not the mystery that we remember. Rather, it is the portrait of yet another richly drawn Richler rogue, an imperfect hero making his compromises with an imperfect world. As usual, Richler has peopled his novel with fully developed minor characters. Some of them, like McIver Senior or Clara's idealistic brother, Norman, exist not only in their own right but as yardsticks by which we may measure Barney's shortcomings – and our own.

Of course Richler has attacked all his usual targets, especially the Parti Québécois, but I detect a kinder, gentler, more forgiving Richler. I have heard Richler say that inside every fat satirist there is a thin moralist, and certainly he still shows his sorrow and anger that the world is not better than it is, but – and it's a big but – with the exception of the swinish cantor, Richler's people are treated with more compassion than Richler has ever displayed before. It is even more evidence to support my claim that he is by far Canada's greatest living satirist.

CINNAMON GARDENS

by Shyam Selvadurai
(Toronto: McClelland & Stewart, 1999)

Shyam Selvadurai, the author of *Cinnamon Gardens*, was born in Colombo, the capital of Sri Lanka, in 1965.

Like another Sri Lankan expatriate, Michael Ondaatje, Selvadurai now lives in Toronto. I met him in November of 1998. We were both giving readings at the opening of the new Indigo bookstore on Bloor Street in Toronto. I was reading from the poetry of Dylan Thomas and he was reading from his then new novel, *Cinnamon Gardens*. Since I hadn't yet read his new work, I spoke to him about his first novel, *Funny Boy* (1994).

It wasn't really a novel, it was autobiography thinly disguised as fiction. First novels often are. It was about growing up in an upper-middle-class home in Sri Lanka in the seventies and eighties, with all the political turmoil going on, and discovering that you were gay and that your family couldn't understand you. It's a wonderful memoir of the loss of political and sexual innocence.

By the way, those of us who are no longer young will remember Sri Lanka as Ceylon, its name even after independence from the British in 1948, right up until 1972 when it became the Republic of Sri Lanka. Many felt that "Ceylon" was too reminiscent of a colonial past. Since the novel is set in the period 1927-1928, I will use the old name, Ceylon, when discussing the events of the book.

An island just off the southern tip of the Indian subcontinent, Sri Lanka is about two-thirds the size of Newfoundland, with a population of just over

263

eighteen million, two million of whom live in the capital city, the port of Colombo, down on the southwest coast.

That's the country and the city the Selvadurai family left in 1984 when Shyam was nineteen. They came to Toronto and Shyam pursued his studies at York University where he took a B.F.A. in creative writing. He now lives with his partner, Andrew Champion, whom he acknowledges at the end of *Cinnamon Gardens*.

You may be wondering why the Selvadurai family left Sri Lanka in 1984. After all, they were well-off, and Sri Lanka is among the most developed of the Third World nations. The average life expectancy is seventy-two, the literacy rate is a remarkable 92 percent, and unemployment runs at about 11 percent, not much more than Canada's. It has a warm climate, lush vegetation, and beautiful and historic cities. It really isn't a bad place to live. Why leave it?

The answer is simple. The Selvadurais left because their lives were in danger. The riots that had begun in Colombo in 1983 were continuing, and Shyam's father was of the Tamil race.

Why did riots begin in 1983, and why was it dangerous to be a Tamil in Colombo? The answers to those questions lie in the history of Sri Lanka, and once we understand that history we will understand the background of *Cinnamon Gardens*. And so, without further ado, I am going to give a brief potted history of the Republic of Sri Lanka.

At the moment there are two distinct peoples living in Sri Lanka, the Sinhalese and the Tamils. The Sinhalese, 74 percent of the population, were the first to settle the country. They came from the northeast of India about twenty-five hundred years ago. Their language is Sinhala and they are Buddhist.

The Tamils are a 17 percent minority who came over from the south of India in two great waves, the first a spontaneous movement about a thousand years ago and the second as part of the British importing of cheap labour in the nineteenth century. The Tamils are Hindu and their language is Tamil. The remaining 9 percent of the population is made up of people of European descent, usually called Burghers, and a small number of Moslems from India.

From the beginning, the Sinhalese and the Tamils established their own separate little kingdoms all over the island. The main Tamil presence was in the north in the kingdom of Jaffna.

In the sixteenth century the Portuguese invaded and occupied most of the country, both Sinhalese and Tamil. In the seventeenth century the Dutch took over from the Portuguese, and in 1802 the British took over from the Dutch as part of the Napoleonic Wars. In 1815 the British annexed the last little independent Sinhalese kingdom, the kingdom of Kandy, in the centre of the island, and from then on Ceylon was a British colony, ruled by a British governor who was advised by executive and legislative councils. The members of both councils were appointed by the governor, not elected by the Ceylonese.

During more than a century of British rule, a whole class of Ceylonese were educated as doctors, lawyers, and administrators. This upper class, both Sinhalese and Tamil, included also the hereditary aristocracy of both cultures. They were referred to condescendingly by the British as "brown sahibs," and many of them, especially from the Tamil minority, converted to Christianity and took English names to identify more closely with the British. We have an example in *Cinnamon Gardens* in the family of Annalukshmi Kandiah and her mother, née Louisa Barnett. This indigenous upper echelon felt little in common with the hoi polloi on the rubber, cinnamon, and tea plantations.

By the end of the First World War, there was a growing movement both on the Indian mainland and on the island of Ceylon for independence from the British. Imitating their Indian cousins, the nationalists in Ceylon organized the Ceylon National Congress in 1919. Just as Hindus and Moslems united in the call for independence in India, so did the Sinhalese majority and the Tamil minority unite, temporarily, in their demand for self-rule.

The British responded by allowing a limited franchise in 1921, but there was a property and education qualification, which meant that only 4 percent of the population could vote – no women of course – and for only a few of the seats on the legislative council. The rest of the seats, and all the seats of the more powerful executive council, continued to be filled by appointees of the British governor.

The concession did nothing to solve the problem. The Tamils felt underrepresented on both councils. They also realized that if the British ever gave Ceylon independence on the basis of one person-one vote, they would be in danger of being swallowed up by the Sinhalese majority. Accordingly, the Tamils broke away from the Ceylon National Congress and formed their own Tamil Association.

In the 1920s the British were becoming a little more sympathetic to the idea of self-rule in the Empire. Remember that this was the decade that saw two socialist governments elected to Westminster.

In 1927 the British sent an investigative commission to Ceylon to discover how best they could help the colony evolve to independence. Led by Lord Donoughmore, the commission would take evidence for a year – the year during which *Cinnamon Gardens* is set. The Donoughmore Commission will play a very important role in the narrative.

The commission took evidence from the Sinhalese majority and the Tamil minority, as well as from the rich and the hereditary aristocrats, including the Tamil *mudaliyars*. One is the Mudaliyar Navaratnam, the father of Balendran, one of our two protagonists. The Mudaliyar, typical of his class, wants independence, but with no nonsense about enfranchising the poor. He wants government by hereditary aristocrats like himself, together with constitutional guarantees to protect the Tamil minority.

The commission also took evidence from the Ceylon National Congress, who wanted universal franchise because it would empower the Sinhalese majority, and from the labour unions, who wanted universal franchise because it would empower the poor. And the commission took evidence from women, because British women had already been given the vote in 1920.

It is against this background of testimony that the novel takes place. At the end of the novel we are told that the commission recommended universal franchise, to include both sexes, and a cabinet of ten ministers, each in charge of an executive committee. Seven of the ministers would be elected native Ceylonese, with an additional three British ministers to oversee the key areas of defence, external affairs, and banking. All activity would be subject to the veto power of the British governor.

For the period, it was a step forward, and the recommendations were implemented in a new constitution for Ceylon in 1931 – after the end of our novel. But the new constitution contained no guarantees of adequate representation for the Tamil minority, and that omission would have terrible repercussions much later, repercussions that would ultimately cause the Selvadurais to flee for their lives in 1984. I shall deal with those repercussions at the end of my discussion.

Let us now examine the novel itself. The author begins by conjuring up for us the city port of Colombo, one of the great junctions of the shipping world ever since the Portuguese first colonized the island in the sixteenth century. I know that in my reviews I focus very often on the characters and themes of the novels and I do not spend enough time on the purely descriptive abilities of the writer. Let me remedy that a little now by reading Selvadurai's description of Colombo in 1927:

> The city was flanked on one side by the ocean, and its inhabitants were never very far from the salty smell of the sea air and its cooling breezes. In the middle of the city was the extensive Beira Lake, from which tributaries snaked their way through the city, forming smaller lakes at various junctures. The waters of the lakes were bordered by foliage of unrivalled beauty, palms of every variety, masses of scarlet flamboyant blossoms, the waving leaves of plantain trees. . . .
>
> The only part of Colombo that possessed the chaos and scramble of other large cities was the Pettah, where the colourful bazaars were always raucous with the cries of vendors, the fierce bargaining of women shopping. Here the streets were narrow, the buildings huddled together, the shops and domestic dwellings often open to the streets, the activity of selling and living going on on the streets themselves. The air was pungent with the odour of fruits, spices, dried fish, meat, the blood from butcher shops running into the open drains. (p. 10)

What colourful detail, what clean prose! Only one metaphor and no strained similes.

Then our author narrows his focus to one of Colombo's suburbs, Cinnamon Gardens, where the indigenous wealthy live. Now Selvadurai will narrow his focus even further, on just two homes. It is in these homes that most of our narrative will take place. I should say two narratives, separate but ultimately connected.

One of the two stories will be about a young woman, the only one of three sisters to reject the traditionally subordinate role of women in Ceylon society. The other story will be about a forty-one-year-old man, utterly dominated by his father, who will have to make a terrible choice. The two stories will be told in alternating chapters, finally coming together as each of our protagonists, in his or her own way, decides to choose freedom.

Let me begin at the larger of the two homes, the palatial mansion of the seventy-year-old Mudaliyar Navaratnam. One of the native leaders appointed by the British governor to the legislative council, his wealth derives from the family rubber and tea plantations and from the offerings at the Hindu temple founded by his grandfather. The temple houses a statue of Shiva, one of the Hindu gods, a statue allegedly brought up out of the sea after his grandfather had a vision. (I have no problem with the miraculous appearance of the statue. It strains my credulity much less than the Parting of the Red Sea or the Liquefaction of Naples.) The Mudaliyar is a Hindu Tamil leader with the strong political views I have already indicated.

To his family he is a despot. One of his two sons, Arul, has long gone. Twenty-eight years before our novel begins, Arul ran away to India with Pakkiam, a low-caste maid in the Mudaliyar's house. There has been no communication between father and son since, although a small monthly allowance is sent to Arul and his wife and son in Bombay via the Mudaliyar's bank manager. The mother, Nalamma, still yearns for her lost boy. She has her other, younger son make frequent offerings at both the Hindu temple and the local Catholic church for the well-being of her first-born. Mother love, as always, touchingly, wears its religion very, very lightly and tries to cover all the bases.

But our first story is not about the Mudaliyar or about his far-away older son. It is about his second son, Balendran. For twenty years Balendran has managed his father's affairs. It is he who runs the plantations and the family temple. It is he who dismissed embezzling managers and priests.

When we meet him in 1927 he is forty-one, with legal training taken in England when he was twenty. He is married to Sonia, half-Tamil and half-English, and they have a much-loved son, Lukshman. As a matter of fact, Sonia and Balendran are bound together by more than marriage and their son; they are also first cousins. The Mudaliyar's brother had married into a titled English family during his studies in England, and Sonia is the result of that union.

The Mudaliyar had been pleased when his son had married his niece, in fact he'd arranged the union. It was a common practice in Tamil families for cousins to marry; it forestalled divided loyalties, and more important it kept the money in the family. Very sensible.

Sonia has come to love her husband and even to tolerate her domineering father-in-law, whom she knows to be an intellectual fraud. The Mudaliyar has literary pretensions, writing on Tamil history and Tamil faith, but is well-received only in the United States, where he is seen as something of a guru.

(The gullibility of the North American regarding self-appointed spiritual leaders from the Indian subcontinent never ceases to amaze me.)

Sonia is a very intelligent, very insightful woman, and she sees herself and her situation very accurately. Because Salvadurai has chosen to use an omniscient narrator we are also made privy to Sonia's reflections. She realizes that she married this brown man at least partially as a protest against the rigid class system of British society. What she had not known is that she would find with Balendran in Ceylon a society more stratified, more feudal, than anything she left behind in England.

Balendran and Sonia represent the most progressive element in Ceylon. Firm believers in democracy, they want a new Ceylon in which the old community loyalties, whether Tamil or Sinhalese, would give way to a genuine desire to improve the miserable lot of the poor. United by their ideals, they appear to be a perfect family. Their grown-up son, Lukshman, is away at his studies in England, staying at the home of Sonia's aunt, Lady Boxton. Balendran is the successful administrator of his father's affairs. What more could one ask for?

It is at this point that Shyam Selvadurai reminds us that nothing in any family is what it appears to be. Families are very complex entities. I remember what a friend once said to me, "Don't speak of that particular family as dysfunctional, there is no other kind!" A little cynical perhaps, but not, I suspect, very far from the truth.

The Mudaliyar tells Balendran he has heard that an advisor to one of the members of the Donoughmore Commission is a Richard Howland, Balendran's fellow student when he was in London twenty years earlier. The Mudaliyar wants Balendran to make contact with his friend and ensure that the Mudaliyar's political views are properly presented. (pp. 30-31)

Balendran cannot believe what his father is asking of him, for it touches on the most painful of memories. And we share his pain as he remembers.

As his father is well aware, Balendran did know Richard in London – they were lovers. It had been a profound physical and emotional relationship, and they had dreamed of a lasting, idyllic union. But that was in 1907, only twelve years after Oscar Wilde had been sent to prison for homosexual activity, and they knew the risk they were taking. Yet in spite of that, Richard and Balendran had such faith in the future of their love.

But reality arrived in the person of the Mudaliyar, alerted to the situation by an anonymous letter. He confronted the lovers, beat them both, and

drove Richard out of the flat. (p. 141) Balendran had a complete breakdown, complicated by pneumonia. For weeks he was nursed back to health
by his father, who never spoke a word to him. Finally, the Mudaliyar proposed that they put the matter behind them, that Balendran marry his
cousin Sonia, and that they return with him to Colombo.

What the Mudaliyar is now asking him to do seems incomprehensible,
but as Balendran watches his father he sees the request as a confirmation
that the Mudaliyar "completely trusted him, that anything there was to
forgive was forgiven." (p. 39) Balendran at forty-one is as much under his
father's thumb as he was at twenty-one. This is a man with a long road to
travel before he can be free. Balendran accepts his father's instruction, as
he always does, and agrees to meet Richard Howland.

Richard in turn is apprehensive about the meeting. He has brought
along his lover of seven years, James Alliston, "Alli," a pretty young man,
fourteen years younger than Richard. Richard is afraid that Balendran
will laugh at him; he "could not help remembering the way Balendran
and he used to make fun of those middle-aged men with their pretty
young things." (p. 105)

But when Richard and Balendran meet, time slips away and they are
young again. I found it impossible not to be moved by both the moment
and their whole love story. "As they held each other's hands, there passed
between them the understanding of their history together, of the life that
had been theirs. It settled on them like fine dust." (p. 106)

Within days Richard declares his love: "'I have fallen in love with you.
All over again,'" (p. 188) and a little later, "'I would willingly leave my
life with Alli for you.'" (p. 207)

And thus begins Balendran's agony. His first reaction to Richard's declaration is one of shock: "'I am married with a child. How can you
compare what I have with what you have.'" (p. 207)

But the temptation is very great, and Richard and Balendran sleep
together. Balendran's torment intensifies. A life with Richard would mean
leaving Colombo, and in Colombo he has so much. Leaving would mean a
parting from his beloved mother and the showpiece he has made of the
family plantations. It would mean giving up the book on the Tamils of Jaffna
he is planning to write. It would mean an end to his relationship with his son
and with his wife, Sonia, whom he has come to value for her decency
and her intelligence. It would mean giving up his whole Tamil way of life,

and there would be no more aristocratic connections in England. To go with Richard would mean to give up everything – except Richard's love.

The Mudaliyar is not an intelligent man, but he is a cunning one. He realizes his mistake in bringing his son and Richard together, particularly since his discovery that Richard is not an advisor to the commission, merely an observer. Pleading the necessity that he testify before the commission far up north in Jaffna, the Mudaliyar asks Balendran to stay at the mansion and to keep his mother company. This would serve two purposes for Balendran, reasons the duplicitous Mudaliyar. It would take him at least temporarily away from Richard, and his mother's tender care and cooking would remind him of all that he would give up.

It's a terribly painful choice that Balendran must make between love and his duty to his wife, his son, his work, his family, and his Tamil community. If he goes to England with Richard, he will be just another under-employed immigrant lawyer moving on the fringes of society.

To further complicate the situation, the family hears that Balendran's older brother is dying in Bombay. Even the Mudaliyar agrees that Balendran must go to him. Balendran will finally meet his brother's twenty-seven-year-old son, Seelan, the grandson the Mudaliyar has never seen. Balendran sets off for Bombay, on the other side of India, with one firm instruction from his father. He is to bring his brother's body back for burial "with full honours" in the ancient Tamil city of Jaffna. (p. 242) Balendran is to bring back nothing and no one else.

Now let us leave Balendran on his way to Bombay and turn to the second narrative of the novel, in chapters alternating with those dealing with Balendran.

Next door to the Mudaliyar's mansion is the house of another Tamil family, the Kandiahs. Their home, Lotus Cottage, is more modest, a simple bungalow. The Kandiahs are related to the Mudaliyar, the great man who lives next door, and Balendran always refers to himself as the uncle of the oldest of the three Kandiah daughters, Annalukshmi, the protagonist of the second narrative.

(I worked out, by the way, that our two protagonists are not, in fact, uncle and niece but second cousins twice removed. In the tightly knit Tamil minority culture of Colombo, however, that counts as close family.)

The Kandiah family consists of the mother, Louisa, the oldest daughter, Annalukshmi, twenty-two, and her two sisters: Kumudini, twenty-one, and

Manohari, just sixteen. Unlike the Mudaliyar and Balendran, the Kandiahs are Christian. There is a father, Murugasu, but he and Louisa are estranged and he lives far away in Malaya, managing the family's rubber plantation outside Kuala Lumpur. He sounds like a fascinating character and I'm sorry we never meet him. When Louisa fell in love with him, twenty-five years before our novel begins, they eloped to the rubber plantation where they had three daughters. Murugasu converted to Christianity to please Louisa, but when the marriage grew stormy and the physical attraction lessened, he reverted to Hinduism and Louisa brought her three daughters back to Colombo. But Murugasu still supports the family and is just as patriarchal as the Mudaliyar himself.

We are introduced to Annalukshmi in the early pages.

> For a young woman of twenty-two from a good Tamil family, living in the year 1927, her achievements were remarkable – or, depending on your conviction, appalling. She had completed her Senior Cambridge, an accomplishment fairly rare in that time for a girl; she had stood first islandwide in English literature, much to the discomfiture of every boys' school. Then she had gone on to teachers college and qualified as a teacher.
>
> Annalukshmi's qualification as a teacher was held to be her greatest crime by her mother's relatives, the Barnetts. A career as a teacher was reserved for those girls who were too poor or too ugly to ever catch a husband. (pp. 3-4)

Annalukshmi has much to rebel against!

Annalukshmi teaches at a private Christian girls' school in Colombo, the same school where she had been a student. Her hero is the British headmistress, Miss Lawton, unmarried and a career educator, who had first encouraged Annalukshmi to become a teacher. It's a career Annalukshmi loves, and she dreads her family pushing her to marry. Miss Lawton points out to her that there is loneliness in the single life: "'choices are never easy. . . . But what is life without its regrets?'" (p. 92) Miss Lawton has attempted to assuage her own loneliness by adopting Nancy, an orphaned Tamil child.

Annalukshmi's chapters in the novel will centre on her mother's fierce attempts to marry her off and her own equally fierce attempts to resist her mother's choices. Her first revolt against her mother will be to ride the bicycle the assistant headmistress gave her. Her mother points out that "'decent, respectable girls don't ride bicycles,'" (p. 7) but Miss Lawton does and that's enough for Annalukshmi.

The clock is ticking for Annalukshmi. Her younger sister Kumudini has her eye on someone, but Tamil convention dictates that she cannot marry before her older sister. The pressure on Annalukshmi becomes greater when telegrams arrive from her father that she is to marry her cousin Muttiah, who will arrive in Colombo in ten days, accompanied by his mother, Murugasu's sister, who will supervise the arrangements and then bring the couple back to Kuala Lumpur. From her childhood in Malaya, Annalukshmi remembers Muttiah as a lout, and anyway she doesn't want to marry. She finds an unlikely ally in her mother. Louisa doesn't want her husband to do the choosing; besides, Muttiah is a Hindu. Louisa and Annalukshmi have only ten days to find a solution. What to do? What to do?

Then fate intervenes in the person of Louisa's cousin, Philomena Barnett, a very proper, middle-aged Christian Tamil lady. She will act immediately as Annalukshmi's matchmaker. Anyone would be better than Muttiah. Philomena warns Louisa that it won't be easy, since Louisa's own elopement twenty-five years earlier had given the Barnett girls the reputation of being "flighty."

"Flighty"! – I haven't heard that word, or seen it in a novel, for very many years. I can't imagine what lengths one would have to go to nowadays to be seen as "flighty."

Philomena also points out that Annalukshmi is over-educated; she would diminish her husband. And what about the scandal of the bicycle? Worst of all, Annalukshmi has shown interest in the suffragette movement, in the real possibility of the Donoughmore Commission recommending votes for women. To Philomena this is horror. As she points out much later, "'Only manly women get involved in men's affairs. Normal women think of their husbands and of their homes and nothing else.'" (p. 117)

In spite of all her misgivings, Philomena decides to soldier on in the cause.

"Well, there's that Worthington boy who's just got a good position in the Postal Services. The Lights are looking for someone for their son and so are the Macintoshes."

Louisa clasped her hands together. "How wonderful!" (p. 46)

I adored Philomena and her life so full of intrigue. Yet I had the oddest feeling that I'd met her before. It took me a long time but finally it came to me. She is right out of a Jane Austen novel – and so is Louisa! Here are two women plotting the marriages of their daughters (Philomena still has her youngest, Dolly, to marry off). I should have realized it sooner; there were lots of clues. When Annalukshmi points out to her younger sister how unsuitable are her mother's choices, Kumudini teases her: " 'This is not *Pride and Prejudice*. . . . Your Mr. Darcy isn't going to ride up on a horse.' " (p. 89)

There are many references in the novel to the Kandiah sisters reading the Victorians: Dickens, Thomas Hardy, and particularly Jane Austen.

What I finally realized was that in the Annalukshmi chapters Selvadurai has written a nineteenth-century novel – a Jane Austen novel – where the concern is to marry off young women to suitable young men.

Then I realized something else. In the Balendran chapters, Salvadurai has written another nineteenth-century novel, this time about the traditional struggle between love and duty. It is true that Selvadurai has put a modern spin on it, Balendran's love being homosexual, but the struggle is essentially the same.

I gasped at Selvadurai's audacity to hide two nineteenth-century novels behind a colonial background and a different kind of love.

Annalukshmi is appalled by the suitors suggested. The best of the bunch would appear to be Chandran Macintosh, the painter. At least he is sensitive and intelligent. Annalukshmi even agrees to meet him. But it is Chandran who fails to keep the appointment. He apologizes later: "He waved his hand to his canvases. 'I am married to this and no woman would agree to take second place to it. I hope you understand.' " (p. 298)

Honest? Certainly, even admirably honest, but Annalukshmi, a very healthy, attractive young woman, is understandably piqued that it was he and not she who decided they had no future. It doesn't help when her youngest sister, Manohari, comments, " 'Deserted like Miss Havisham in *Great Expectations*.' " (p. 177)

For a while, Annalukshmi becomes interested in Mr. Jayaweera, the new clerical assistant at her school. She admires him for his concern for the poor, for his respect for his own rural traditions, and for his nobility in supporting his mother and his sisters on a minuscule salary. But nothing comes of Annalukshmi's interest, since Mr. Jayaweera falls in love with Miss Lawton's adopted daughter, Nancy.

With Muttiah's arrival imminent, Annalukshmi panics and takes the train to stay with a friend of Miss Lawton's, her absence making it possible for Muttiah to fall in love with Kumudini, Annalukshmi's younger sister. As the older sister, Annalukshmi graciously waives her right of first marriage and first choice and she is free!

She is also liberated from her hero-worship of her headmistress. Nancy confides in her that Miss Lawton is in Ceylon because her father was accused of embezzling church funds. Rather than stay in England as the poor daughter of a disgraced clergyman, she came out to a colony to condescend to the natives. (p. 220) How often, in the time of the British Raj, did the Empire offer the chance to second-rate people to assume first-rate positions among the colonized!

For the first time, Annalukshmi understands that Miss Lawton has a very marked racist attitude. Now she understands why there are no Ceylonese natives in senior positions at Miss Lawton's school. Now she understands why Miss Lawton is opposed to Nancy marrying Mr. Jayaweera. Now she understands why Miss Lawton dismissed Mr. Jayaweera when he was arrested for pro-union activity, even though the charges were dropped. Miss Lawton is terrified of scandal, of anything that might endanger her position and send her back to the life of a nonentity in England. Now it all becomes clear. "Something that had been there all along had now moved into the foreground." (p. 287) It is the mark of a very fine novelist to endow a secondary character like Miss Lawton with such a textured personality.

Annalukshmi is now free of Miss Lawton's benevolent maternalism, but before the novel ends Annalukshmi has one more obstacle to overcome. This is when Selvadurai will draw his two narratives together to a common conclusion.

You will remember that we left Balendran on his way to his dying brother, Arul, in Bombay. When he gets there he learns how Arul and his Pakkiam have lived together for twenty-eight years in love and squalor, how they have sacrificed everything to send their son, Seelan, to England to become a doctor, and how the Mudaliyar had debauched Pakkiam's mother, a poor widow, and then brought Pakkiam at fifteen into his home as a maid so that he could debauch her too. His dying brother challenges Balendran to face the truth about their father. " 'You have been blind to the reality of life, Bala. You have spent your whole life living by codes every-one lays down but nobody follows.' " (p. 273)

Balendran decides to assert himself. He has his brother cremated in Bombay and then returns to face his father's wrath. And wrath there is. But Balendran sees his father enter the bedroom of his American secretary, Miss Adamson, and realizes that Pakkiam and her mother were not the only women the Mudaliyar had debauched. He realizes how many lives his father has controlled and ruined. Balendran is now ready to advance another step on the road to freedom, and invites his nephew Seelan to come from Bombay to Colombo. Initially, however, Balendran suggests that Seelan use an alias, "Dr. Govind." Balendran hopes to win his father over slowly to the idea of receiving his grandson.

The two narratives come together as "Dr. Govind" and Annalukshmi meet and are attracted to each other. There is a brief, delicious courtship. The highlight is when they bump into each other in a bookstore. They discuss their favourite author – who else but Jane Austen? – and "Dr. Govind" offers to buy Jane Austen's *Mansfield Park* for Annalukshmi, who accepts the gift "with a flutter of excitement at his gesture." (p. 346) Her sister Manohari is shocked at her forwardness. At home, Annalukshmi reads the inscription on the flyleaf: "May our joy of reading strengthen our regard for each other. Dr. Govind." (p. 348)

How lovely! I thought. How delicate! How innocent! How Jane Austen! How different from the vulgarity of courtships nowadays, where the hesi-tant phrases of Miss Austen's characters are replaced by a few guttural grunts. The relationship blossoms and "Dr. Govind" is invited to tea at Lotus Cottage. But the Mudaliyar has found out about the liaison and the impersonation and goes to Lotus Cottage to expel Seelan forcibly. Annalukshmi is reduced to tears.

Seelan hurries to Balendran to tell him what has happened, and Balendran remembers the terrible scene in London twenty years earlier. "He vowed now that he would not let his father dictate Seelan's destiny. At least one of them would escape from his clutches." (p. 363)

Balendran confronts his father with all that he has done to Arul, to Pakkiam, to Pakkiam's mother: "'And for those things you hate your grandson. . . . Why didn't you leave me alone in London? . . . I might have been truly happy.'" (pp. 366-67)

It is a powerful confrontation, and Balendran realizes that he has won: "He saw that by confronting his father with his true nature, unashamed, assured, he had taken something away from him. . . . He had come looking for his nephew's freedom and, unwittingly, he had achieved his own." (pp. 367-68)

Now that Balendran is free of the code of the Mudaliyar, he must make his choice. He writes to Richard, offering friendship but not a life together. The friendship he offers is total: "Perhaps it is enough to have one person to whom nothing is a secret, to whom one can lay open the inner workings of one's heart." (p. 385)

He acknowledges his love for Richard, but it must exist within the limits of that to which Balendran has committed himself: his wife, his son, and his work.

A Freudian would make much of the fact that Balendran writes this final offer at his father's desk, on his father's stationery, and with his father's pen. A victory indeed! Sometimes a pen is just a pen, but sometimes it really can be a phallic symbol. In the final line of the novel, the phallic symbolism continues, "Balendran straightened his tie and went to take his place amongst the family," not the place assigned to him by his father, but the place *he* has chosen.

Annalukshmi, free of Miss Lawton, must also make a choice. She too will write a letter. (I thought it a lovely touch by Selvadurai to conclude both his narratives with a letter.) Hers will be to Seelan, ending their relationship. Seelan had cooked his own goose during that ill-fated visit to Lotus Cottage when, as "Dr. Govind," he had said to Annalukshmi, "'Has British imperialism been such a terrible thing for us? It has brought so many advantages, railways, rule of law, postal services, electricity. I, unlike so many others, would be very unhappy to see the British go.'" (p. 359)

If and when Annalukshmi marries, it will be to a free man and not an imitation Englishman. For the moment she will move to the Tamil city of Jaffna to teach and to reclaim the identity she almost lost to Miss Lawton. And that is, for the moment, the end of her story. I must confess that, as a great admirer of Miss Austen, I still have high hopes for Chandran

Macintosh. He and Annalukshmi might still come together. Who knows what happens in a novel after the covers are closed?

Both our protagonists have made choices of their own free will, at last liberated from a person and a code that had shaped them into something not true to themselves. I was a little sad that Balendran finally chose duty over love, but I respected his choice; it is never a simple one to make. I respected even more Selvadurai's permitting him to make that choice. It would have been so easy to let the decision go the other way. I admired Selvadurai's resisting the temptation to let love conquer all. It very rarely does.

I admired so much about the novel: Selvadurai's control of the two narratives, the movement from the tight, airless world of the Tamil aristocrat to the squalor of Bombay, and the fully drawn minor characters like Miss Lawton and the divine Philomena.

Perhaps this is the moment to bring ourselves up to date on Sri Lankan history after the novel ends in 1928. You will remember that the Donoughmore Commission failed to recommend that guarantees of Tamil representation be written into the new constitution. After Ceylon received its independence on February 4, 1948, all the Tamils' worst fears were realized. Five of the Sri Lankan prime ministers and presidents since 1948 have come from just two Sinhalese families, the Senanayakes and the Bandaranaikes. It was Solomon Bandaranaike who declared Sinhalese the only official language in the country and Buddhism the only religion to receive a state subsidy.

The Tamils demanded without success some measure of autonomy for their community in the north, centred on the city of Jaffna. Some demanded outright independence. No concessions were offered by the Colombo government, and the north exploded into violence in 1980. The Tamil Liberation Front, the "Tamil Tigers," seized Jaffna. They would hold the city for fifteen years against repeated attacks by soldiers of the central government.

There was a backlash in Colombo against all its Tamil residents. They were told to join their rebel brothers in the north or to get out of the country. Shyam Selvadurai's mother was Sinhalese, but his father was a Christian Tamil and the family name was enough to damn them. By 1984 the situation in Colombo was intolerable and Sri Lanka's loss became Toronto's gain.

Even now, there is fighting in Sri Lanka. The future seems very bleak. The current president, Mrs. Chandrika Bandaranaike Kumaratunga, is very unlikely to offer an acceptable compromise solution.

But let us not end on a negative note. Let me conclude with a startling piece of information. In a speech to the Book Publishers' Professional Association, Selvadurai revealed that *Cinnamon Gardens* is not the novel he had intended to write.

He had planned to write about his grandmother's sister, a remarkable woman who had wanted to become a lawyer but who was married off at nineteen to a rubber planter in Malaya. She discovered that her husband was weak and inefficient and so took over the estate, teaching herself to drive and to shoot,

> just the type of person who would make a wonderful character in a novel. Thus, in the winter of 1994 and again in 1995, I went to Malaysia and Sri Lanka to discover more about this woman and also to get a sense of the time in which she had lived. . . .
>
> Armed with all my research I sat down one fine summer day in Toronto to begin the novel. The novel was to start in Sri Lanka and then, about a third of the way through, move with the heroine to Malaysia. Imagine my dismay then when I came to the point where my heroine simply folded her arms to her chest and refused to get married! Refused to have anything to do with even the notion of marriage! I coaxed, I pleaded [but she refused to get married and move to Malaysia]. . . .
>
> Before my very eyes, two-thirds of the novel I had intended to write was washed away, taking with it all those hard months I had spent in Malaysia trekking around in the hot sun collecting information.

Thus it was that Selvadurai ended up, not with his great-aunt, but with Annalukshmi, who would liberate herself in a very different way.

Balendran, Selvadurai explained in the same talk, was just there one day. Selvadurai believes that Balendran may be "my phantom self."

> There's a question I always ask myself. I ask myself what would have happened to me if I had continued to live in Sri Lanka and never gone to a Western country. What would I have done? Would

I have married? Would I have continued to have been celibate? The obvious answer is, I don't know. Balendran is, in a way, an exploration of that possibility for myself.

How fascinating it is to hear an author discussing the genesis of a novel as complex and fine as this one. And there is a treat in store for us. Mr. Selvadurai told me that his third novel will be about Toronto. Given his demonstrated ability to dissect the tensions and expose the hypocrisies of whatever society he is examining, I can hardly wait!

SACRED HUNGER

Barry Unsworth
(Toronto: Penguin, 1992)

Barry Unsworth was born in England in 1930 and has spent a large part of his life teaching English literature all over the world, with long periods in Greece and Turkey. For the last several years he has lived in Finland with his Finnish wife.

Sacred Hunger was the joint winner of the 1992 Booker Prize. (The other winner was Michael Ondaatje's *The English Patient*.) It is his tenth novel, but I have so much to say about it that I cannot give the attention I would wish to his earlier work. Let me just say that he is a master of detailed historical background and draw your attention to his sixth novel, *Rage of the Vulture* (1982), a superb novel set in the old Ottoman Empire.

Before we can explore *Sacred Hunger* in any depth, we must first have before us an overview of the slave trade, that obscenity in which Great Britain played such an important role.

Sacred Hunger spans the years 1752 to 1765, a time when Britain was taking over the leadership of the world in all matters military, political, and commercial. It was during this period that the British crushed the French and thereby took control of India, North America, and most of the West Indies. And it was also during this period that the British established themselves as the world's most industrialized nation.

The British people paid a terrible price for their Industrial Revolution. Children began to work in the new factories at five or six years old. They worked from dawn to dusk, twelve hours a day, six days a week. In the newly industrialized cities like Liverpool, Manchester, and Birmingham living conditions were abominable. The overcrowding resulted in massive wife and child abuse, incest, and early death. As late as 1845, nearly a century after the period of the novel, the great social reformer Lord Shaftesbury discovered that the average age of death in the great industrial cities was twenty-one. There was no social legislation, no maximum work hours, no minimum wage, no minimum working age. Unfettered as they were by parliament, which they controlled anyway, British industrialists were able to produce cheap goods in abundance. Parliament was no more than a collection of industrialists and rich landowners with special interests. There was the Cotton Interest, the Coal Interest, the Wool Interest, the Iron Interest, and the Sugar Interest. Seats in parliament were bought and sold in an electoral system designed for a medieval, agricultural economy. A village whose population had departed to the new industrial centres might still elect a member of parliament, even if the village now had only one or two inhabitants. It was thus possible for a few rich men to buy and control large blocks of these so-called "rotten boroughs." Erasmus Kemp, one of the characters in the novel, controls fifty-three seats in parliament on behalf of the Sugar Interest.

One result of Britain's Industrial Revolution and the ensuing commercial expansion of the eighteenth and nineteenth centuries was the need for colonies. The British required both raw materials and new markets for the vast quantities of factory-produced goods. With the colonies acquired, a new need arose for cheap labour to help build those colonies, and so British merchants and shipowners entered wholeheartedly into the already existing slave trade.

Participation in the slave trade put Britain into a commercial struggle with all the other slave-trading nations, particularly Spain, France, Holland, Denmark, and Portugal. To guarantee a safe passage for English slave ships from Africa across the Atlantic to the West Indies, Britain had to control the seas, and so the English navy – both the Royal Navy and the merchant navy – was given, under law, extraordinary power. Sea captains who needed to make up a crew had the right of impressment. Their press gangs had the power to seize any able-bodied man who did not own property – gentlemen were naturally exempt – and to compel him, to "press" him, to sign on for a voyage. He owed total obedience to the captain of the ship. The punishment for minor offences was flogging and the punishment for mutiny was death. We have several examples in the novel of men being pressed, sold, or kidnapped. Billy Blair and Michael Sullivan are both kidnapped from a tavern and forced into service on the slave ship *Liverpool Merchant*. One poor woman sells her husband's friend to the press gang for two pounds, enough to buy a little food and a lot of gin.

The eighteenth century, and the century that followed, was a period in British history of enormous economic growth and of enormous greed. The rich endowed themselves not only with political but with religious authority. They argued that since the bounty of the earth is God's gift, those who use this bounty most productively are those who are most effective in doing God's work. According to the concept of the good steward, the most successful capitalist must therefore be the most successful servant of God. The argument can be taken even further, as it is in the following passage, which also makes clear the genesis of the title of the novel.

> "Money is sacred, as everyone knows. . . . So then must be the hunger for it and the means we use to obtain it. Once a man is in debt he becomes a flesh and blood form of money, a walking investment. You can do what you like with him, you can work him to death or you can sell him. This cannot be called cruelty or greed because we are seeking only to recover our investment and that is a sacred duty." (p. 325)

Slavery becomes not only an economic activity but the righteous response to a commandment. Over and over again in the novel, both industrialists and slavers will use the same expression: "The commerce is lawful." Not only was the trade permitted by British law, it was the teaching of organized religion at the time.

Slavery had existed in most cultures since the beginning of time. The slavery that our novel is concerned with – that of the African Negro from the west coast of Africa, below the Sahara – had been going on for at least a thousand years and was largely in the control of Moslem Arabs. The Arabs came down from North Africa, crossed the Sahara, and bought slaves from the leaders of various tribes along the West African coast. It was the habit of victorious African chiefs to enslave subjugated peoples and to sell to the Arabs any slaves surplus to their own requirements. The Arabs then took the slaves back north across the Sahara and sold them, particularly in the great slave-trading centre of Alexandria.

In the fifteenth century, Europeans made their appearance in the slave trade. The first to come were the Portuguese, who needed labour in the sugar plantations of their island colonies like Madeira. The Portuguese were soon joined by the Spanish, the Danes, the Dutch, the French, and the English.

There was never any question of religious opposition to the practice of slavery. It had the blessing of both Islam and Christianity. The Church of England, for example, was the largest single slave-owner on the island of Barbados until the British abolished slavery in the Empire in 1833. The Anglican Church in Barbados had the interesting habit of branding the word "Society" on the chests of its slaves. It was an abbreviation of "Society for the Propagation of the Gospel."

It sometimes seems to me that if there really is a Day of Judgment, organized religion is going to have a lot to answer for. Fortunately, it's had a lot of practice in defending the indefensible.

Finally, to our novel. The year is 1752 and William Kemp is building his ship, *Liverpool Merchant*, to participate in the Triangular Trade.

The first side of the triangle was the voyage from a British port to the west coast of Africa. Trade goods, firearms, cheap jewellery, and cloth would be exchanged for slaves. Then began the Middle Passage, the second side of the triangle, the voyage from West Africa to the West Indies or the American colonies. There the slaves would be sold at an immense profit and the proceeds used to buy West Indian sugar and rum or American cotton and tobacco. The third side of the triangle was the return to a British port and a second massive profit. It is for such a voyage that William Kemp is preparing *Liverpool Merchant*.

William Kemp had come to Liverpool as a penniless, barefoot boy and had prospered through hard work, saving, and speculation. Supporters of unrestricted capitalism would hail him, even now in certain quarters, as living proof that the system works, that anyone who wants to hard enough, anyone who has "the sacred hunger" in sufficient quantity, can and will prosper.

Erasmus, Kemp's twenty-three-year-old son, will remain in England with his father during the voyage. As firm a believer as his father in the capitalist ethic, Erasmus Kemp is a singularly unlovable young man. His only weakness is his passion for Sarah Wolpert, the daughter of a wealthy neighbour, and the courtship of Sarah will serve, in the first half of the novel, as a counter-narrative to the voyage of *Liverpool Merchant*.

William Kemp has appointed his nephew, Matthew Paris, as the ship's doctor. Slaving was a physically demanding and physically dirty business, and few doctors were interested in serving on slave ships, but Matthew Paris has little choice. He had run afoul of the Church. A hundred years before Darwin, Matthew Paris had published his reflections on the origin of man. He had questioned the literal truth of the Book of Genesis, that man was created in a moment as an immutable species. He had thus incurred the wrath of the Bishop of Norwich, who incited a mob to attack and vandalize Matthew Paris's home. The violence caused his pregnant wife to miscarry and the miscarriage caused her death. Matthew himself was put into the stocks and exposed to public ridicule and then sent to prison. By the way, once in prison, Matthew was able to rent a private room and buy acceptable food through the generosity of his uncle. There weren't many prisons in the mid-eighteenth century, and those that did exist were mostly short-term, privately owned, and run for profit. You could pay for private or semi-private accommodation and you could even bring a servant if you could afford to pay for his board and lodging. (If you had no money, then prison life was miserable indeed.) This was, after all, the time of uncontrolled capitalism. You were allowed to make a profit on anything. As a matter of fact, the prison Matthew was in was owned by his accuser, the Bishop of Norwich.

Of course, we have come a long way since then. Can you imagine anyone in this day and age who would seriously propose privatizing prisons?

Once freed into his uncle's custody, what better way to overcome his grief and humiliation than to slip away on a long sea voyage? And so Matthew Paris accepts his uncle's offer and comes aboard as ship's doctor under the command of Captain Thurso. William Kemp's generosity to his nephew was not entirely altruistic. He believed that God was as careful a businessman as he: "Kemp held a moral view of the universe. God balanced the ledgers. Nothing went unrecognized. A good deed was an entry on the credit side." (p. 29)

Captain Thurso is a marvellous literary creation, a direct ancestor of Captain Ahab. Captain Thurso believes that the universe speaks to him, that storms and calms are Heaven's personal message. When two men fall from the masts during the building of the ship, there is a small look of satisfaction on the captain's face. Heaven has confirmed his power of life and death over the crew. (p. 59)

The omniscient narrator makes it clear that Captain Thurso is no simple sadist: "Thurso despised cruelty, as he did compassion. . . . He knew he was not himself cruel but merely practical and obedient to the counsels of necessity." (p. 114) That necessity will cause him to have men flogged until the flesh hangs off their backs, but it is Captain Thurso's sincere belief that this is a necessary sacrifice to the heavens to call up the wind he needs. (p. 122)

In addition to his mystical belief in his communion with the elements, Captain Thurso has embraced the morality of his age, that wonderfully convenient marriage of religion and private enterprise. When the slaves are taken on board in West Africa, the captain forbids the crew to have sexual congress with the women: "'I will not have my ship turned into a sink of iniquity. A girl still intact is worth a good ten guineas more in Jamaica.'" (p. 216)

The juxtaposition of the two sentences is a master stroke by the author in illustrating the hypocrisy of the age.

The early pages of the novel contain a fascinating, detailed account of the building and outfitting of a ship. (Remember that since its inception, the English novel has had a didactic tradition.) Just as fascinating is the way the author puts together a crew. Every man is an individual and every man contributes a piece to the portrait of the age.

The seaman Hughes is a perfect example. He loves solitude and it is his joy to climb up and up and up into the loneliness of the topsails. He is a man who "from adolescence had been unsettled by people coming too close, had once scarred a man terribly in the hysteria of contested space." (p. 131)

What a magnificent phrase to describe the claustrophobic reaction of someone born into an intensely crowded English slum, "the hysteria of contested space."

We meet the fiddler Michael Sullivan and his friend the pugnacious, proud little Billy Blair, both of them shanghaied from the same tavern in one of the most exciting scenes in the novel. (pp. 80 ff) We meet the simple-minded boy Calley, one of the few who signed on willingly, flattered by the first mate into believing he was being given worthwhile employment. We meet the kindly Deakin who tries to protect Calley from the worst of the crew's practical jokes. There are the two homosexuals, Evans and Johnson, who find comfort in each other in the hold at night. There is the loutish Wilson and the thieving and sycophantic first mate, Barton. There is Haines, the bosun, who proves that the vision of religious capitalism has trickled down to the lowest classes. Haines has understood the motivation of the age: "'Him that has got something already must always try to get hold of more. . . . An' the more he gets, the more will be given to him. That is in the Gospels.'" (p. 242)

We have on board the whole spectrum of humanity, from the thinker to the brute. Barry Unsworth has created a self-contained little world, a microcosm of the greater society on land.

When this little floating world reaches the Guinea coast and the penned slaves waiting for it, we are treated to one of Unsworth's many passages of descriptive brilliance.

> Three of the dungeons were occupied now, two with men handcuffed together in pairs and one with unshackled girls and women. Sunlight for this hour was caged there with them. Motes of dust moved with gauzy flies through the bright air. The bodies of the slaves were flecked and stippled and the straw that covered the earth floors was luminous gold. The smells of excrement and trodden straw seemed like a release of this flooding warmth of sunshine. Through the barred embrasures in the walls, Paris heard the hammering again, much closer now, a double-stroke, impatient and swift, metal on wood. Then he saw that one of the women had come forward and was standing pressed against the bars in a shaft of sunlight. She was looking directly at him – he saw the gleam of her eyes. But her face was shadowed. Sunlight fell on her from the window behind, her face and head were edged with fire. (pp. 313-14)

I am sure you noticed that, throughout the passage, while the word "gold" itself is used only once, gold is suggested all through the scene in the bright air, the straw, the gleam, and the fire. "Sunlight" is used three times and "sunshine" once. It is the most accomplished use of language, reinforcing so delicately and subtly the terrible truth that these imprisoned human beings are, to the slavers, no more than walking gold. We will also remember later in the novel that this is the shining moment when our protagonist, Matthew Paris, first lays eyes on Tabakali, the Fulani woman who will later become his wife.

In the white exploiters of the slave-trading settlement, Unsworth adds further specimens to our list of the varieties of the human species, from the diet-obsessed governor to the factor, dying of drink and loneliness. We are also given another horrendous example of Captain Thurso's response to the demands of necessity: he uses thumbscrews on a slave trying to fast to death to escape his fate.

After the assembling and embarkation of two hundred slaves, *Liverpool Merchant* begins the second leg of the triangle, the infamous Middle Passage across the Atlantic to the West Indies. Unsworth devotes chapter after chapter to the horror of the conditions. The slaves are shackled below decks in tiers, lying head-to-toe, covered in their own excrement, and brought on deck and into fresh air only to exercise, jumping up and down, still in chains, to the sound of Sullivan's fiddle. The description is of the ultimate degradation of man by man. Some slaves starve themselves to death and others, in their chains, jump overboard.

Both crew and slaves begin to die of malaria, scurvy, blackwater fever, and what they call, graphically, "bloody flux." Tensions are at breaking-point, and the horror is enhanced by Unsworth's superb descriptions of the beauty of sea and sky, descriptions worthy of Joseph Conrad at his best. The misery of the ship is a gripping portrait of mankind at its most abysmal, and the author uses the portrait as a background to a fascinating discussion of the very nature of man.

It is a three-way conversation between Thurso, Paris, and the painter Delblanc, a French passenger they took on in Guinea. The discussion is ongoing, with each man arguing from one of the three dominant philosophic positions of the age.

Thurso asserts the prevailing point of view, that of Thomas Hobbes, that life is nasty, brutish, and short, that man is vicious by nature and must be chained by law and authority in order for society to function.

Delblanc, embodying Rousseau's belief in man as "the noble savage," represents the opposite extreme. He believes that man is innately good and that all of society's evils would disappear if the coercion of authority were lifted. As he says to Matthew Paris, "'Do you think for a moment that men would enslave one another if they lived in a state of nature?'" (p. 329)

Mathew Paris takes a middle view, that of John Locke, who believed that man is born neither good nor bad, but an empty tablet, *tabula rasa*, on which experience would write. As a rational being, the thinking man would realize that a just society is in his own self-interest. Paris has already understood the failure of unrestricted capitalism. As he says to Thurso about the slaves in Guinea, "'You are admirably clear in your mind . . . as to who is caged and who is free. I . . . cannot always see the difference.'" (p. 153)

Matthew Paris causes the reader to reflect, not only on the Guinea slavers, but on the whole of English society, shackled to the profit motive, the rich protected only by the threat of the whip and the hangman's noose.

The second half of the novel will put the competing beliefs of the three to the test, but before that we have the tremendous climax of the first half. Paris is already prepared to make common cause with the crew, surviving on putrid salt beef and daily flogging, and with the slaves. The moment of truth comes when he sees Captain Thurso, "an incarnation, really, of the profit motive," (p. 382) throwing overboard sick but still living slaves. They are going to die anyway, and Thurso wants not only to save the expense of feeding them but to collect the 30 percent of their value the insurance company will pay. The reaction of Matthew Paris is immediate: "'No!' he shouted. 'No!' . . . With all the strength of his lungs, aiming his voice at the sky, he shouted again: 'No!'" (p. 384) It is a piece of beautifully concise writing. Paris is shrieking not at Thurso but at a world, a heaven, that would permit such inhumanity.

The crew will rise up in mutiny, Captain Thurso will be destroyed, and *Liverpool Merchant* will disappear from the shipping lanes, believed lost.

While we have been experiencing the agony of the slaves and the torment of the crew, a parallel narrative has been developing in England. Matthew Paris's cousin, Erasmus Kemp, has been wooing Sara Wolpert. Since she loves amateur theatricals, Erasmus has had to attend rehearsals in order to see her. Of the two keys to a full understanding of the novel, the debate on the nature of man on *Liverpool Merchant* is one, and the choice of the play is the other.

The play is *The Enchanted Island*, a bowdlerized version of Shakespeare's *The Tempest*. The fastidious eighteenth-century upper crust loved performing Shakespeare's plays, but only after all the negative thoughts and dirty bits had been taken out. It is vital that we have in mind the essentials of *The Tempest*, and since it may have been some time since you read it at school, permit me to make a very brief synopsis.

Prospero, the rightful Duke of Milan, has been deposed by his brother and marooned on a desert island with his daughter Miranda. Using his book of magic, Prospero frees the spirit Ariel, the maker of music, long imprisoned by the local witch, the mother of the wretched Caliban. Using his magic again, Prospero causes his brother and his brother's son, Ferdinand, to be wrecked on the same island. Under the influence of Ariel's music and the love that develops between the cousins Miranda and Ferdinand, an enchanted atmosphere is created in which the old enemies reconcile, the young people marry, and Prospero is restored to his rightful position.

If all this reminds you of some paradise in nature where enmity fades away, enemies find peace, and love triumphs, then Unsworth has succeeded. This is the Rousseau-inspired state of nature of which the artist Delblanc spoke to Captain Thurso and Matthew Paris.

Having said all that, let me now move to the second half of the novel and the year 1765, twelve years after the mutiny and the disappearance of *Liverpool Merchant*.

Erasmus Kemp has triumphed after two setbacks. Sarah Wolpert had finally refused him, and for the most interesting of reasons. Erasmus had been ruined when his father committed suicide after the loss of his ship, but Sarah did not refuse him because he had become poor, but rather because he saw her as no more than property. In her own words, " 'It is not because you have nothing to offer me but because you have nothing now to add me to.' " (p. 391)

Erasmus Kemp has restored his fortune by speculation in sugar and has just been elected president of the West India Association. His inauguration takes place, by the way, in a scene of debauchery that is very, very explicit. I will not go into detail, but it involves a dancer and a phallus made from sugar, which must surely cause many readers' eyebrows to raise. For those who would like to check the details, the scene is on pages 418 and following. It is certainly intended by the author as an illustration of the moral corruption that lay beneath the precious pretensions of the wealthy classes of the time.

Erasmus is informed that the beached *Liverpool Merchant* has been seen on the Florida coast and leaves to seek revenge on the cousin who caused his father's death. When he finds Matthew Paris's journal on the abandoned ship with the entry, "*I have assisted in the suffering inflicted on these innocent people*," (p. 451) we, the readers, understand that Paris had left behind the diary with his old life and gone inland with the crew and the slaves to try to forge a more moral society.

With the soldiers afforded him by the British governor of St. Augustine, Erasmus sets off to confront his cousin.

Let us examine in some detail the commune established by Matthew Paris, the crew, and the slaves. They have been living in a state of nature for twelve years. We shall see if Delblanc's belief in the goodness of man and Matthew's belief that rational man will act justly in enlightened self-interest were justified.

What will a group of individuals do, isolated from conventional society and freed from the constraints of any legal authority? You will remember that William Golding made the same exploration in *Lord of the Flies*, and you will remember the comment of Erasmus Kemp on Sarah Wolpert's play, "'the nonsense of an enchanted island where divisions could be healed and enemies reconciled.'" (p. 355)

Our first impressions of the commune are reassuring. Racial differences have fallen away. The pugnacious, verbose Billy Blair, for example, has found a soulmate in the black Inchebe. They dispute trivialities interminably as they hunt together and share the same wife. There were relatively few women among the slaves on *Liverpool Merchant* and the commune has established a system of polyandry in which one wife has several husbands. The system seems to have provoked no lasting disharmony and we are far from Erasmus Kemp and his like, who see women only as property.

The women of the commune are fully developed characters who are perceived by the men in their full humanity. Sallian, the wife shared by Billy Blair and Inchebe, is wise and nurturing and full of love. Tabakali, the beautiful Fulani woman with whom Paris fell in love and by whom he has a son, has a second husband, Nadri the hunter, but the relationship between Matthew Paris and the fiercely intelligent Tabakali is no less profound because one of them has sufficient love to give another. Social rank has been abandoned and Sullivan, the fiddler, and Matthew Paris, the doctor, have become intimate friends. Young Calley has been taught how to comb the beaches by the hunter Nadri after the death of Deakin, Calley's first protector. They all live by barter, and each contributes his own special skill. The strong protect the weak and each takes only according to his need. As I first read about the commune, my reaction was, "Thank heavens! Thank heavens! Mankind, or a fair cross-section of it, has been given a second chance in this new Garden of Eden, and this time they're not buggering it up!"

Hughes, the solitary man, spends his life alone as the lookout in the tree-tops. I must admit that he is the character, although minor, to whom I was most drawn. There is one moment of his which is particularly beautiful:

> He watched the woodpecker until it disappeared among the lower foliage and then, with the same attention, a honey-coloured bee at the flowers of a smooth-barked tree which grew almost as tall as his own, ending some feet below his platform. He followed the movements of the bee as it clambered among the drooping white spikes of blossom, observing how the insect vibrated its body each time it entered one of the flowers. His mind moved slowly over possible explanation. Could the bee do this to help the flower spread its pollen? From time to time he glanced across the short space of clearing towards the black water below him. In this dry season, when the levels sank below the roots of the saw-grass, the deer came more often to these pools in the jungle islands. He knew they came to this one: he had seen their traces in the soft earth at the edge and the nibbled-off tops of the spider-lilies. (p. 500)

How tender is the passage! We are compelled to wonder how great a natural scientist Hughes might have been if his youth had not been so distorted by the overcrowding of England's slums.

The island – I always think of the commune as an island like Prospero's island – is indeed beautiful, but it is a very fragile world. Hughes, the lookout, had once saved them from the intrusion of slavers who had captured local Indians, and although the result of that encounter had been friendship with the Indians, we are reminded of how vulnerable the commune is.

But the greatest danger is from within. Some of the white men brought the sacred hunger with them. Barton and the seaman Haines try to escape with Captain Thurso's gold dust, and Haines is caught and scalped by Indians, who throw away the worthless dust. The scene seems to me to be a very clear borrowing from its counterpart in *The Treasure of the Sierra Madre* and it makes the same point. Gold is valuable only if society attributes value to it. Of what value is gold dust in Paradise?

The brutish Wilson is executed by a mixed-race firing squad because he wouldn't share a woman and because he kills his rival. The point that Unsworth makes here is the perennial thorn in the side of those who dream that humankind can make a heaven on earth. What do you do with dis-senters, people who don't agree with you, who don't like the rules? Prospero faced the same problem in *The Tempest* when Ariel threatened rebellion and Prospero counter-threatened imprisonment.

I don't have an answer. It was the problem that nagged at me when I was young and I dreamed of a socialist millennium. I leave you with the problem. If you come up with a solution, do let me know.

But the greater danger within is that identified by the charismatic black leader Kireku, with whom several have allied themselves. First, as even Matthew's friend Nadri points out to him, the commune is a *white* dream, the dream of Rousseau, the dream of Matthew Paris. "'[Y]*ou* are here by accident. I am here because you bringed me. . . . First you bringed us, say we are free, then you want to make us serve some idea in your head. But the people cannot serve your idea, you cannot make them do that.'" (p. 563)

Kireku argues with Matthew Paris even more directly. In a pidgin superbly reproduced by Unsworth and remarkably easy to understand, he says, "'I no ask come here. Now I here I fight for place. Strong man get rich, him slave get rich. Strong man make everybody rich.'" (p. 581)

Kireku restates the belief in trickle-down economics – embraced by the eighteenth century, Margaret Thatcher, Ronald Reagan, and George Bush – that man is competitively capitalist by nature, and as the rich get richer, the wealth will eventually trickle down to the poor.

The debate is, in any event, academic. Erasmus Kemp arrives with his soldiers. He hears Sullivan's music as he advances, but it does not win over his heart as the music of Ariel won over the heart of Prospero's brother on Shakespeare's island. Many are killed, Matthew Paris is mortally wounded, the blacks are re-enslaved, and the whites are put in irons.

Erasmus Kemp remains to the end the personification of capitalism without conscience, but there is something in his cousin's tranquillity on his deathbed that causes Erasmus to blurt out the emptiness of his life. In the most delicate of exchanges, Matthew comments on the futility of revenge: "'Nothing that becomes of me can mend these things. You will still be where you were.'" (p. 620) Erasmus's response is to think, "Of all the injuries that Paris had done him it seemed to him for a moment that this kindness of tone was the worst." (p. 621)

In my sentimental way, I like to think that a tiny seed of hope has been planted in the heart of Erasmus Kemp; his last action in the novel is to slip into his pocket one of Sullivan's precious brass buttons. An emblem of love and friendship, it had been Sullivan's gift to the dying Matthew Paris, and now Erasmus takes it from the hand of his dead cousin.

But perhaps I am being too optimistic. Perhaps it is just another example of an unrepentant entrepreneur slipping something of apparent value into his pocket.

With the death of Matthew Paris and with what I hope is a tiny chance of redemption for Erasmus Kemp, we move to the epilogue of the novel. It picks up on the very brief prologue. We are in New Orleans in the year 1832, nearly seventy years after the extinction of the Florida commune. We meet again an old, dying black man, a former plantation slave in the South who had been freed and turned off the land when he was no longer capable of productive work. "Sometimes one of the customers will set him off, winking round at the others: 'Come on, old Sawdust, what's the news from Paradise?'" (p. 628)

The Paradise Nigger, as he is cruelly known, always rises to the bait: "'Red-colour fish in them pool . . . an' leather-shell turtle. I kin see it now. It never snowed nor frosted neether. . . . That place nobody boss man. . . . My fadder a *doctor*. I born in a paradise place. You hear me?'" (p. 629)

We know that the Paradise Nigger can only be Kenka, the son of Tabakali and Matthew Paris, and that this is the end of the dream.

We know that Barry Unsworth was driven to write *Sacred Hunger* by looking around at Thatcher's England and Reagan's America in the 1980s, when greed was again sanctified as ideology – Unsworth said as much in an interview with *Books* magazine in March of 1992. We can admire the author's control of language, the thoroughness of his research, his evocation of the extremes of wealth and poverty, his intricate psychological portraits, his lofty debate, the excitement of his narrative, and the beauty of his descriptions, but surely our dominant feeling as we put the novel down cannot be one of admiration for the author, however well-deserved. Surely our feeling must be one of pity – pity for the English poor, pity for the wretched slaves, pity for the brave, doomed commune, and, above all, pity for what Mark Twain called "the whole damned human race."

A TRIBUTE TO ADELE WISEMAN

*(from the Michael Lauter Memorial Lecture delivered at
the Montreal Jewish Public Library, March 30, 1993)*

I want to pay tribute to the life and work of Adele Wiseman, whom I regard as the most neglected of all our great Canadian writers.

She was not a prolific author. She wrote only two novels, *The Sacrifice* (1956) and *Crackpot* (1974). In 1978 she wrote a memoir of her mother, Chaika, *Old Woman at Play*; in 1982 her impressions of a visit to China, *Chinada: Memoirs of the Gang of Seven*; and in 1989 a children's story, *Kenji and the Cricket*. There were two plays, *The Lovebound* and *Testimonial Dinner*, neither of which, I believe, was ever professionally produced. Her essays were published as a collection in 1987, *Memoirs of a Book-Molesting Childhood*, and apart from writing the text for an illustrated study of old Winnipeg markets, that was it. Her literary reputation is based almost entirely upon the two novels, *The Sacrifice* and *Crackpot*. In my opinion, they are both masterpieces.

Adele Wiseman never intended to write more than she did. In the blurb on the dust jacket of *The Sacrifice*, she makes it clear that she intends "to go on writing at a moderate pace and only what I want to write . . . to travel about, read and continue as long as possible." Regrettably, her odyssey ended on June 1, 1992, when she finally succumbed to complications related to sarcoma after a long and courageous battle with cancer.

Adele Wiseman was born the third of four children in Winnipeg on May 21, 1928. She was the child of Jewish immigrants from the Ukraine who had come to Canada because Pesach Wiseman, Adele's father, had decided to accompany his frightened, illiterate sister to the unknown country to which her husband had preceded her.

The early years in the Depression were very difficult. In an interview with *Time Magazine* on May 13, 1957, Wiseman remembered that the family lived in Winnipeg in a former showroom, partitioned into four rooms and a tiny tailor and dressmaking shop.

> "In the mornings we four children would get up to go to school and find our parents had fallen asleep on their arms, huddled over the shop machine. . . . Their fixed idea was that we children should not have to go through the same thing."

Her parents had only one dream, that their four children would all study at a university, and that dream came true. Two engineers, a biochemist, and a writer.

There will never, ever, be another generation like that of Adele Wiseman's parents, working so hard, so many hours a day, sacrificing everything so that their children should see a better life. I think of my own background. One of my grandfathers was a blind man and the other an illiterate stonemason. Because of economic circumstances, neither of my parents was able to finish school. Yet because of the loving home they gave us and the values they taught us, my brothers and I are all university graduates. The credit does not belong to me or my siblings, it belongs to that incredible generation of which Adele Wiseman's parents and my parents were a part. I fear, I fear greatly, that we shall not see such giants again.

Adele Wiseman always knew she would be a writer. She saw it as her inheritance from her mother, her grandmother, from all the women of all the generations of her family. As she wrote in "Word Power," one of the essays in her 1987 collection,

> Indeed, I know that at least one of my grandmothers was unlettered, analphabetic. But even those unlettered generations of women were, in fact, the traditional tale-bearers of cultures, transmitting their accepted values to the very young. How many writers have told tales learned "at my mother's knees," brave tales of absent fathers, stories told by all the grannies of all the ages? . . .

In a sense we have always been the transmitters of the raw material of cultures, the third world of literature.

But how to go from being a traditional teller of tales to one who can make a living from the written word? Adele knew the obstacles that the double standard placed in the path of the woman writer. In the same essay, she wrote,

> No one has ever suggested to our male counterparts that they must choose between devotions and suffer guilt if they appear to make what is considered the wrong choice. Indeed, it is considered somewhat heroic and even a sign of genius in a man if he behaves with irresponsible selfishness in his personal life. He is considered redeemed by his utter devotion to his art. The exact reverse is usually true for a woman artist. The writer who also wants to live her life fully as a mother and wife is constantly faced with largely artificial choices and has her guilts set out for her. The writer who, for whatever reason, avoids the prescribed course of marriage and motherhood is an even more suspicious object, behung with guilt-inducing stereotypes which often effectively neutralize, even for herself, the suspicion that she has gained something of freedom.

With a full understanding of all the difficulties that faced a woman who chooses a career, Adele Wiseman, at the age of seventeen, enrolled at the University of Manitoba in 1945 to study literature and psychology. It was there that she would meet Margaret Laurence, who would become her life-long friend, and their great teacher Malcolm Ross.

> I showed my earliest work to Malcolm, and the great sensitivity and wonderful delicacy with which he handled one of my tentative stories in fact led me to the writing of my first novel. He was also of enormous assistance to Margaret in the edition and publishing of her earliest stories.

Wiseman also speaks of the invaluable influence of those fellow students who had just returned from the war, the ex-servicemen whom Wiseman calls "death-hardened" men: "They vastly expanded my education. There was no bullshit from these men. If you thought clearly and wrote well they respected you for it, and told you so."

Adele Wiseman's next problem was what to write about. Would it be what so many westerners had chosen before her, the lonely prairies, the silent expanses of snow? Wiseman had very ambivalent feelings about her native Manitoba. In a wittily sardonic essay she wrote, on request, in honour of the province's centennial in 1970, Wiseman was less than affectionate.

> Everybody knows midwesterners are a friendly, hospitable lot. They're notorious for it. You will find, for instance, that about the only people Manitobans could not stand in those days were those who got there before them: Indians and Métis . . . and the people who got there after them (27 other ethnic groups).

Rejecting a culture she found narrow and bigoted, Wiseman decided to look elsewhere, and she found somewhere to look. In a lecture she gave to a Royal Society symposium in June 1967, she told her audience what she had discovered during her university days: "To produce first-class work requires not only courage but skill on the part of the writer. He has to be able to look into himself and into his world and to risk setting down what he finds."

As a university student, she made her choice. Her subject matter would be the world she knew, the world of the Jewish immigrant community. But she saw it as no more than a vehicle in the search for universal truth, the permanent realities of existence. She would write of the parochial, but the truths she hoped to illuminate would be truths general to the whole of humanity. In bearing witness to the world of her parents, the *shtetl* recreated in the North End of Winnipeg, she would speak to the hearts and minds of readers of every culture.

In 1949 she began to develop a short story idea she had discussed with Malcolm Ross. She thought she could develop it into a novel. The writing took seven years, during which time she visited Margaret Laurence in England. Wiseman felt she needed travel to understand better the variety of the human animal. She sustained herself by odd jobs and unemployment insurance, and in 1956 *The Sacrifice* was ready.

It was a sensation, and Adele Wiseman became the crown princess of Canadian literature. *The Sacrifice* won her a Governor General's Award and a Canada Foundation Award. It also got her a Canada Council grant and a Guggenheim scholarship. These permitted her to travel extensively, and the prestige helped her to get teaching appointments in Montreal at Sir George Williams College, later Concordia University, and at McGill. She would teach right up until her marriage to the environmental consultant Dmitry Stone in 1969.

The genesis of *The Sacrifice* is interesting. Adele Wiseman explained it in an article about her in *Books in Canada* in October 1964.

"When I was 15 or 16, working for the summer in a fruit shop near the market, there was the first murder committed by a Jew in Manitoba. An old man had axed a woman who had apparently led him on. He was someone from our district, a deaf old man, lonely, paying court to a somewhat younger woman. My mother and aunt knew him." That incident triggered her thinking. It was not the action itself but the psychological kernel – the moral implications of behaviour – that fascinated her. "I wanted to find the best possible reason that a good man could have for committing such an atrocity."

The novel is the story of Abraham and Sarah, Jewish immigrants to a prairie city, probably Winnipeg, some time after 1920. After losing two sons in a pogrom in the Old Country, Abraham and Sarah have come to the New World with their remaining son, Isaac. Abraham is a patriarchal figure, huge, fork-bearded, and devout. On the shoulders of his remaining son he places all the hopes and ambitions he had had for all three of his children.

Isaac grows up and marries the orphan Ruth. They have two sons, Moses and Jacob, but then Isaac dies while saving the Torah from a fire in the synagogue. Abraham is crazed with grief and his sanity wavers. Irritated by the advances of the kindly but promiscuous Laiah, to whom he is delivering meat, he finally loses his reason and cuts her throat. My own belief is that, driven mad by all his bereavements, in that moment he sees, not Laiah, but his own dead Isaac standing before him. In a recapitulation of the Biblical story, Abraham honours his promise to his God and sacrifices the figure he believes to be his son.

Another of the many interpretations of this wonderfully powerful scene is that, driven mad by loss, he takes a life as an act of revolt against the terrible barrenness of the future. I know that eventually Ms. Wiseman was unable to remember which interpretation she had had in mind when she wrote the scene.

Abraham is confined to an asylum, and there is a moving reconciliation at the end of the novel between Abraham and his grandson Moses. Moses finally comes to understand the agony that had brought the old man to stand alone, mad with grief, at the edge of Creation, face to face, as he believed, with his God.

The Sacrifice is a brilliantly crafted piece of work, combining a chronicle of the immigrant experience, with all its sweatshops and dreams, with a retelling and a revision of the Biblical epic.

The novel also works as a fine study of inter-generational conflict, in particular the dilemma of the son born in the New World, unsure of how much of his heritage he should cling to or discard.

This theme of the conflict between father and son is one Wiseman would explore in her play *Testimonial Dinner*, published privately in 1978. The play is about a family of three generations of publishers in which the grandson wants to add a soft-porn element to the family's Yiddish-language newspaper. The play is interesting but doesn't begin to compare with *The Sacrifice*.

The Sacrifice made it clear that Wiseman had her own voice, a voice very different from those of other North American Jewish writers. There is none of the moral outrage of Mordecai Richler and none of the urban neuroses we find in Philip Roth or Saul Bellow. Also, in spite of the fact that *The Sacrifice* covers three generations, there is not a single significant Gentile character. There are no comparisons drawn, flattering or otherwise, between Jews and other people. What Wiseman is trying to do is examine the whole of humanity by examining one tiny part of it, complete in itself, closely and well.

While paying tribute to the craftsmanship of the whole book and to the compelling horror of the sacrifice itself, I must say that there is one scene in the novel that haunts me, that is always with me. I notice it is the same scene that Adele Wiseman chose to read when she visited the Montreal Jewish Public Library. I have listened to the tape.

It is a scene after the death of Isaac and before the murder. Abraham fears that his daughter-in-law, Ruth, will take his grandson Moses away, possibly so that she might marry another man. Ruth and Abraham have a confrontation in which each of them drags out all the old slights, all the old hurts. In my hardcover edition, it's on pages 290 and following.

First, Ruth:

"You may throw my miserable life up to me. I know I'm nothing to you. But I tried. Every one of your crazy ideas, because you were Isaac's father; I didn't say anything; I didn't mix in. How many times did Isaac come to me, even before we were married, and tell me –" Ruth choked on the words, covered her face.

And now Abraham's response:

He pounded one fist into the open palm of the other. "You lie," he whispered hoarsely. "Tell me you lie! What would my son say about me? It's you who tricked him into marrying you with your nice words and pretenses. You think I haven't noticed how, after he was dead, almost on his deathbed, you were painting your lips already and dressing and fussing over yourself?"

And on it goes and I thought how well Adele Wiseman understands the human condition, how well she understands that terrible account book of other people's behaviour that each of us, from whatever the culture, seems to carry. How easily we dip into it to take out spite that we can throw to hurt.

After the spectacular reception of *The Sacrifice*, the world waited for Adele Wiseman's next novel. The world had to wait for a long time. It would be eighteen years before *Crackpot* appeared in 1974. The plot is easily summarized.

The marriage of a blind man and a hunchbacked woman is arranged in their European *shtetl*. The little Jewish community believes that it can ward off a nearby plague only by uniting two of God's most forsaken creatures, thus reaffirming their belief in the continuity of humankind. The couple move to Winnipeg where their daughter, Hoda, is born.

After her mother's death, Hoda prostitutes herself as the only means of supporting her blind father. Hoda grows larger and larger, both in body and soul. She is a life force, an elemental figure. This wonderful, blowsy, courageous woman contains a world within herself, all our need to give and receive love, all our need to belong. Finally she will accept the marriage proposal of a "Displaced Person," appropriately named Lazar, who had crawled back to life out of a German death pit. This perfectly constructed novel begins with the union of two of life's victims and ends with the union of two unlikely survivors. Hoda who has suffered so much is the cracked pot of the title, the vessel of life shattered by life into little pieces. At the end of the novel, the cracked pot is made whole. Hoda has come to know who she is; the exile of the self from the self is over.

I found the novel profoundly moving. As I read about Hoda I fell in love with her innocence and her dream that the Prince of Wales, the only Prince Charming she had ever heard of, would one day come and choose her as his Queen Esther. I wept for her when she had to masturbate the butcher to get scraps of meat for her blind father. I wept for her when she told her class at school of her parents' wedding, believing that the teacher who had rejected her would now see her as special, resulting as she did from a union that carried such import. I wept for her when she let boys touch her because she could make no other human contact with her peers. When we read of the fat, ungainly child looking in from the outside, yearning for acceptance, yearning to be loved, is there any one of us who is not touched? Which of us has never stood outside the charmed circle, wanting with all our heart to be invited in and accepted?

Hoda has a child whom she must leave at a foundlings' home. We share Hoda's pain when, years later, this same son comes to her, like all the youth of the neighbourhood, for his sexual initiation. She knows of the relationship between them; he does not and must not. He has been rejected so many times, how can she reject him now? This is not Hoda the child, this is a mature Hoda, who has learned compassion through pain. She understands rejection. She thinks back to the butcher who abused her: "You don't do that to a child." What can she do to her son that will hurt him least?

We have all faced terrible existential choices, not between good and evil, but between bad and worse. How can we judge Hoda when she held her son tenderly and tried, in the only way she knew how, to make up for all the harm she had done?

Margaret Laurence in an afterword to the novel calls the sexual meeting of mother and son one of the most devastating scenes in contemporary literature. I agree, but I know one even more likely to tear your heart out, and it also comes from this novel. I would read the scene aloud except that I can never get through it without tears.

The scene is when the child Hoda gives birth to her son. Little Hoda had heard the story of the Ugly Duckling and had come to believe that she too would one day turn into a new and beautiful version of herself. Hoda, covered with rolls of fat, has no idea she is pregnant. She has let every local boy molest her; all they had to say was, "I love you." With no understanding of biology and no mother to guide her, she has no idea what is happening to her when her labour pains begin. Then she remembers the story of the Ugly Duckling. Her moment has arrived!

I can remember no scene in modern literature that moved me as profoundly as this one did. Hoda is alone and in agony, but is absolutely convinced that the time of her transformation has come and that her beautiful new self will emerge out of the unbearable pain.

If you did not already know, you will be amazed to be told that *Crackpot*, every bit as fine a work as *The Sacrifice*, received almost universally poor reviews. Critics sneered at the cliché of "the whore with a heart of gold." I did not understand the reaction then and I do not understand it now. Any work can be dismissed with a facile phrase. Lear becomes a parent with ungrateful children. Is there anything more clichéd than that? Anna Karenina becomes a bored wife who kills herself over a love affair gone bad. The stuff of soap opera!

I cannot discuss the adverse reaction, because I truly do not understand it. *Crackpot* has humour, pathos, and an exquisitely balanced structure. The critics were wrong. If you have read the novel, you will agree with me. If you haven't, please do so.

We come now to Adele Wiseman's memoir of her mother, Chaika, in *Old Woman at Play* (1978). It's about Adele's mother and her doll-making. It's also about Adele's own childhood and the hardships of her parents' lives and their memories of the Ukraine. It is also an explanation of Adele Wiseman's theory of the process of creation, using her mother's doll-making as the vehicle. In the words of Margaret Laurence, "We share in a revelation, that the dolls that Chaika Wiseman makes are not only made to please children but to enable their creator to make some kind of sense out of the chaos of her experiences. Art is then both celebration and healing. And I see a great parallel between Chaika Wiseman making her dolls and her daughter Adele Wiseman making this book."

In 1981, Adele Wiseman and six other Canadian writers were invited to visit China by the Chinese Writers' Association. A number of Chinese writers were invited to Canada shortly afterwards. In 1982 Adele Wiseman published her impressions of both visits under the title *Chinada: Memoirs of the Gang of Seven.* My favourite paragraph refers to a gift made to the Chinese writers visiting Canada. They were presented with a painting by Hing Mak, a young Chinese Canadian, of a Chinese immigrant woman in Toronto.

> The woman in the painting is bent over a sewing machine, in the dim light. At the same time as she is sewing she is rocking her child with the bare foot which she has hooked under its cradle. Somehow, in the bold, strong strokes one can feel the long hours, the double work, the anxious, divided attention. I was startled and moved by the painting. Its subject was so familiar to me. It is the story of my mother's life as an immigrant too. (p. 112)

This paragraph demonstrates Adele Wiseman's unique achievement. She could look at a single moment in a human life and see in it the universality of the human condition with all its pain and its mystery.

In her essay "Word Power," Adele Wiseman wrote her dream review, the review she always wanted. It is now my pleasure to read it. I am only sorry that it is being read posthumously.

> *Miss Wiseman's profound insight into human character, her grasp of the implications of human behaviour, the scope of her imagination, her fearless exploration of the human condition, her fascinating story line, the fine balance and movement of her narrative, her wit, her delicious sense of mischief, her timing, her unerring choice of the significant moment, her vivid descriptive powers, her picturesque but exact use of language, her inventiveness, her rich purity of tone, her absolute pitch; all of these convince us that she knows us better than we know ourselves, and assure us, from the first moment, that she is taking us where we must have always wanted to go. This writer is a natural force who writes because she has to write for us. How grateful we are that Miss Wiseman is one of the new generation of women who have been allowed to learn how to read and write.*

And I say Amen, and again Amen, to that.

PUBLISHER'S ACKNOWLEDGEMENTS

Excerpts from *The Tortilla Curtain* by T. Coraghessan Boyle, copyright © 1995 by T. Coraghessan Boyle. Used by permission of Viking Penguin, a division of Penguin Putnam Inc.

Excerpts from *A Private View* by Anita Brookner. Copyright © 1994 by Anita Brookner. Reprinted by permission of Vintage Canada, a divison of Random House of Canada Limited.

Excerpts from *Jack Maggs* by Peter Carey. Copyright © 1997 by Peter Carey. Reprinted by permission of Vintage Canada, a division of Random House of Canada Limited.

Excerpts from *Wise Children* by Angela Carter. Copyright © Angela Carter 1991. Reproduced by permission of the Estate of Angela Carter c/o Rogers, Coleridge & White Ltd., 20 Powis Mews, London W11 1JN

Excerpts from *The Farming of Bones* by Edwidge Danticat, copyright © 1998 by Edwidge Danticat. Reprinted by permission of Soho Press

Excerpts from *Captain Corelli's Mandolin* by Louis de Bernières, published by Martin Secker & Warburg. Reprinted by permission of The Random House Group Ltd.

Excerpts from *Paddy Clarke Ha Ha Ha* by Roddy Doyle, published by Martin Secker & Warburg. Reprinted by permission of The Random House Group Ltd.

Excerpts from "The Love Song of J. Alfred Prufrock" from *Collected Poems 1909-1962*. Copyright © 1964 by T.S. Eliot. Reprinted by permission of Faber and Faber Ltd.

Excerpts from *Birdsong* by Sebastian Faulks, published by Hutchinson. Reprinted by permission of The Random House Group Ltd.
Excerpts from *The Poisonwood Bible* by Barbara Kingsolver. Copyright © 1998 by Barbara Kingsolver. Reprinted by permission of HarperCollins, Inc.

Excerpts from *Palace Walk* by Naguib Mahfouz. Copyright © 1956 by Naguib Mahfouz. English-language translation copyright © 1990 by The American

PUBLISHER'S ACKNOWLEDGEMENTS

Excerpts from *The Tortilla Curtain* by T. Coraghessan Boyle, copyright © 1995 by T. Coraghessan Boyle. Used by permission of Viking Penguin, a division of Penguin Putnam Inc.

Excerpts from *A Private View* by Anita Brookner. Copyright © 1994 by Anita Brookner. Reprinted by permission of Vintage Canada, a divison of Random House of Canada Limited.

Excerpts from *Jack Maggs* by Peter Carey. Copyright © 1997 by Peter Carey. Reprinted by permission of Vintage Canada, a division of Random House of Canada Limited.

Excerpts from *Wise Children* by Angela Carter. Copyright © Angela Carter 1991. Reproduced by permission of the Estate of Angela Carter c/o Rogers, Coleridge & White Ltd., 20 Powis Mews, London W11 1JN

Excerpts from *The Farming of Bones* by Edwidge Danticat, copyright © 1998 by Edwidge Danticat. Reprinted by permission of Soho Press

Excerpts from *Captain Corelli's Mandolin* by Louis de Bernières, published by Martin Secker & Warburg. Reprinted by permission of The Random House Group Ltd.

Excerpts from *Paddy Clarke Ha Ha Ha* by Roddy Doyle, published by Martin Secker & Warburg. Reprinted by permission of The Random House Group Ltd.

Excerpts from "The Love Song of J. Alfred Prufrock" from *Collected Poems 1909-1962*. Copyright © 1964 by T.S. Eliot. Reprinted by permission of Faber and Faber Ltd.

Excerpts from *Birdsong* by Sebastian Faulks, published by Hutchinson. Reprinted by permission of The Random House Group Ltd.
Excerpts from *The Poisonwood Bible* by Barbara Kingsolver. Copyright © 1998 by Barbara Kingsolver. Reprinted by permission of HarperCollins, Inc.

Excerpts from *Palace Walk* by Naguib Mahfouz. Copyright © 1956 by Naguib Mahfouz. English-language translation copyright © 1990 by The American